QUEST

FOR

DISCOVERY

QUEST
FOR
DISCOVERY

THE REMARKABLE SEARCH FOR NOAH'S ARK

richard carl bright

New Leaf Press

First printing: September 2001

ISBN: 0-89221-505-4
Library of Congress Catalog Number: 00-110208

Biblical references are from the King James Version unless otherwise stated.

Cover illustration by Bryan Miller

Printed in the United States of America.

Please visit our website for other great titles:
www.newleafpress.net

For information regarding publicity for author interviews contact Dianna Fletcher at (870) 438-5288.

DEDICATION

Written for the skeptic, but dedicated
to those of us who have trouble,
yet have faith and hope
in the Saving Grace of the Lord Jesus Christ.
I am one of those.

These things I have spoken unto you, that in me
ye might have peace.
In this world ye shall have tribulation;
but be of good cheer;
I have overcome the world
(John 16:33).

SPECIAL THANKS

It is appropriate to render appreciation and special recognition to the government of Turkey for allowing the search for the existing remains of the ancient ocean-going vessel . . . NOAH'S ARK. We are thankful for their help to insure our safety through military protection provided us during times of trouble.

To the former astronaut Colonel James B. Irwin, who has passed on from this earthly life into God's eternity. As the president of the High Flight Foundation of Colorado Springs, Colorado, Irwin allowed me to join his team on three separate occasions. This was the beginning of what has been the greatest adventure of my life. I am thankful and deeply indebted. Also to Mary Irwin, whose belief has proven to be a tremendous support.

To the authors of the books whose material they graciously allowed me to quote.

To Eryl and Violet Cummings of Farmington, New Mexico, who have also passed on from this earthly life into God's eternity. Their writings and years of dedication in the search for Noah's ark provided inspiration for me.

To Ronald L. Lane of Ranger Associates, Inc., formerly of Longwood, Florida, who too has passed on from this earthly life to God's eternal kingdom. Ron not only devoted many personal hours assisting me in the advising, editing, and publishing of the original text of this book, but also left his own blood and sweat on the mountain in this search for truth. I can truly say that he was my friend. The original text was titled *The Ark, a Reality?* You may find references to this title within the text of this new book.

In addition to Jim Irwin and Ron Lane, to all the people I climbed with over the years, alphabetically: Ahmet Arslan, Dave Banks, John Christensen, Bob Cornuke, Ole Honnungdalanes, George Kralik, Dave Larsen, John McIntosh, Bob Stuplich, Paul Thomas, and the many others not mentioned, which include the Turkish and Kurdish climbers who helped in this effort; to Ray Anderson, whose research and own work proves him to be a giant part of this search. I thank all of you for being there when you were needed.

To my parents, Ray and Louise Bright, who gave me their heartfelt support in this endeavor; they have my eternal appreciation. Ray Bright has since passed on into God's eternity.

To my daughter Courtney, who waited for me to return, I love you.

To Betsy McCreary of Littleton, Colorado, whose talent, skill, belief, and dedication to the work helped make the original printing possible. To Audrey Fitzgerald of Voorheesville, New York, for typing skills and assistance. To Sammie Brown of Humble, Texas, who worked with me on the report of the 1993 expedition. Sammie, too, has passed on to eternity.

To Mary Bielby of Aurora, Colorado, whose computer and office skills made possible much of the rewriting of the original draft, and the distribution of the first printing, and to Jim Bielby who proofread it.

To the staff of New Leaf Press for the work of this printing, and everyone who has helped in any way.

God bless you all!

CONTENTS

Foreword

JOHN MORRIS

A survey was taken in the early 1970s by a Hollywood-based film company, to discern which subjects were of most interest to American viewers. What subject would they most like to see documented on film? The answer? The search for Noah's ark!

Several expeditions, including some of my own, had journeyed to that fabled mountain in the preceding years, and had received significant press coverage. The adventure had seemingly captured the imagination of the nation, and while the newness of the search has waned somewhat, the adventure continues.

I was captivated as a boy of nine, when my father showed me a newspaper clipping regarding Fernand Navarra's discovery of hand-tooled lumber high on the slopes of Mount Ararat in 1955. My interest was rekindled in 1969 by the tales of Dr. Clifford Burdick and an intriguing early manuscript by Violet Cummings, which was eventually to become her 1972 book *Noah's Ark: Fact or Fable?* I couldn't put that manuscript down. Such an adventure! This input led to my personal involvement in the search and to the addition of even more evidence to the already convincing case.

On several of my 13 trips to Mount Ararat, I had the distinct privilege of working with Mr. Dick Bright. While many were the distractions and roadblocks, I found him to be a man of unusual concentration and focus on the job at hand. He has now been to the mountain more often than I, cooperating with larger, more visible groups at times, and working quietly with little fanfare at others. This search has been his life's passion, and he has been involved at every turn. Thus, he is uniquely qualified to write this summary book.

Some might ask — why hasn't the ark already been discovered? Surely, it can't be that hard. Of course, that question has crossed all of our minds at times, but the ark, assuming its remains do exist, seems well hidden and perhaps fortified. The hazards are many. The dangers on the treacherous mountain, from glacial crevasses, to rock avalanches, to wild animals, to violent storms, etc., are multiplied by continual threats from many other directions. And ever since the invasion of Kuwait by nearby Iraq, the mountain has been overrun by terrorists. This endeavor is not a simple search.

So why search at all? What good would it do? Briefly put, I think a successful search would change the world. It would rewrite archeology and refute uniformity (the principle upon which evolution is based). Furthermore, it would demonstrate the accuracy of the early chapters of Genesis. More could derive from this discovery than any other, and it deserves our attention and support.

God's blessings be upon you, Dick Bright. May He grant you success in your arduous search, and may eternal fruit abound from your selfless labors.

INTRODUCTION

WHY?

As I write this introduction, there are those of us who are convinced that Noah's ark is on Mount Ararat. There are also those who are skeptical, at best. If the ark is on the mountain, then as you read of the efforts to find it you may wonder just what the problem has been in locating the proof. You may even wonder why we keep at it if we seem to be continuously spinning our wheels. You may question our motives and wonder what scientific evidence exists in the earth's history for a biblical flood. By the end of this report, I trust you will have those questions answered. Up to the time of this writing, we've had a certain amount of trouble in our quest. You will read of it in this book. However, even though we have had trouble in our search to find the ark, there is a level of commitment to make every effort, every attempt to reach it and document the location for all to see. Why?

I imagine each person who gets involved in this quest has his own personal reasons for his desire to do so. Maybe it's the adventure. Maybe it's more than that. Could it be to do what we believe is the will of God in our lives? Maybe. Is it to do something to show where we stand in our belief? Maybe. I've heard it said that people may doubt what you say in your life, but they will believe what you do. Is it a leading by the Spirit of God? Is it because of the love for others as well as the love and belief in the Lord? Maybe, but the skeptic will have a tough time with that. He will probably think there is a selfish reason somewhere, or else we must be just a bunch of religious fanatics who happen to be scientifically ignorant. Well, skeptic, I may just understand where you get your point of view. I was once there. This book was written for you. If you have the courage, read it. Then perhaps you will be able to better decide.

So then, why? Why the commitment to this search? Is it to do a good work, to get "points" from God? No. The Scripture tells us, "For by grace are ye saved through faith; and that not of yourselves: it is the gift of God: Not of works, lest any man should boast" (Eph. 2:8–9). We can't work our way into heaven. Still, is it to hope God will say, at the appointed time, "Well done, thou good and faithful servant"? Maybe. Is this being selfish? I don't think so. I think the action taken demonstrates faith, even belief. Is it that in doing this we hope to reach the lives of other people? Is to to help get the word out? Is it to do our best to make a difference — a good, positive difference? Maybe. Is it just something we have to do for reasons we don't really seem to fully understand? Maybe.

I think most of us have reasons that are similar, and those reasons are, for the most part, good, and hopefully acceptable to God. To my way of thinking, some of the people mentioned here are giants in this undertaking. Among them were such people as Eryl Cummings, who inspired and led people to seek the resting place of the ark. He climbed and felt the pain of injury in the efforts. In addition, Eryl researched the ark stories for over 40 years. We also remember Violet Cummings, who wrote two tremendous books on the subject. Colonel Jim Irwin, who was an astronaut, evangelist, and a great man of faith, belief, and accomplishment, led expeditions to Ararat. He left some of his blood on the mountain. These three passed on from this earthly life, but the example they set remains. Dr. John Morris, a creation geologist, author, and veteran of Ararat, was once struck by lightning while on a climb. He survived, and is a leader in this effort. Barry Setterfield of Australia has now taken a leadership role in the search for the ark and scientific truth. There are others not mentioned here, but their contributions and efforts, according to their own beliefs and reasons, I think will be accepted as gold.

I was taught in college that theories of evolution, particularly the Darwinian theory, natural selection, and chance, were responsible for my existence and the existence of every plant, person, and type of animal. In essence, life was an accident.

I was taught that the doctrine of uniformitarianism was the guiding geological principle in the history of the earth. There was no room for cataclysm. (These things are dealt with in this book.)

In college, I sat in anthropology classes and listened to the way anthropologists, paleontologists, and other scientists of one name or another could take a tooth, a jawbone, or a portion of a skullcap determined to be of great age, and then build a model of some gigantic beast to fit the fragment. They even put fleshly and hairy exteriors on the products of their imaginations and sold it to the student as part of our heritage. I didn't buy it.

I took the classes, passed the tests, giving the appropriate answers, and I graduated. But down deep I didn't believe that which I had been taught was, in fact, the complete truth.

Some things such as mathematical probabilities of chance, the laws of thermodynamics, the fossil record, and especially the possibility of creationism were not fairly or even at all discussed. I had trouble with that. Gradually a search for truth began in me. This report deals with that search for truth.

The bottom line is that I am of the belief that we are not here by random chance, having accidentally evolved from a simple form such as unicellular organism. Accidents and random chance cannot be the Creator. I believe there is a purpose to life. I believe each of us have a purpose and we can fulfill it if we choose to ask for God's guidance, believe, and take the appropriate action. Life was not built by accident, there is someone with a "blueprint." We were created by purposeful design. "Chance" is not my God.

Based on my study of earth's history, I have come to these conclusions: *Geology has not been uniform throughout history. The geologic column in its entirety does not exist outside of the textbook. The history of the earth has the signature of cataclysm all over it. The earth has the signature of cataclysm by water.* All of this is obvious as we open our eyes and do our own study apart from the college classroom. This is my opinion, and I was heading in this direction even before I opened page one of the Bible.

As I look back on that college experience, I appreciate the science instructors and their desire to teach what they believed to be the truth of history. However, what I did learn from those teachers, and throughout much of my college classroom experience, was to be skeptical. I was skeptical of what I was being taught in the classroom.

The science teachers were, and are, educated in evolutionary and uniformitarian theories first taught by only a few learned men. The teachers then teach that which they were taught. This is to be expected. However, it is my opinion, and I believe the opinion of many highly educated people today, that the evolutionary and uniformitarian theories being taught to students who become the new teachers, are highly inaccurate. The theories are based on old information and incorrect interpretation of the scientific data. Possibly, new scientific discoveries by such people as astronomer Barry Setterfield on the "speed of light" will shed a new light on the time factor concerning the past, present, and future. His work is discussed in this book. So is work by Drs. Gentry, Brown, Morris, Macosko, and others.

The problem, I think, is also a spiritual problem. Because of the college curriculum, I was inevitably being taught to be skeptical about anything to do with religion. Obviously, if we had evolved, over a long period of time, we could not have been suddenly created. I carried this point of view for several years. Still, I had trouble with what I had been taught in the college classroom. I was quietly troubled over the conflict in my mind. Then, as the experiences of life began to fill the passing years, I admitted to myself that something was gently tugging at me from somewhere deep down inside. I had to deal with the conflict in my mind — which also seemed to be a conflict in my own spirit. I certainly did not understand that. At age 35, I asked Jesus Christ into my life. It was at that time that I started to read the Scripture. I believe that by this decision I found truth. It's hope and promise; it's a spiritual connection; it's God's grace; and it just makes sense. A couple of years or so later I read Violet Cummings' book *Has Anybody Really Seen Noah's Ark?* I then met her and her husband, Eryl. I also met Jim Irwin. These introductions were the beginning of this story.

During the years since I read that first book concerning the ark, I have read as much as I could find on the subjects of Noah's ark and the Genesis flood. In some of the books, I have read many accounts of reported sightings of the ark. I have even spoken with people who claim to have seen the ship several years ago as it lay in the ice and rocks of Ararat. By the vast numbers of reported sightings alone (200 or more since antiquity), one would then tend to believe there is something to the legitimacy of the reports. When a person considers the similarities of many of the reports, then the tendency to believe is further strengthened. You will have the opportunity to read many of those reports in this book. Some of the reports may have no basis in fact, or there may have been a misidentification of what was seen. However, understand this — it takes just one true sighting to put the ark on Ararat. Ultimately, truth is the object of our search, and it is by God's grace we will find it.

Maybe "God's grace" is the "why." It is not of ourselves, but of God's grace, a Creator with grace for all who accept the truth. I think this is the "why."

WHAT HAS BEEN FOUND?

Sunday, August 26, 1984, Denver, Colorado *Rocky Mountain News*

NOAH'S ARK FOUND ON TURKISH PEAK, AMERICAN-SPONSORED TEAM CLAIMS

ANKARA, Turkey — Five Americans and one Turkish explorer believe they have discovered Noah's ark on the southwestern face of Mount Ararat, a team spokesman said Saturday.

Colorado Springs astronaut James Irwin, leader of a fundamental Christian group, has tried unsuccessfully to find the ark over the past two years.

"Members of the team arrived at the site of a boat-shaped formation clearly visible at the 5,200-foot level on Wednesday and Thursday," said Marvin Steffins, the president of International Expeditions, based in his hometown of Monroe, La., and the head of the team.

"We believe further archeological investigation and scientific evaluation will prove this to be the site of the remains of the ark of Noah," he told a news conference.

On the same day the *Indianapolis Star* reports:

SITE OF NOAH'S ARK FOUND, EXPLORERS SAY

ANKARA, Turkey — U.S. explorers, including former astronaut James Irwin, have found a boat-shaped formation on Mount Ararat they believe is the site of the legendary wreck of Noah's ark, the group's leader said Saturday.

Marvin Steffins, president of International Expeditions, told reporters his group located the site Thursday 5,200 feet up the southern slopes of Mount Ararat in eastern Turkey.

"We cannot say that this is Noah's ark, but we believe we have found the site of it," Steffins said.

The news reports go on and on. Now to answer the question, "What has been found?"

Geologist Clifford Burdick, who in 1973 went to the site, believes the object is nothing more than a clay push-up in what some think is an old lava flow. After he saw it those many years ago, he wrote a report of his finding, some of which I will include here. I will show there are two opposing views, by at least three learned and scientifically educated professors. Each are highly influential men in their fields of expertise.

THE INITIAL DISCOVERY

About 1959, aerial photographs of parts of the Tendurek Mountains of eastern Turkey were brought to public notice. The point of interest was an elliptical formation, having an outline roughly that of a ship, which appeared in the photographs. Captain Sevket Kurtis, a Turkish flier, had taken these photographs and he brought them to Ohio State University where he was doing advanced work in connection with aerial surveying.

A specialist at Ohio State University, Arthur Brendenberger, upon examining the photographs believed that the object could be none other than the ark of Noah.

A picture was published in several magazines and newspapers. It appeared in *Life* magazine. The *Stats Zeitung and Herald*, Woodside, New Jersey, 15 November 1959, published the picture, with a caption: "Stereo-airphotos at Mount Ararat show a petrified boat in a field of lava, possibly Noah's ark of the Bible." About the same time, a writer in a newspaper in Columbus, Ohio, commented in part:

Discovered with stereoplanograph, the air photos were taken a year and a half ago on behalf of the Geodetic Institute of Turkey. But a curious object was recently discovered in one of the photos. It was discovered when in Ankara. Captain Ilhan Duripinar used a stereoplanograph in order to prepare maps. The size corresponds with the description of the ark in the Bible and in the Koran. The object has the form of a boat, 450' long and 160' wide. . . . Kurtis said that the object is sunk in a field of lava. A member of the Geodetic Institute of Ohio State University [Arthur Brendenberger] after he had seen the sterophotographs, said that he was convinced that the object could not be a product of nature, but was possibly "a petrified boat."

"There is a ship on Ararat," he declared positively, "and someone had better find out how it got there."[1]

It must be noted that the measurements included in this observation give the object what appears to be a 3 to 1 ratio, length to width. Remember this point as we read further. This next opinion by Clifford Burdick gives another explanation for the object:

THE ACTUAL FORMATION

The elevation of the formation in the Tendurek Mountains is about 6,000 feet. That seemed to us too low to agree with the reports of eyewitnesses, according to whom the ark is at an elevation of about 14,000 feet. . . .

The phenomenon in question lies along a broad, well-peneplaned contour. What had looked like a flow of lava in the aerial pictures turned out to be a deep deposit of clay, intermixed with small breccia, along the bed of a stream.

From a tectonic standpoint, apparently what had happened was that a small fault or fracture of about 450 feet (approximately the length of the ark) occurred along the bed of the stream. Actually, by pacing, I estimated 500 feet. The "prow" of the formation was uphill from the stern.

Apparently a granitic or rhyolitic type of intrusive lava had pushed up through the clay along the center of the formation, making an elevation ridge along the center. The ridge does look something like the keel of a ship — but upside-down. The outcrop of rock should have been an obvious clue to the nature of the phenomenon.

Apparently the extrusion widens a few feet below the surface. Along the center part of the formation, thus giving the whole thing the outline of a "ship." Possibly as the molten or plastic rock mass rose through the clay bed of the wash, it raised the hardened clay with it. The hardened clay did actually simulate the sides of the ship, and from a distance one could easily accept such an interpretation.

Although in an aerial view [a] formation may look quite ship-like, it does not take a geologist on the site long to dismiss the notion that the strange phenomenon is an actual ship.[2]

William H. Shea, Professor of Old Testament, Andrews University, Berrien Springs, Michigan, has this to say about the object and refers to both Burdick and Brendenberger. Shea relates:

> The expert in aerial photogrammetry (Brendenberger) from Ohio State University who read the film said of it before going to the field with the expedition, "I have no doubt at all that this object is a ship. In my entire career I have never seen an object like this on a stereo photo." This formation certainly does have the outline of a hull of a ship, which is a fact that no one has denied; and even Dr Burdick, who visited the site but does not relate it to the ark, was impressed with some of its ship-like characteristics, i.e., a prow "like the Queen Mary."
>
> The logical question that stems from this is, if this is the place where the ark landed, then where is the ark? Aerial photographs of this area in 1959 show that this formation lies in a lava flow, and this interpretation has been confirmed by surface observation since that time. Burdick, however, said it was a clay push-up. The answer to this question seems rather evident, therefore, since a ship constructed of wood in such a situation would have burned.
>
> In view of the hypothesis that wood may have burned where the soil lies within the confines of the walls of this "ship" is of some great interest. According to the color photograph of the outside of this clay wall above the crevasse, around its base shows a rather brown color mixed with the red of some iron oxides, as a geologist has pointed out to me.
>
> One might suggest, therefore, that the gray color of the soil inside this formation may be significant and the color could be an indication that the soil contains considerable ash.[3]

Burdick said it was "clay intermixed with small breccia along a stream bed." Breccia is simply a conglomerate ... pebbles of any type mixed and cemented together.

So we have diverse opinions and interpretations, and back and forth we go. We have an example that clearly shows us how the inaccurate science of geology in its findings is open to the individual interpretations of the geologist.

To further consider diversified opinions, let us investigate another possible explanation for the boat-shaped object and how it measures up.

Jim Irwin, while on one of his trips abroad, was told that the

Roman emperor Constantine was reported to have built a copy of the ark in approximately A.D. 300. Ron Wyatt had mentioned to me something to this effect, also. In his reading while on a trip to Jerusalem, Ron came across information indicating the Armenians may have built a copy of the ark also in approximately A.D. 300. An accurate source for this information cannot be pinpointed, but for the purpose of considering this possibility, let's assume an element of truth in this report.

Since Armenia was part of the Roman Empire in that time period,[4] I would imagine that both pieces of information could be based in fact, with Constantine in charge of, or giving the order that the Armenians do the labor. However, this possibility does bring about a question. Why would a Roman emperor be interested in Noah's ark? If even interested, why would he go so far as to build a copy of it?

Researching the answers to these questions came about almost unexpectedly when Bob Lambert, a well-read friend of mine, and at the time a flight dispatcher working for the same airline I do, loaned a book to me entitled, *Caesar and Christ*. On page 662 of this brilliantly written history by Will Durant, it says, "Constantine was known as the first Christian emperor."[5] Let us for a moment, take a brief look at Constantine.

Constantine fought in the British campaigns and was proclaimed emperor in A.D. 306, but accepted the lesser title of Caesar because he felt his life would be safer with the army at his back. On October 27, 312, Constantine saw a flaming cross in the sky with the Greek words, *en toa toi nika* — "in this sign, conquer." Constantine dreamed that a voice commanded him to have his soldiers mark upon their shield the letter X, with a line down through it curled around the top — symbol of Christ. On arising he obeyed, and then advanced into the forefront of battle carrying the initials of Christ interwoven with a cross. Constantine cast his lot with the Christians, who were numerous in his army, against the Roman Emperor, Maxentius. Constantine won this battle, the battle of the Mulvian Bridge, and Maxentius and thousands of his troops perished in the Tiber River. Constantine entered Rome as the undisputed victor.[6]

Constantine became the sole emperor of Rome at the end of a period when Christians had suffered much persecution and death at the hands of the Romans. Constantine put an end to the persecution:

> [Constantine] recalled the Christian exiles, and restored
> to all "confessors" their lost privileges and properties. While

still proclaiming liberty of worship for all, he now definitely declared himself a Christian, and invited his subjects to join him in celebrating his new faith.[7]

It was Constantine who ordered a church of the Holy Sepulcher to be built over the tomb of Christ in Jerusalem. At the time of his death at age 64 due to illness, Constantine called for a priest to administer to him the sacrament of baptism, which he had purposely deferred to this moment, hoping to be cleaned by it from all the sins of his crowded life. Then the tired ruler laid aside the purple robes of royalty, put on the white garb of a Christian neophyte, and passed away.[8]

Yes, I think this "defender of Christianity" could possibly have had an interest, and ordered a copy of the ark to be built. If in fact he did, and whether or not it was an exact copy, is another question to be dealt with. If, indeed, there was a copy built, then it should have been built in the exact measurements as the original ark.

Keep in mind, if we are to believe the accuracy of the facts as given to us in the Bible, then the Bible is the blueprint we must go by. Genesis 6:15 gives the measurement of Noah's ark as 300 x 50 x 30 in terms of cubits. If the measurement of 300 cubits long is accounted for in the boat-shaped object, then the width of 50 cubits must also be accounted for when reading the measurements of the same blueprint. Professor Shea says this about the measurements of the boat-shaped object:

> According to a second set of more accurate measurements taken from the aerial photographs, this formation is said to have measured 500 feet long and 160 feet at its widest point. Though the ground measurements have not been reported in detail, they were said to confirm the measurements made from the photographs. (Author: This set of measurements gives us approximately a 3 to 1 ratio.)

> It is necessary to estimate the length of the cubit employed in the biblical record of the dimensions of the ark, in order to find any correlation in modern measurement.

> The length of the cubit varied from place to place and time to time in the ancient world. While the use of an antediluvian (before the Flood) cubit cannot be ruled out, it is just as likely, if not more so, that these measurements were given in terms of postdiluvian (after the Flood) cubits. It is suggested by the very use of the Semitic word for cubit here,

since it derives from a particular postdiluvial language family. If one compares the Mesopotamian cubit of 19.6 inches for the ark's cubit with the original measurements of 150 meters for this formation, they are just about the same, at 490 feet.

In the times of the Israelite monarchy, the Hebrew cubit varied from the "old" cubit of 17.5 inches (2 Chron. 3:3) to the "long" cubit (Ezek. 40:5, 43:13) which was approximately equivalent to the Egyptian cubit of 20.6 inches. Moses has been credited with the authorship of this passage of Scripture and the cubit with which he was familiar during Egyptian education may well have been the standard by which he set down these figures.

The longer Egyptian cubit, as reported here, would give the ark a length measurement of 515 feet, and the shorter cubit a length of only 437.5 feet. The boat-shaped object measures 500 feet long. Understand this point — we do not actually know how large the cubit was at that time. Robert W. Faid, a nuclear scientist and author, tells us "The cubit was a measurement from a man's elbow to the tip of his middle finger."[9]

Genesis 6:4 tells us, "There were giants in the earth in those days" (before the Flood). This may indicate the cubit was much larger than the measurements of the postdiluvian cubit. Noah and his sons could have been physically big men, consequently, a bigger cubit, a bigger ark. We do not know. However, we do know the Bible gives us measurements of a 6 to 1 ratio in the ark's construction.

Dr. Shea continues the discussion of the cubit in terms of the width of the ark:

> In the first place, we do not know precisely how this biblical measurement for the width of the ark was made. The ancients practiced mathematics differently than we do now in some respects. The use of inclusive reckoning whereby any fraction came to stand for the whole is one example (cf. 2 Kings 18:9–10). If some sort of averaging was employed to measure the width of an elliptical hull, then that figure must have come out differently than the way we now measure the widest points on this formation.
>
> We also should allow for the possibility that this formation may now be wider than it was originally. It is interesting to note in this connection what marine archaeologists have

learned about shipwrecks that have rested on the bottom of the Mediterranean Sea for centuries and millennia. As ships have disintegrated, in some cases sections of their hulls have fallen outwards. While the conditions under which these ships fell apart were not identical to those obtained in the Tendurek Mountains, it is possible that any remains of the ark here could have suffered a similar fate.

Another possibility is that a geologic event(s) could have caused some spreading or fracturing. We now know that an earthquake damaged this formation between the summers of 1977 and 1979. Since this formation is located in a geologically active region, such damage could have also occurred in the more remote past.

Perhaps the most important point about this comparison of measurements is that its length corresponds quite closely with the measurements given in the Bible. Since the ark was only 1/6 as wide as it was long, however, destruction or disintegration could have altered its configuration and dimensions more significantly in width. The 160-foot width of the boat-shaped object gives it a 3 to 1 ratio. In other words, when compared with the biblical measurements of the ark, the length of this formation is of greatest significance, its width is of intermediate significance, and its height is of least significance. In the dimension that counts the most — the length — the fit between this formation and measurements of the ark in the Bible is most precise.[10]

Keeping in mind that the boat-shaped object in question has a length to width ratio of 3 to 1, a comparison should be made from another source.

LaHaye and Morris state in their book *The Ark on Ararat*:

It is interesting to note that many modern-day vessels are built on design specifications similar to those of the ark. Modern-day mathematical studies have shown that the ark must have been a remarkably stable ship. Experienced designers will recognize that the ratio of length to width of 6 to 1 is considered to be the optimum design for stability, and is used in construction of many different types of ships, from warships to racing sailboats.

It would appear that in order to build a racing sailboat, which is much the same shape as the boat-shaped object, with a 6:1 ratio, then

as Dr. Shea previously indicated, some form of mathematical aver-
aging may be used. This is to say that the racing sailboat is not a
parallelogram barge. I believe the stability of the ship gives us a key
to understanding the mystery.

Lahaye and Morris continue:

> The length of the ark, 450 feet or so (using an 18-inch
> cubit), would tend to provide insurance that the ark would
> not be subjected to any wave of equal magnitude acting
> throughout its entire length. The ark's chances for capsizing
> were, therefore, lessened.
>
> The cross section of 75 feet by 45 feet (18-inch cubit) is
> also significant. The center of gravity for such a section can
> be calculated as well as the buoyant forces of the water for
> any given degree of tilt, and conclusions drawn. It can be
> shown that for any degree of tilt up to 90 degrees, the ark
> would tend to right itself. Noah's ark was indeed optimally
> designed to perform under adverse conditions.[11]

The idea promoted here is that the ark is a parallel-sided barge-
like construction.

Mrs. Violet Cummings, in her book *Has Anybody Really Seen
Noah's Ark?* says this in reference to measurement of the ark:

> Leading Bible scholars have come to some remarkable
> conclusions on their own regarding the appearance and
> construction of the ark. For instance, according to
> McClintock & Strong's Cyclopedia, "The original Hebrew
> word for Noah's vessel, as used in the biblical account of the
> Deluge, is *tebah*, denoting a chest, or ark, which is differen-
> tiated from the term describing the sacred ark of the cov-
> enant, in that it denotes something designed to float upon the
> waters." Another source describes it like this: "If we examine
> the passage in Genesis 6:15–16 we can only draw from it the
> conclusion that this ark was not a boat or a ship; but . . . a
> 'building in the form of a parallelogram' . . . that it was not
> a 'regularly built vessel,' but merely intended to float at large
> upon the water. We may, therefore, probably with justice,
> regard it as a large, oblong, floating house, with a roof either
> flat or only slightly inclined. It was constructed with three
> stories and had a door on the side.

Alexander Heidel points out that the Hebrew word
tebah is related to the Egyptian *db't*, which is sometimes

translated "coffin." Heidel states, "Outside of the Flood account it is used only as Moses' ark in the Nile . . . as evidenced by its dimensions and the names by which it was designated in Greek and Hebrew, (it) was a flat-bottomed, rectangular construction, square on both ends and straight up the sides." However, since a coffin is usually designed with slightly sloping sides, this conclusion fits in very well with Lee's drawing of the ark.[12]

I'll let you come to your conclusions on this matter, but for me it seems as though the engineers have given ample reason for the size of the ark as reported in the Bible.

I suggest we stick to what is recorded in the Holy Bible, which is considered by most believers to be the true Word of God. I suggest we use the biblical blueprint, because we must have a place to start. For instance, if a 6 to 1 ratio is indeed considered by modern shipbuilders to be the most stable of dimensions for ocean-going vessels, then one must wonder why the intelligence of God would choose any other than what would be the most suitable to withstand the turbulent waters during the cataclysmic event of the Genesis flood, especially in a ship with such an important cargo.

To answer the question of this chapter, "What has been found?" — possibly only a geological formation that looks like a ship; possibly only dirt. Excavation is needed to find the truth. Turkey has not allowed it. The next question is, "What is reported to have been seen?" Let's start in Russia.

RUSSIAN ACCOUNTS

From the pages of *The Genesis Flood*:

Rumors of the reported discovery of the ark, preserved high on the snow-covered slopes of Mount Ararat, have been published from time to time. These have never been confirmed, however, and more than one expedition to the area has failed in the attempt to locate it. We fear that any hope of its preservation for the thousands of years of postdiluvian history is merely wishful thinking. Even if it had been preserved through burial and freezing, it would be so hard to find that nothing less than divine direction should ever lead explorers to its true location.[1]

Now to the question of *Where is Noah's Ark?* The true facts in any of the following sightings is subject to guesswork, but this is what we have to go on.

Violet Cummings' book, *Has Anybody Really Seen Noah's Ark?* contains the Roskovitsky story. His real name could have been "Zabolotsky," but for possibly his personal reasons, the name "Roskovitsky" is used in this report from Violet Cummings:

For the benefit of readers unfamiliar with this widely circulated story, so often branded as false, we produce it here just as it appears in the *New Eden* magazine, circa 1939. The Editor's Note, following the title of the article, "Noah's Ark Found," with the by-line Vladimiar Roskovitsky, explains: "The following story by Mr. Roskovitsky, a converted Russian, speaks for itself. He is now engaged in selling Bibles, etc. and is an American citizen, having severed all ties with Godless Bolshevism, from which he so narrowly escaped with his life, after discovering the ark. He gives this discovery credit for opening his eyes to the truth of the Bible, and we pass it along trusting that you will find it of interest and value."

The now-famous story follows, just as it appeared in *New Eden:*

It was in the days just before the Russian revolution that this story really began.

A group of us Russian aviators were stationed at a temporary air outpost about 25 miles northwest of Mount Ararat. [The report by LaHaye and Morris in *The Ark on Ararat* gives the air outpost 25 miles northeast of Ararat — this could be significant.]

The day was dry and terribly hot, as August days so often are in the semi-desert land.

Even the lizards were flattened out under the shady sides of rocks or twigs, their mouths open and tongues lashing out as if each panting breath would be their last. Only occasionally would a tiny wisp of air rattle the parched vegetation and stir up a choking cloudlet of dust.

Farther up on the side of the mountain, we could see a thunder shower, while still farther up we could see the white snow-cap of Mount Ararat, which has snow all year round because of its great height. How we longed for some of that snow!

Then the miracle happened. The captain walked in and announced that plane number seven had its new supercharger installed and was ready for high-altitude tests, and ordered my buddy and me to make the test. At least, we could escape the heat!

Needless to say, we lost no time getting on our parachutes, strapping on our oxygen cans, and doing all the other half-dozen little things that have to be done before "going-up."

Then a climb into the cockpits, safety belts fastened, a mechanic gives the prop a flip, and yells, "Contact," and in less time than it takes to tell it, we were in the air. No use wasting time warming up the engine, when the sun already had it nearly red hot.

We circled the field several times, until we hit the 14,000-foot mark, and then stopped climbing for a few minutes to get used to the altitude.

I looked over to the right at the beautiful snow-capped

peak, now just a little above us, and for some reason that I can't explain, turned and headed the plane straight toward it.

My buddy turned around and looked at me with question marks in his eyes, but there was too much noise for him to ask questions.

After all, twenty-five miles doesn't mean much at a hundred miles an hour.

As I looked down at the great stone battlements surrounding the lower part of the mountain, I remembered having heard that it has never been climbed since the year 700 before Christ, when some pilgrims were supposed to have gone up there to scrape tar off an old shipwreck to make good luck emblems to wear around their necks, to prevent their crops from being destroyed by excessive rainfall. The legend said that they left in haste, after a bolt of lightning struck near them, and they never returned. Silly ancients. Who ever heard of looking for a shipwreck on a mountaintop?

A couple of circles around the snow-capped dome, and then a long, swift glide down the side, and then we suddenly came upon a perfect little gem of a lake, blue as an emerald, but still frozen over on the shady side.

We circled around and returned for another look at it.

Suddenly my companion whirled around and yelled something, and excitedly pointed down at the overflow end of the lake. I looked and nearly fainted!

A submarine! No, it wasn't, for it had stubby masts, but the top was rounded over with only a flat catwalk about five feet across down the length of it. What a strange craft, built as though the designer had expected the waves to roll over the top most of the time, and had engineered it to wallow in the sea like a log, with those stubby masts carrying only enough sail to keep it facing the waves. [Years later in the Great Lakes, I saw the famous "whaleback" ore carriers with this same kind of rounded deck.]

We flew down as close as safety permitted, and took several circles around it. We were surprised when we got close to it at the immense size of the thing, for it was as long as a city block, and would compare very favorably in size to modern battleships of today. It was grounded on the shore of the lake with about one-fourth of the rear end still running out into the water, and its extreme rear was three-fourths under water. It had been partly dismantled on one side near the front, and on the other side there was a great door nearly 20 feet square, but with the door gone. This seemed quite out of proportion as even today ships seldom have doors even half that large.

After seeing all we could from the air, we broke all speed records back down to the airport. When we related our find, the laughter was loud and long. Some accused us of getting drunk on too much oxygen, and there were many other remarks too numerous to relate.

The captain, however, was serious. He asked several questions and ended by saying, "Take me up there. I want to look at it."

We made the trip without incident and returned to the airport.

"What do you make of it?" I asked, as we climbed out of the plane.

"Astounding," he replied. "Do you know what ship that is?"

"Of course not, Sir."

"Ever hear of Noah's ark?"

"Yes, Sir, but I don't know what the legend of Noah's ark has to do with us finding this strange thing 14,000 feet up on a mountaintop."

"This strange craft," explained the captain, "is Noah's ark. It has been sitting up there for nearly 5,000 years. Being frozen up for nine or ten months of the year, it couldn't rot, and has been in cold storage, as it were all this time. You have made the most amazing discovery of the age!"

"When the captain sent his report to the Russian government, it aroused considerable interest, and the czar sent two special companies of soldiers to climb the mountain. One group of 50 men attacked one side and the other group of 100 men, attacked the mountain from the other side.

Two weeks of hard work were required to chop out a trail along the cliffs of the lower part of the mountain, and it was nearly a month before the ark was reached by the 100, and seen by the 50.

Complete measurements were taken and plans drawn of it, as well as many photographs, all of which were sent to the czar of Russia.

The ark was found to contain hundreds of small rooms and some rooms very large with high ceilings. The large rooms usually had a fence of great timbers across them, some of which were two feet thick, as though designed to hold beasts ten times as large as elephants. Other rooms were lined with tiers of cages somewhat like one sees today at a poultry show, only instead of chicken wire, they had rows of tiny wrought iron bars across the fronts.

Everything was heavily painted with a wax-like paint resembling shellac, and the workmanship of the craft showed all the signs of a high type of civilization.

The wood used throughout was oleander, which belongs to the cypress family, and never rots, which of course, coupled with the facts of it being painted and it being frozen most of the time, account for its perfect preservation.

The expedition found on the peak of the mountain above the ship, the burned remains of the timbers that were missing out of the one side of the ship. It seems that these timbers had been hauled up on the top of the peak and used to build a tiny one-room shrine, inside of which was a rough stone hearth like the altars the Hebrews used for sacrifices, and it had either caught fire from the altar, or been struck by lightning, as the timbers were considerably burned and charred, and the roof was completely burned off.

A few days after this expedition sent its report to the czar, the government was overthrown and godless Bolshevism took over, so that the records were never made public, and were probably destroyed in the zeal of the Bolsheviks to discredit all religion and belief in the truth of the Bible.[2]

This same *New Eden* account is quoted in the book *Doomsday 1999 A.D.* by Charles Berlitz; Berlitz puts the date of this Los Angeles magazine article as 1940.

As I considered this report and its validity, I decided to investigate the possibility of an aircraft of World War I vintage having the capability of reaching an altitude of 14,000 feet, and more. The question to be answered is, what was the ceiling of the aircraft used? The ceiling or service ceiling, is calculated to be the maximum altitude the airplane is capable of attaining under standard conditions; standard conditions pertaining to variables such as air density, altitude, ambient temperature, gross width, etc. In late November 1984, I discussed this briefly with Russ Tarvin, a member of the Order of Daedalians, an elite organization of ex-military pilots. Mr. Tarvin told me that in past conversations with World War I pilots, they had said they could get their planes to 17,000 feet or more.

Reggie Sinclair, a World War I pilot, flew the French-made Spade (he describes it as the finest aircraft in WWI). I spoke with Mr. Sinclair by phone on December 7, and he told me he was able to climb his Spade, powered by a 220 horse-powered engine, to 18,000 feet with "no strain."

I had the opportunity to visit with Dr. Jim Parks of Parker, Colorado, and toured his WWI museum.

Dr. Parks, a gynecologist by profession, has accumulated, in what has been a lifelong pursuit, what is probably one of the finest collections of WWI records and memorabilia in existence today.

Jim has made this museum very personal. He has displayed the uniforms of many of his friends, and the fathers and relatives of his friends, among others, from all over the world, on manikins constructed expertly to look like the person the uniform originally belonged to. At least 40 uniformed manikins, complete with medals, awards, and photographs, line the walls of his museum. It is impossible for me to accurately describe what Jim Parks has accumulated over the years — one would have to see it for himself. It will be sufficient for me to say that in the near future the museum will be given a proper place for displaying in a special hall at the U.S. Air Force Academy in Colorado Springs, Colorado.

In Jim's vast library, he was able to find the information I was seeking pertaining to the performance of the aircraft used in WWI. I wanted to read the manufacturer's specifications, and see on paper the answer to my question: How high could those planes go?

I was not disappointed. There were nine pages in one book alone, listing the various aircraft flown: models, engine types and horse-power ratings, dimensions, and operating altitudes. The service ceilings of the many planes flown were all there, plus much more.

The Russians flew mainly French-made aircraft: Moranes, Nieuports, and Spades pretty much dominated the scene, and these planes had ceilings (depending on which model and engine) of 15,000 feet up to, in one case, 27,000 feet. Most were in the area of 18,000 to 21,000 feet, and of 17 models I read about, only 2 had a ceiling less than 14,000. Superchargers are not mentioned. If there was a newly designed supercharger installed in any of the planes, the altitudes certainly could have been increased. Any of these vintage aircraft could have been used. An American-built or British-built plane, the

American Thomas-Morcse, or the Standard or LePere, were certified from 15,000, 14,800, and 20,000 feet respectively. The British Bristol and Austin-Ball had ceilings from 15,500 feet to 22,000 feet.

There are many others I could mention, such as the Sopwith or Vickers, and of 13 British or American models, the service ceilings of only two are calculated to be below 14,500 feet and they were low-powered trainers.

Most of the WWI aircraft had engines capable of developing 200 to 400 horsepower.

I have no trouble at all with the technical possibility of WWI aircraft reaching altitudes of 14,000 feet and above. It was done on a regular basis.

For the purpose of added credibility to this reported sighting, I am including a weather report, based on a study by C. Allen Roy formerly of Touchet, Washington, now living in Beaver Creek, Oregon. Mr. Roy is a student of archaeology. The results of this particular study were published in a *Bible Science Newsletter* of July 16, 1978: "Was It Hot or Not?" Mr. Roy says:

> To further probe into the trustworthiness of the reported sightings of Noah's ark, I decided to study the past weather conditions to see whether the date of the claimed sightings corresponded with favorable weather conditions. The first thing I discovered was that there is no data available from any point within 100 miles of Mount Ararat. This eliminated the hope that absolute values of precipitation, temperature, and snow accumulation would be available. That leaves only relative values from year-to-year to work with.

> The general weather conditions for a 500-mile diameter region about Ararat has been calculated from an average of seven stations per year. These stations were chosen from most of the various types of climate found in the area — high and low altitudes, dry and wet, hot and cold — in order to get the general conditions by eliminating local variation.

The ideal conditions would have been years with low precipitation and high temperatures, that is, hot and dry. "From 1916 to 1917 (the WWI period) there are five separate reports from Turkish and Russian soldiers concerning Noah's ark in the midst of the Great War. Since both of these years were hot and dry, they surely pass the test with flying colors."[3]

I conclude my comments about this sighting with this summation:

The air outpost was 25 miles northwest of Ararat (according to Mrs. Cummings' book), so Rotskovitsky probably approached the mountain from that direction. He circled the mountain two times; the question is, which way? Since he mentions cockpits, and being that it was 1916, I'm sure it would have been a tandem seating aircraft, so the pilot could get a good view from either side, circling either direction. I'm going to assume that the winds were not a real factor as he circled around the mountain, so down drafts on the leeward side must not have been much. I'm also going to assume that he circled to his right. First, because he initially turned to the right to get to the mountain. Also, because as he descended, he may have planned a descent in a right turn around the mountain in order to return to his airfield. Or in other words, a clockwise direction. I think this is the way I would have approached the mountain in this case. However, we don't know what he did, and in a tandem seating aircraft, it would make no difference which way he circled as the view would have been just as good from either side for either pilot.

If the airbase was on the "northeast of Ararat" (as is stated in *The Ark on Ararat*, by LaHaye & Morris),[5] then a descent down the northeast side makes sense. However, almost anything seems possible. About all we know for sure is that he circled the dome and glided down. The sighting was somewhere down from the top, in a lake.

The two groups of soldiers which were sent after him "attacked" the mountain from two sides. On the northeast is a rugged area. It took two weeks to chop out a trail in the lower part of the cliffs. There is also a very difficult and rugged area on the southeast side of the mountain. The glide down the south side before his sighting, according to Mrs. Cummings, makes this area a real possibility. There is also a rugged canyon on the north.

Other WWI reports of Russian origin have filtered down over the years. Violet Cummings reports, "Captain Benjamin Franklin Allen, a retired army officer and creation geologist, had letters from a relative and a friend (who had never chanced to meet), who had told the same story of two men, both now deceased, who had served in the czar's army during WWI, and had participated in expeditions to Mount Ararat, where the ark had been sighted in a remote canyon of the peak."[6]

If peak means near the top, then this could be significant.

In a casual conversation with a neighbor, Capt. Benjamin Franklin Allen had learned certain "basic facts" concerning two former soldiers in the czarís White Russian Army, who claimed that they had taken part in two separate expeditions to verify a report that an aviator had sighted a "suspicious looking structure in one of Ararat's obscure canyons." They had later escaped to the northwestern United States at the time the Bolsheviks took over the czar's regime. It was claimed that these two men had never met; nevertheless, their stories agreed. Since these two former soldiers, Georgenson, a Dane, and Schilleroff, a German, were both attested by their relatives to be "sober and reliable men," their information had, without question, been accepted as accurate.

While in the Russian Army, the story goes, they were ordered to pack for a long tramp up into the mountains of Ararat. A Russian aviator had sighted what looked to him like a huge wooden structure in a small lake. About two-thirds of the way up, probably a little farther, they stopped on a high cliff, and in a small valley below them was a dense swamp in which the object could be seen. It appeared like a huge ship or barge with one end under water, and only one corner could be clearly seen from where these men stood. . . . Georgensen, the man who gave this account, obviously had made this trip in company with the czar's fifty-man expedition who sighted the ship, but who were unable to reach it from where they stood.[7]

To comment on this, I can say I have a little problem with the "dense swamp" which was mentioned. There simply is no such thing on Ararat. Of course, my own definition of a "swamp" may be different than theirs. Perhaps in their definition it simply means an accumulation of water.

In quoting directly from Violet Cummings:

The also-famous Rosseya story parallels the Roskovitsky accounts. The story was published in the White Russian publication *Rosseya*, around 1945 or 1946. (*Rosseya* had offices in New York.) Eyrl Cummings first learned of this story from a Mrs. Larabee-Platt, a former missionary at the Presbyterian College in Persia (now Iran) who, because of her contact with Cummings, had become vitally interested in ark research. Translated into English, the 4,000-word article contained details of one of the czar's two-phased ground expeditions to which Roskovitsky, Schilleroff, and Georgensen had only alluded. These details, too, could only have been recounted by one who had personally accompanied the group. The article in *Rosseya* had been authored by a Col. Alexander A. Koor, formerly an officer in the czar's White Russian Army stationed in the Ararat region in November of 1915, during WWI.

The *Rosseya* story concerns the second group described by Roskovitsky, in which a number of scientists and specialists took part. It begins by briefly reiterating the account of the initial discovery by air, describing the huge structure resembling a submarine, with the remains of a superstructure still visible in the center. The vessel leaned on one side toward the shore of the little lake in which it was partly submerged; and on this side, near the nose of the ship, was an asymmetrical opening, or hole, broken by accident or, perhaps, by necessity. On the other side was a great doorway with the door itself missing.

According to this account, it had taken some time for the report of the aviator's discovery to reach the ears of the czar, who ordered an immediate and scientific ground expedition to verify the exciting report. It was not until the end of December 1917, according to the article, that the two research divisions of 150 infantrymen, army engineers, and specialists reached the site after a month of the most difficult and arduous work. In time the hardy, winter-injured Russians did reach the lake and the ark. They had traversed a "wild and inaccessible locality," braving severe snowstorms and falling ice. It had been necessary to clear a trail and cut steps to the site; they endured the incredible hardships of sleeping in the snow, of hunger and freezing, as well as the shortage or delays of receiving food supplies.

The rigors of the difficult campaign were all but forgotten, said the story, when the men finally reached the object of their search. As the huge ship at last loomed before them, an awed silence descended. . . . "Without a word of command everyone took off his hat, looking reverently toward the ark; everybody knew, feeling it in his heart and soul . . . that they were in the actual presence of the ark." Many "crossed themselves and whispered a prayer," said an eyewitness account. It was like being in a church, and the hands of the archaeologist trembled as he snapped the shutter of the camera and took a picture of the old boat as if she were "on parade."

The investigating party found that the ship was, indeed, of a "huge size"; measurements disclosed it to be about 500 feet in length. These dimensions, when compared with a twenty-inch cubit, fitted "quite proportionately" with the size of Noah's ark as described in Genesis 6:15. The entire rear end of the ship was in ice. Through the broken hatchway near the front of the boat, however, the investigating party was able to enter first the upper room, a "very narrow one with a high ceiling." From here "side by side to it, stretched rooms of various sizes; small and large ones."

There was also "a very large room, separated as if by a great fence of huge trunks of trees," possibly "stables for the huge animals," such as elephants and hippopotami. On the walls of the rooms were cages, arranged in lines all the way from the floor to the ceiling, and they had marks of rust from the iron rods which were there before. There were very many various rooms, similar to these, apparently several hundreds of them. It was not possible exactly to count them, because the lower rooms and even a part of the upper ones — all this was filled with hard ice. In the middle of the ship there was a corridor. The end of this corridor was "overloaded with broken partitions."

The story went on: "The ark was covered from inside as well as from outside with some kind of a dark brown color resembling wax and varnish." The wood of which the ark was built was excellently preserved except (1) at the hole in the front of the ship, and (2) at the door-hole in the side of the ship; there the wood was porous and it broke easily.

This analysis of the wood showed it to be similar to the cedar and the larch tree, which are related to the family of the cypress trees "which cannot decay." [It might be interesting to mention that the controversial "gopher wood" mentioned in Genesis as the material form which Noah constructed the ark, is described in *Strong's Exhaustive Concordance of the Bible* as coming from "an unused root, probably meaning to house in: a kind of tree or wood — as used for building — apparently the cypress."]

The *Rosseya* article went on to state, as had the Roskovitsky account, that the description and measurements of the ark, both inside and out, together with photos, plans, and samples of wood, were sent at once by special courier to the office of the chief commandant of the army "as the czar had ordered." The article concluded, "But not so . . . had Fate destined. By the time the courier had been sent on his way, the Bolsheviks had taken over the old czarist regime. The courier was intercepted and, if the rumors were correct, he was shot, and his important documents eventually fell into the hands of Trotsky himself."[8]

The author of this account, Col. Alexander A. Koor, had first been contacted by Eryl Cummings in Seattle, Washington. Cummings had spent ten days in the New York offices of *Rosseya*, anxiously awaiting information as to the author's whereabouts. Understandably suspicious at first, the publishers finally provided the information. Col. Koor was at the home of General Jacob Elshin. Cummings was soon on a plane flying across an entire continent to the northwest. Here another careful screening took place before General Elshin had satisfied himself of the sincerity of his guest, and — at last — Cummings found himself face-to-face with the man he had come so far to see. A warm friendship soon developed between Cummings and the two highly cultured White Russian families who were so far from their original homes in the Ukraine.

The 80-year old Elshi, a four-star Russian general, proved to be a much-decorated veteran of two great wars, a man considered as a "great humanitarian and scholar." He held honorary memberships in both the American International Academy in Washington, D.C., as well as the Andras Research University in Andras, India. Colonel Koor, a much younger man, and a close friend, had been commander of troops guarding the Araratsky Pass in a remote area near the base of Aghri Dagh during the closing years of the First World War. He had fought against the Bolsheviks, escaped into Manchuria, and with his wife and child, eventually reached asylum in the United States.

Both General Elshin and Colonel Koor were personally acquainted with members of the czar's ground parties sent to the site of the ark. They were delighted to learn that further investigation to verify the discovery was underway.

Colonel Koor immediately offered the assistance of his own years of personal research. On March 1, 1946, he supplied "data" from the "official records of the Russian Caucasian Army, 1914–1917, by General E.B. Mavlovsky."

To quote Colonel Koor:

> The 14th battalion came to the front in the summer of 1916 from Russia. I understand that the discovery of Noah's ark was in the end of 1916, with the scouting parties having to wait until the summer of 1917. I know that Sergeant Boris V. Rujansky belonged to the 14th battalion. I understand, and it is logical, that the first and second parties of the expedition to Mount Ararat were formed from the local force of the 14th battalion . . . by order from the local brigade headquarters. Sergeant Rujansky was sent to join the party because he was a specialist. In 1916 the 3-D Caucasian Detachment, under the command of 1st Lt. Zabolotsky, served air duty over the region at Mount Ararat, Lake Van, and Lake Urmia. This aviation detachment served the 4th Caucasian Corps, and the Army Aviation Inspector was Captain Koorbatoff. I hope 1st Lt. Zabolotsky is the man you are looking for, for he, from an airplane, sighted the ark and started the investigation. Captain Koorbatoff was his supervisor.

How does this fit in with the story told years later by a man claiming to be Vladimir Roskovitsky, the Russian flier who had discovered the ark? This plausible explanation is suggested: After making their escape, the four Russian fliers may very well have changed their names (as many of the refugees did) to avoid pursuit and the vengeance of their Bolshevik foes. It seems entirely possible that "Zabolotsky" became "Roskovitsky." Of course, if we may assume this to be the case, the name on his report to the czar would have appeared in the official records as "Zabolotsky," since the Revolution had not yet taken place, and he had not made his escape.

In a certified "To Whom It May Concern" statement, Colonel Koor provided the following additional information:

> This is to certify that I, Alexander A. Koor, former colonel and Chief-in-Command of the 19th Petropaulovsky regiment, heard the following concerning the discovery of Noah's ark:

(1) 1st Lt. Paul Vaslivich Rujansky of the 156th Elisavewtpolsky Caucasian Army. I knew all of Rujansky's family for years. I met them in the city of Kazan, Russia, where I attended the government Military Academy. 1st Lt. Rujansky was wounded in Erzurum when his regiment took Chaban Dede, central fort of the Erzurum fortifications. He was relieved from active duty and sent to work in the Commandant's office, in the city of Irkutsk, Siberia. After the Bolsheviks made an uprising he moved to the city of Harbin, Manchuria, where I found him in 1921.

(2) Lt. Peter Nicolovich Leslin of the 26th Ahichinsky regiment, also the Caucasion Army. During the Bolshevik uprising he was arrested, but escaped from them, and in December 1918, joined my Petropaulovsky regiment.

(3) About July or August 1921, Lt. Leslin and I met 1st Lt. Rujansky in Harbin. During one of our conversations, 1st Lt. Rujansky told me about the discovery of Noah's ark. He (1st Lt. Rujansky) didn't know about the details because he was wounded and sent to Russia, but he knew because his brother, Boris Vasilivich Rujansky, Sergeant of the Military Railroad Battalion, was a member of the investigating party which was sent to mount Ararat to corroborate the discovery of Noah's ark.

Lieutenant Leslin admitted he had also heard about the discovery of Noah's ark, not as a rumor, but as news, from the Senior Adjutant of his division, who had told him that Noah's ark was found in the saddle of two peaks of Mount Ararat.

This is all I heard from these two officers, and I am sure both told me the truth.

(signed) Col. Alexander A. Koor[9]

Something additional about Col. Koor:

To Colonel Koor — scholar, researcher, author, historian, and expert in ancient languages, a specialist in the ancient history of Russia and the Far East guages, a specialist in the ancient history of Russia and the Far East — belongs the important discovery in 1915 of the Sumerian inscriptions at Karada. This is a small peak in the foothills of Greater Ararat on the remote Araratsky Pass. Some of the pictorial figures on the cliff have been defaced by the passing

of centuries of time, but an inscription clearly tells the story
of the Great Deluge:

> God sowed the seeds of the word into the waters
> . . . the waters filled the earth, descending from above
> . . . his children came to rest on the mountain or peak.[10]

Included in this section is a slightly different account, related by
an aging Russian woman named Eva Ebling. As a young woman she
barely escaped with her life after the death of her father, a high-
ranking medical officer in the czar's White Russian Cossack Army
prior to the Bolshevik Revolution. Intimate details could have been
related to her only by someone personally acquainted with the
circumstances surrounding the story. Her account shows sincerity
and carries a ring of truth and is worthy of inclusion at this point.

Responding to a Noah's ark interview with Eryl
Cummings on the NBC "Tomorrow" show in 1974, one
listener stated that the father of an elderly relative had seen
the ark in or about 1917. Arrangements were quickly made
to visit and to ascertain the facts from this relative — Eva
Ebling — in her adopted Canada, where she had lived for
many years.

[Author: While attending a convention of ark enthusi-
asts in Farmington, New Mexico, June 1986, I met Al
Holderbecker from Appleton, Minnesota, a nephew of the
late Mrs. Ebling. He confirmed this story to me, and also told
of her escape from Russia and the journey which eventually
led her to Canada.]

Briefly, her story is this:

A second expedition to the ark had taken place sometime shortly after it was learned that the report of the czar's
first ill-fated expedition to the ship had been confiscated and
the courier reported shot. It is impossible to pinpoint the
exact date of this second attempt, but we can assume this
daring group braved incredible dangers, not only from the
difficult climb, but also in successfully eluding the revolu-
tionary Bolsheviks who were overrunning the land.

This second group included medical personal evidently
associated with the royal household, and Eva understood
that the czarina herself went along. Her father, a medical
officer, accompanied the group. There is some confusion in
the story, since history informs us that the empress was a

partial invalid, sometimes confined to a wheelchair because of the heart condition which later caused her death. She certainly would not be a likely candidate for such a strenuous undertaking as a climb up the rugged Mount Ararat.

However, the empress' youngest daughter, Anastasia, in her late teens, was described as "a loner and a tomboy . . . daring," and was regarded by her parents as "self-reliant enough to wrangle out of any scrape she got herself into."[11]

Mrs. Ebling informed us that this second expedition actually succeeded in reaching the mountain and attempted to climb the steep steps so recently hacked in the rocks by the 100-man group. It seems that the female member of the party, whoever she may have been, was more agile than her companions and outdistanced them on the climb. Unfortunately, the party was not able to complete the ascent, but the group did reach a point where the ark was plainly visible and they were able to photograph it before starting their descent.

Eva Ebling explained that her father died a year later from typhoid fever. Before his death he entrusted his precious pictures of the ark to his wife and her stepmother, who later joined the Bolsheviks and turned the photographs over to them. But of course, Eva had already seen the pictures many times.[12]

There are other reports of Russian origin listed on the pages of Mrs. Cummings' book. These have been some of them. A question that must be considered is to ask if the evidence of these sightings, and subsequently the locations of Noah's ark is somewhere locked away in the Russian archives, hidden there with no intention of ever being brought forth to reveal to the world the truth it represents.

EARLY SIGHTINGS

In 1840, there was a devastating earthquake which greatly altered the appearance of the northeastern side of Mount Ararat. Reported sightings of Noah's ark before and after this event, which by some was termed an *explosion,* are recorded in this chapter.

WORLD WAR I AMERICAN

An aerial sighting in the World War I time frame by an American is worthy of consideration, especially since our previous discussion of aircraft performance tells us that technically this was a real possibility.

Related by a clear-minded gentleman of eighty-seven (since deceased), it contains his flight to Ararat in 1918 with an Army pilot who had bought and reconditioned a used plane at the close of WWI. Mr. Guillford Officer, a casual acquaintance, was invited on the flight. They took off on a furlough that included Greece, Turkey, and the biblical peak in eastern Turkey. When the men reached the mountain, recalled the old gentleman, they had flown clockwise around the peak three times before they gained the necessary altitude.

As the men crossed the Ahora Gorge at approximately 14,000 feet and turned south, they were surprised to find themselves nearly level with a great ship in a small lake valley, half-exposed and protruding from a melting glacier, with deep snow still piled on the back. It was about noon on a hot July day, and the ship stood out clearly in the bright sunlight.

According to Officer's description, the vessel resembled a submarine, listing to one side, with a superstructure (or *deck-house*) on top. As they passed, the men noted a door on one side, as well as openings for windows around the top.[1]

This report comes from the pages of Cummings' book, but the

source of the report was Mr. Guillford Officer himself. I listened to a taped interview of Mr. Officer, by Mr. Eryl Cummings. Unfortunately, the tape had been accidently and partly recorded over; and I was unable to hear all of what Mr. Officer had to say with regard to the ship's location and the extent of his flight. Because of this, I was left somewhat confused by the end of the tape. However, the description and position of the ark does fall in line with other reported sightings.

I found some difficulty in retracing Mr. Officer's flight path, and this is somewhat of concern to me. Still, in fairness to Mr. Officer, with the tape being partially recorded over, some of what he said was lost. Also, the line of questioning during the interview did not appear to focus on the details of his trip, but rather on his reported sighting of Noah's ark.

According to what I could understand from the tape recording, Mr. Officer was stationed in Scotland and on leave to London where he apparently made friends with an airman who was also on leave.

The airman had his own plane, or had access to one, and the two men took off on a flight which led them to a great discovery. They traveled from London, and Mr. Officer remembers crossing over Italy and parts of the Mediterranean to Greece, and apparently they landed in Athens. During much of the flight, Mr. Officer admits to being airsick, and in this condition, he wasn't sure at times where he was. I can understand that, but what bothers me is that the further extent of his flight is not clear. He does not mention a destination east of Athens, but he says on his way back they then flew by Mount Ararat, circled the mountain to gain altitude, and found the ship.

Mount Ararat is a considerable distance to the east of Athens, and not on the way back to London, unless, of course, they had flown to a destination east or south of Ararat, which he doesn't mention. The question I have is the extent of their flight after Athens, and where were they *coming back* from? This could put a shadow of doubt on the Officer experience, but I must keep in mind that the line of questioning in the interview did not lead in this direction, rather it concentrated on the reported sighting.

In listening to the tape recording of Mr. Officer relating his story, I really would like to believe him, as he sounds so genuine.

Something that must be considered is that the flight took place in 1918, and the interview took place in 1972 — 54 years had passed. The passage of time could certainly have clouded the memory of the entire trip, yet he remembered fairly clearly seeing the ship. I can understand that; I have trouble remembering some of the countries I have flown over in Europe, and for me it has not been nearly so long. I would certainly remember, in far greater detail, the sighting of a great ship on a mountaintop, than I would all the places along the way.

Mr. Officer died shortly after the interview with Mr. Cummings. This report is all we have of his experience.

YOUNG BOY AND HIS GOAT

This report begins like a fairy tale, but it is reported to be a factual account and what it says is of interest.

> The story is given by permission of the young Lutheran minister to whom it was told, but for many valid personal reasons, further identification may not be revealed. Apparently, the personal safety, or at least the privacy of his source would be in jeopardy should his name be known. It is possible that this story also is true because of its marked resemblance to the many other reports.

> Many years ago a young boy followed a stray goat up the sides of Mount Ararat and came unexpectedly to the end of the trail. There he was astonished to see below him in a small valley a huge ship encased in ice. The object sat in a small lake on the mountainside and rested on a sort of ledge or cliff which dropped off very rapidly on the front side. The valley was surrounded on the other three sides by walls of rock and small jagged peaks and terrain. The lad saw the ship on other occasions when the ice melted back. At these times the ship had a reddish-brown wood appearance, its construction resembling a houseboat with a flat deck surface.[2]

I recently read a transcript of an interview with the son of the *young boy*. Obviously, the reported sighting took place quite some time ago, as the son is now an elderly gentleman. Because I will remain true to the desire for secrecy, I will not mention names, regardless of what this action does to the perceived credibility of the report.

The son of the one-time *young boy* who reportedly saw the ship, gives us some information on how to reach the ship. Again, the passage of time and secondhand information to begin with adds confusion, and clarity suffers. The direction of the ship does not necessarily coincide with other reports, and its location is not clear. However, this particular reported sighting increases my level of interest when I read of the three walls of rock and small jagged peaks surrounding the ship which rests on a cliff in the edge of the ice in a small mountain lake.

The Russian reports mention a small lake and they also indicate a rugged terrain with statements like *a wild and inaccessible locality,* and the fact that they *chopped out a trail along the cliffs,* and a high cliff is mentioned in one soldier's account.

Other information that I have read indicates that the highest pastures for grazing sheep and goats are located on the south and east sides of the mountain, although there are also pastures on the west side. If this is based on a true account, then I find it somewhat of a relief to read there must be an easier route to a point where the ark can at least be seen — a point above it. Now all we have to do is find that route.

I think perhaps the goat could well have climbed high to come to the end of the trail above the pastures near the edge of a very rugged area near the edge of the ice.

WORLD WAR I TURKS

Near the end of WWI, five Turkish soldiers climbed Ararat and reportedly saw the ark. Mount Ararat was still in Russian territory at the time, and what the Turks were doing there behind enemy lines (in 1915 the Turks joined the Central European powers in the war against Russia and their British allies),[3] and how they by chance decided to climb Ararat is not clear, yet so the story goes. We'll pick up the story some 30 years after the possible discovery took place.

In 1946 one of the five Turkish soldiers, a man named Sakir, with the help of Duran Ayranci, a Turkish scribe, sent a letter to leaders of a proposed American expedition called the *Sacred History Research Expedition* and offered to lead them to the site. The expedition never materialized, and the letter was in the care of Dr. Lawrence Moore, attache in charge of the American Embassy in Turkey at the time.

Mr. Moore must have been impressed by the contents of the letter, and kept it in his file until August of 1966. Mr. Eryl Cummings had heard of the letter, he contacted Mr. Moore, and the letter was given to him, some 20 years after it had been written. It reads as follows:

> When returning from World War I, I and five or six of my friends passed by the Ararat. We saw Noah's ark leaning against the mountain. I measured the length of the boat. It was 150 paces long. It had three stories. I read in the papers that an American group is looking for this boat. I wish to inform you that I shall personally show this boat and I

request your intervention so that I may show the boat.

It was signed by Duran Ayranci, the scribe.[4]

Further investigation by Mr. Cummings found that by this time the five army soldiers were now dead, but the scribe was still alive, a healthy man in his seventies. Communications between Mr. Cummings and Ayranci were pursued, and a letter was sent to Mr. Cummings. The report continues:

"Near the top of Aghri Dagh," he wrote, "was a decayed boat put together with wooden nails. It was resting on a rock. It extended from north to south." Although he himself had never seen the ark, he recalled Sakir's story so vividly that he could lead a party directly to the great ship.

Now a frustrating period of several months began. Most important, the problem of communication must be solved. Translators were hard to come by. At last a charming young Turkish exchange student, who declared that she herself was from Adana, was located in an Albuquerque, New Mexico, university. She agreed to help.

The situation became complicated at times with Miss Habiba Mir in the center doing her best to keep the lines open between Farmington, New Mexico, where Cummings now lived, and far-off Adana in Turkey, where Duran Ayranci still operated his little shop. Thanks to her sincere interest and desire to be of help, Miss Mir translated information containing more facinating details which were gradually being disclosed: the Turkish soldiers (according to her translation of Ayranci's letters) had climbed onto a mountain called *Gudi* — a hill — very close to the mountain of Ararat.

It must have been difficult for Miss Mir, herself a busy student in an alien land, to find words to convey correctly the proper meaning of Ayranci's letters in a foreign language. As she explained, it was mentioned in the Koran (or Qur'an), the Moslems' Holy Book, that "the ark rested on Mount Judi" (The Holy Qur'an, SURA XI 44). According to Sakir, "The ark is on that hill facing north-south, and the body is on the west side of the hill."

In 1966, these descriptions were puzzling. *Gudi? Ararat? Aghri Dagh?* Did Ayranci and Miss Mir actually know what they were talking about?[5]

The Koran tells me that *Gudi, Judi,* and *Kudi* (a name believed to be connected to Kurdistan) are interchangeable, and all mean the same thing. Hence, the ark landed on *Judi;* it also landed on *Gudi,* and *Kudi.*

A translation of SURA XI 43-44 in the Koran doesn't promote a landing of the ark on Mount Ararat, or Aghri, but on a lower peak.[6]

Cummings says, "In time a more detailed description followed: *Gudi* mountain is not as high as Mount Aghri and it is attached to Mount Aghri. They are both the same mountain." [Author comment: I don't know what that description is, unless it is that *Judi* is simply a smaller peak on Mount Ararat.]

"As Sakir told me," explained Ayranci, "the boat is very large. One of the wood [timbers?] measures about four meters [13+ feet]. The northeast side is leaning on a big rock and it has decayed a bit. He said it is all ice. That is why it will not decay . . . the position of the boat is close to the top of the mountain. One can climb from the west of the mountain." Ayranci seemed perfectly familiar with the route the five soldiers had taken to reach the site.

At this point in our bewilderment, Habiba Mir offered a helpful clue. The Aghri Mountain area is very mountainous, she wrote. The local people give different names to each small part of the mountain. *Gudi* is mentioned in the religious stories I heard as a child. It might be one of the names given to Aghri in these stories. Religious stories? We wondered. About what? Noah, the flood, and the ark? We were not destined to find out, however, for about this time our contact with Miss Habiba ceased. Had she returned to Turkey, or had she merely tired of what must have seemed a fruitless task? We never knew.

Financial negotiations with Ayranci also seemed to reach a dead end. It is difficult to make such arrangements by mail, especially between two individuals of different races, languages, and cultures, whom we have never met. It was arranged for Sergeant and Mrs. Douglas King with the U.S. Air Force in Adana, to look up the old gentleman and send a picture and report, if possible. The Kings secured the services of an Armenian translator and finally succeeded in fulfilling our unusual request. Thus reassured of Ayranci's integrity, Cummings himself made a side trip to Adana on his next expedition to Turkey, but Duran Ayranci was no longer in his shop. No amount of searching ever turned him up; perhaps this old man, too, had died![7]

In considering this story, I find certain problems. First of all, I don't know how the soldier would determine the ship had three stories unless they got inside. They said that the ship had decayed a bit; if they are referring to the damage on one end which has been reported in other sightings, then perhaps they were able to get inside, or they could have used the door, if they were able. The ark having three stories coincides with the Bible. The measurement of 150 paces long would probably be about 450 feet, which would be 300 cubits, using an 18-inch cubit. I think this information is encouraging.

Resting on a rock in a north-south direction, also coincides with other reports we will read on the pages ahead. I find some confusion in its location with reference to other reports. Still, we may have some clues. Climbing from the west, and the ark being on the west side of the hill, with the northeast side leaning on a big rock, close to the top of the mountain. One problem is that this story is written by Ayranci, as told by Sakir — it is second hand. Perhaps the initial letter was written by both of them, but subsequent communication was with Ayranci the scribe, not Sakir, who gave the report.

Of course, if Sakir had still been alive when his long-delayed letter was opened and read, he could have no doubt added many more pertinent details not mentioned in his brief communication in 1946.

It seems unfortunate that Sakir's letter lay so long undelivered in Dr. Lawrence Moore's file, or the ark might have been rediscovered long since. Perhaps God, in His wisdom, only intended to allow another tantalizing glimpse of the great ship whose rediscovery will add the final touch of confirmation that the Genesis account of the ark and a great flood is a true historical account.[8]

Dr. Kasem Gulek, whom I was privileged to meet during my first trip to Turkey, read aloud from the Koran, and he said the ark rested on El Judi. We have quoted this from the Koran (Qur'an) exactly. The translation in the English version of the Koran says *El Judi* and *Gudi* are one and the same.

ANTIQUITY

There are reports that go back before World War I. In fact throughout history, various writers mention the ark of Noah. Berosus, a third century B.C. Jewish historian, said some parts of the ship still remained in his day.[9] But Viscount James Bryce, an English statesman of the 19th century, pointed out that Berosus puts the ark on the mountains of the Gordyaeans, 200 miles to the south. This is the region of the Gordyene. Bryce also points out that the biblical reference to *Kingdoms of Ararat* (Jer. 51:27) could hardly apply to Gordyene. In this chapter of Jeremiah, the Lord is rising up against Babylon and its wickedness, a standard is sought, and the *Kingdoms of Ararat* are called against Babylon.[10] I don't completely understand Bryce's connection here to Noah's ark. What is apparent here is that even in ancient historical accounts, there is controversy as to where the ark landed!

Flavius Josephus, who lived during the time the New Testament was being written, said the remains of the ark "are still shown to such as are desirous to see them."[11] Bryce quotes Josephus in this manner: "For the ark being saved in that place, its remains are shown there by the inhabitants to this day."[12]

Faustus of Byzantium, a fourth century historian, tells of St. Jacob of Medzpin, who when attempting to climb the mountain, was brought a piece of wood from the ark by an angel who told him to try and climb no more.[13] The wood is now reported to be in the Monastery of Echmiadzen, northeast of Ararat near Erivan, and now in Russia. The story of St. Jacob is told in detail in *The Ark on Ararat,* by LaHaye and Morris. The story was told also by Sir John Mandeville, in 1360:

> And there besides is another hill that men clept (call) Ararat, but the Jews clept (call) it Taneez, where Noah's ship rested, and yet is upon that mountain. And men see it afar in clear weather. And that mountain is well a seven miles high. And some men say that they have seen and touched the ship, and put their fingers in the parts where the fiend went out, when that Noah said, *Benedicite.* But they that say such words, say their will. For a man may not go up the mountain, for great plenty of snow that is always on that mountain, neither summer not winter. So that no man may go up there, ne never man did, since the time of Noah, save a Monk that, by the grace of God, brought one of the planks down, that yet is in the minister at the foot of the mountain.[14]

The *minister at the foot of the mountain* is the monastery of Echmiadzen.[15]

Sir John Chardin detailed his travels of the area, and he wrote, "The Armenian traditions relate that the ark is still upon the point of Mount Massis."[16] (The Armenian name for Mount Ararat is Mount Massis.)

Bryce says this of Chardin:

> Whether Chardin, himself, believed the ark to be still on
> the top of the mountain, does not appear. In two views of it,
> which he gives showing also Erivan, an Etchmiadzin, the ark
> appears, in shape exactly the ark of the nursery on Sunday
> afternoons, poised on the summit of Great Ararat. But this
> may be merely emblematic; indeed, I have not found any
> author who says he has, himself, seen it, though plenty who
> (like the retellers of ghost stories) mention other people who
> have.[17]

An early historian, John Chrysostom, mentions the existence of
the ark. In trying to prove a point, he writes, "Do not the mountains
of Armenia testify to it, where the ark rested? And are not the remains
of the ark preserved there to this very day for our admonition?"[18]

In 1647, Adam Olearius in his book *Voyages and Travels of the
Ambassadors,* relates, "The Armenians and the Persians themselves,
are of the opinion that there are still upon the said mountain some
remainders of the ark, but that time both so hardened them that they
seem absolutely petrified. At Schamachy in Media Persia, we were
shown a cross of a black and hard wood, which the inhabitants
affirmed to have been made of the wood of the Ark."[19]

In 1670, Jans Janszoon Struys, a Dutch traveler, tells in detail of
meeting a monk on Ararat who told him, because of the weather on
the summit of the mountain, "The ark is not decayed, and that it is
after so many centuries as complete as the first day it came here."[20]

Jehan Haithon, a monk, wrote in 1254, "Upon the snows of
Ararat, a black speck is visible at all times: This is Noah's ark."[21]

Some of these references I have listed come from the research of
LaHaye and Morris and are detailed to a far greater extent in their
facinating book, *The Ark on Ararat.* There are many more. Mrs.
Cummings in her book *Has Anybody Really Seen Noah's Ark?* also
digs deeply into antiquity, and documents the findings of artifacts and
tablets which give the account of the Deluge, and Noah and the ark.

Mrs. Cummings writes in one chapter of discoveries in Michigan
which lend to the possibility of visitors from Tarshish. Tarshish was
a seaport believed to have been located on the tip of Spain and
founded by Tarshish, the great grandson of Noah. This chapter alone
is worth the price of her book.

In my own research, and in addition to what we've read, as I
paged through *The Travels of Marco Polo,* the 13th century Venetian,

I found this reference to Noah's ark: "In the central part of Armenia stands an exceedingly large and high mountain, upon which it is said the ark of Noah rested, and for this reason it is termed the Mountain of the Ark."[22]

Let us now glance over the reports we have read, which date back to times before the earthquake of 1840, and make an observation. (We will later discuss in greater detail the earthquake of 1840.) There's the monk, Jehan Haithon, who says the ark "is visible at all times."[23] Jans Janszoon Struys was told by a monk that the ark is "on the summit of the mountain,"[24] and Sir John Manville said, "Men may see it from afar."[25] There is also Sir John Chardin, who relates the ark, by Armenian tradition, is still on the *point* of the mountain.[26]

More recent reports we have read tell us the ark is in a rugged area of the mountain, and not in an area from which it is easy for animals to disembark. It stands to reason that if there was an ark, and animals were its cargo, and there was a worldwide flood, the animals had to be able to leave the ship once it had landed, since they are here now. The ship, then, must have moved, or the mountain must have changed, or both. We will discuss that possibility again later.

NOURI

Prince Nouri of Malibar, India, claimed to have discovered the ark on his third attempt at climbing the mountain. The year of this reported discovery was 1887.[27]

In my research I requested and received from the original publisher a copy of the article covering this story as it was published in the *Zion's Watch Tower,* August 15, 1894. In its entirety, it reads exactly this way:

A Remarkable Narrative

The Rev. Dr. John Joseph Nouri, D.D., LI., D., Chaldean Archdeacon of Babylon and Jerusalem, Pontifical Delegate General of Malabar and Ex-grand Secretary of the Metropolitan Archdiocese of India and Persia, has found Noah's Ark! At least he says he has, tells a very straight though somewhat gorgeous story about it and has gained believers among men of piety and learning. He is of the Orthodox Greek Church and his labors have been in Africa and southwestern Asia.

After spending several years in African explorations, Dr. Nouri crossed the east mountains to the coast of Abyssinia, and was received with great honors. His expedition up the Euphrates and over the Ararat was an expensive affair, but he got there, camped on the plateau and climbed the two peaks. Between them there is a valley, and from each side of it rise the peaks — one 16,000 and the other nearly 18,000 feet high. Starting in March, they found the snow-drifts impassible, and waited another month. Then they climbed to within sight of a narrow plateau almost on the summit, and on that plateau they saw the ark.

The bow and stern, says the archdeacon, were clearly in view, but the center was buried in snow and one end of it had fallen off and decayed. It stood more than 100 feet high and was over 300 yards long. The wood was peculiar, dark reddish in color, almost iron colored in fact, and seemed very thick. I think the cold has preserved the wood. I am very positive that we saw the real ark, though it is over 4,000 years old!

Though within rifle shot, they could not reach it, the slope from the bench on which it rested being a glare of ice and snow, and they could not remain till the midsummer thaw. Many educated gentlemen, including preachers, have called upon Archdeacon Nouri and found him a most facinating talker. He speaks ten languages with considerable fluency, having also a smattering of the local dialects of various places. He is by birth a Syrian of the old Chaldean stock, and is a man of great wealth. His credentials are a study in themselves. His commission for Persia and India is signed by Greek bishops of those countries to the number of eighty.[28]

I will assume that this brilliant, honorable, well-traveled man of impeccable accomplishments, would give exaggeration in this story only in the size of the ark as it seemed to him, while he was awestruck at the very sight of it. Consider the clues he gives to us, which fall in line with other reports. The one end had fallen off and decayed. Could it have been just damaged — an opening, as in the report by the World War I Turks?

I think it is highly unlikely that a man of such reknown, would make up the story. It stands to reason that he would be telling the truth as he remembered it. However, he does not tell us how to get to the ship, or just exactly where it sits. Still, this may well be valuable information.

YEARAM

One hot summer day, sometime in mid-1856, three foreigners arrived at an Armenian village at the base of

Mount Ararat and demanded a guide. They let it be known that they were atheistic scientists from London, and that their purpose was to search the mountain to explode the ancient story that Noah's ark had ever landed there.

Consternation spread among the villagers. The elders called a council to determine what to do. If they agreed to these strangers' high-handed proposal, if they disclosed the hiding place of the ark, they might incur the displeasure of God. For centuries, their most sacred traditions had taught them that their knowledge of the whereabouts of the ark was a sacred trust. They believed implicitly that God had concealed it from mortal eyes until the end of time, when it would be revealed again to prove that the Bible and the story of the flood was true.[29]

I do not question the truth to the possibility of the Armenians knowing the whereabouts of the ark. If the ark is on Mount Ararat, then I believe the Armenians, at least a few of them, knew its location. Remember, as quoted earlier in this chapter, of the Venetian travels of Marco Polo: "In the central part of Armenia stands an exceedingly large and high mountain, upon which it is said the Ark of Noah rested, and for this reason it is termed the mountain of the Ark." Also, the ancient scholar Sir John Chardin, who wrote *The Armenian Traditions,* relates that the ark is still upon the point of Mount Massis.

The question I had in reference to this tradition was about the presence of a Bible in this predominately Moslem nation of Turkey. Was the Bible common in Armenian villages?

In *Agathangelos — History of the Armenians,* we read of the early fourth-century conversion of the Armenian king Tiridates, and of the missionary work in Armenia of St. Gregory, the Illuminator. Under the lead of this missionary, and sanctioned by the king, the country of Armenia experienced a conversion to Christianity.[30] Armenia became the first country to make Christianity the established faith. It, in fact, became the state religion. This came about in the early fourth century before the time of Constantine. (Constantine's Christianity was discussed in chapter 2.) This was at a time when the Roman Empire was as yet anything but friendly to the new religion.[31]

However, the spread of Christianity throughout the whole of Armenia was a slow process. Success only became possible after the development of a script in the Armenian language, so that religious services and the Scriptures could be understood. This took place in the fifth century A.D. Until then, Greek or Syriac were the languages of the church, though oral preaching was naturally done in the vernacular. The invention of a national script was the work of an indefatigable missionary, Mastots, also known as Mesrop by latter Armenian writers.[32]

Mastots, or Mesrop, a Persian Armenian Monk, conceived the idea of translating the Scriptures from the Greek and Syriac into Armenian in A.D. 396. He traveled to the Greek city Neopolis and entered into a fraternity of prayer with the monk Issac, to seek divine guidance on the matter. The answer came in A.D. 400 when a Syrian monk, Abel, approached the Armenian king Vramshabouh with an Armenian alphabet he had devised. Testing and instruction of the alphabet began in A.D. 404, and by A.D. 410 the first national alphabet was complete. The task of translating the Scriptures into the Armenian language now became a possibility. The king put Mesrop in charge of the project. The teaching of the alphabet was also ordered by King Vramshabouh throughout all the schools of the country. The initial translation of the Scriptures into the Armenian version was complete by A.D. 433, with minor corrections taking place in the years ahead.[33]

In view of the basic purpose behind the invention of the Armenian alphabet, which was the bringing of the gospel and the Christian faith to the Armenian people in their own tongue, it is hardly surprising that the Bible was the fundamental text studied in the monastic schools. The Book of Proverbs was the book used by those beginning to learn to read and write in Armenian.[34]

Further confirmation of the presence of the Bible in Armenia comes from the pages of *Passages to Ararat,* a documentary by the author, Arlen, on a more recent journey through Armenia: "It was in a large church-like building set against the side of one of the hills. The old manuscripts were locked away in glass cases. There were displays of tiny Bibles no larger than a couple of thumbs, and of huge volumes in ancient, hand-worked leather. The bright colors of the illuminated pages, the tiny, glowing figures in red, blue, and gold, the angular Armenian lettering of the gospels; it was hard to know what it all meant. The manuscripts and old Bibles rested serenely under the glass. Arlen read from a display card. This is part of the Bible from the Armenian Church at Van, which was smuggled away by two sisters when they fled from the Turks. When one of the sisters died by the roadside, the other retained the Bible and brought it here."[35]

Between the time of the translation of the Scriptures in the fifth century, and the time of the Turkish Conquest, when Armenians fled the area or died at the hands of the Turks, before the times surrounding World War I, was the time in which this story of the English atheists and the Armenian guide and son takes place.

In answer to the question, was the presence of the Bible common in Armenian villages? I believe the answer is yes, it most definately was. Let's continue on.

Since the Armenians are no longer living around the mountain, researching the story about Yearam is somewhat difficult. It is easy to poke holes in it, but because this story was apparently carried on for so many years it is worth repeating. Besides, I find the ending of the story to be quite interesting.

It had been only some fourteen years since the great explosion of 1840 had rent the upper part of the Ahora Gorge into seemingly impenetrable canyons, sheer precipices and rocky slopes. Yet it was no great secret to these simple tribesmen that the ark had survived the ordeal, and a few of their hardy guides, at least, knew the hazardous route to its remote hiding place high on the mountainside. But, they reasoned among themselves, perhaps this was the *end of time*. Perhaps God had brought these unbelieving men to their village for a purpose. Perhaps, if they were taken to the ark, if they saw it with their own eyes, they would know the story to be true.

The decision was made. The elders selected a capable guide; the atheists hired his sturdy teenage son, Yearam (Jeremiah) to go along to help carry the gear, and they started off.

After an extremely perilous and difficult climb, perhaps three-quarters of the way up, the small party came to a little valley on Greater Ararat, surrounded by small peaks. Here they found the prow of a mighty ship protruding from a glacier whose melting waters formed a lake, then spilled them over into a little river that tumbled down the mountainside. The summer had been unusually long and hot and the ice in part of the ship had melted out, making it possible to enter and explore some of the rooms. They found the immence structure divided into several floors and stages with compartments and with bars like animal cages of today. The entire ship was heavily coated, both inside and out, with a varnish or lacquer that was very thick and hard. The superstructure appeared much like a great and mighty house built on a hull of a ship. There was a large doorway, but the door itself was missing. From where they stood on the ground, no windows could be seen.

Author: The Armenians had done their job. They had guided the English atheists to the remains of what they said was Noah's ark. It seems logical the three scientists, atheists or not, would have taken a scientific approach to what they discovered, or at least realized the evidence at hand. However, according to the story, they went into a satanic rage, and were anything but scientific in their approach to this discovery. Cummings reports that the scientists went after the structure with an ax, and even tried to burn it. This information puts the story in serious doubt as far as it goes to this point. I have a tough time understanding how a scientist, or anyone, would act this way. Again, let's continue on, remembering that if their purpose was to *explode* the story of Noah's ark, they now had a problem.

If the atheists returned home and reported what they had seen, they would lose face among their colleagues. What if one of them should tell? At last they conceived a diabolical plan. Taking a solemn and fearful death oath, they vowed that if any man present should ever breathe a word about what had taken place that day, he would be tortured and put to death. As for their guides, perhaps it would be better to kill them on the spot. Before they could carry out their idea, however, a little sanity began to creep back into their minds. Their lives were dependent on these two Armenians. If they killed them they would very likely never reach the bottom of the mountain alive. So, from the terrified father and son they also extracted a terrible oath, that if they ever breathed a word of what had happened, they, too would be tortured and put to death.

The three cunning and frustrated atheists returned to their native land, determined at all costs to hide their guilty secret from their friends. That they succeeded beyond their wildest dreams is reflected in subsequent events, but no positive trace of these men has ever been found.[36]

If this is a true story, then in this example we see the amazing power of the devil, and how he can blind the minds of people even in the presence of absolute proof of Biblical truth.

Mrs. Cummings has a lot to say about this in her book:

The nineteenth century is recognized as one of great turmoil and change in the spiritual and scientific worlds. Opposing forces of truth and error fought desperately for the control of men's minds. Eschatological preaching, warning mankind of the imminent approach of Christ and the end of the world, won millions of adherents around the globe. Vying with this biblical concept were the optimistic proponents of a *better world,* of an approaching golden age when strife and wars would cease by mankind's own efforts to pull itself up by its own bootstraps.

In the case of the atheists, the year was 1856. It was only three years before Darwin's *Origin of the Species* was released to the world. These men visited Ararat with the avowed purpose of searching the mountain to prove that the Genesis story was not true.

What if these three men, thus far unnamed, but possibly influential in the scientific field, had accepted this evidence for biblical truth and announced to the world what they had found. What a powerful witness for truth they might have become if they had faithfully taken the story of Noah and his ark back to England! The *Origin of the Species* might never have seen the light of day, and the evolutionary theory might have died a natural death![37]

To tie this up, it is worthwhile to mention that a deathbed confession, quite possibly by one of the three atheists,[38] gives credence to the Yearam story. Notice how it neatly ties in with Haji as he relates this story in the latter days of his life.

As a young man, Yearam had made a trip to Jerusalem from Armenia and gained the title of respect, Haji Yearam, or Jeremiah the Pilgrim, a name carried throughout the remainder of his long life. He had gone to Constantinople (now Istanbul) and opened a business. When religious and political pressures began to mount, he went to Europe and eventually found himself across the Atlantic in the United States, far from his beloved homeland and the mountain he loved. Being both an earnest Christian and a typically astute Armenian businessman, Haji prospered. Several times he amassed a small fortune, intending to return to his far-off home in Armenia, but each time robbers foiled his attempt.

At last he found himself, aging and broke, starting all

over again in a city on the West Coast (Oakland, California). Slowly his fortunes began to mend. Trading in real estate and antiques, he lived frugally in the upstairs rooms of the old mansion where his business was conducted. Respected by all who knew him, he nevertheless must have lived a lonely life.

It was at this time that Harold Williams found him, and from then on the old Armenian knew what it meant to have a family and friends. Williams, a nurse, had been visiting his parents in the bay city area when the pastor of the Oakland Seventh Day Adventist Church of which Haji was a member, approached him with a request. He had missed his elderly member, he said, and feared he was sick. Handing Williams a name and address, he asked him to look up his old friend and check on his situation. Harold Williams had almost given up on locating Haji when he finally found the old man in his bloody bed in the attic room. Haji was much too ill to be moved, so the young nurse cared for him there until he was on the mend. Then Williams took Haji home with him to Angwin, California, where he and his wife, Ida, operated a nursing home while Harold pursued his studies at nearby Pacific Union College.

Under the young couple's skillful care, it was not long before Haji's health was completely restored and he was once again his usual energetic and hearty self. Soon the old Armenian became a much-loved and respected member of the Williams family and often entertained them with stories of his travels and of his boyhood and youth around Mount Ararat in Armenia. Haji was deeply religious and kind, recalled Harold Williams years later, and people who met him were reminded of a veritable saint.

Haji Yearam had a major problem: he was gradually going blind. It soon became obvious to his young friends that some heavy burden was weighing on his mind. One day he called Ida and Harold to his room, telling them he had made a momentous decision. He had an important story to tell them while his mind was still keen and alert. If Harold would bring some paper and a new composition book, he would have him write it down. Thus, 60 years after the event had taken place, the story of the atheists and the ark began to unfold before the eyes of the young couple on the other side of the world.

True to his vow on that terrifying day, Haji had kept the knowledge of the ark locked within his breast ever since his early youth. What a relief — to unburden his heart at last to these dear, new and trusted friends who had given him a home in his lonely old age!

Haji was not satisfied to have the story written only once. With his passion for accuracy and his keen intellect (he spoke seven languages), he insisted that Harold write the story three times with meticulous attention to details. Then he had him read it back to him while Ida followed the reading over her husband's shoulder. Satisfied at last, Haji had the account transferred to the new composition book and signed it, with Harold and Ida as witnesses. He then entrusted the precious document to his new friends. Someday, he believed, his story would serve an important purpose and be an inspiration to brave men who would return to rediscover the great ship he had seen with his own eyes and had examined so many years ago.

Not long after this, Harold Williams accepted a position in the east. They took Haji to Harold's parents' home in Oakland, where he lived for nearly five years until his death on May 3, 1920, at the age of 83. Believed at first to be penniless, Haji had indeed owned several houses, one of which he willed to Harold's mother for caring for him.

Author: Earlier in this Yearam story, I mentioned it was very easy to poke holes in it. I also said that the ending was interesting, I might also add — if it is true.

It was unexpected news to learn that, after so many years, one of the atheists appeared again on the scene of action. One day in his home in Brockton, Massachusetts, Harold Williams noticed a small headline in his newspaper. It included the words "Noah's Ark" and preceded a small "filler-type" item, perhaps a column wide and not more than an inch or two long. It was located probably at the bottom of the front page, as near as Williams could recall.

The item told of an aged scientist in London who, like Haji, had broken a vow made many years before. Fearing to die before unburdening his heart of the guilt he had carried for so long, he confessed to his family the part he had played with the other atheists after they had seen and entered the ark, and had then promised each other never to divulge the truth. Now he, too, could die in peace.

Excited by the news, Harold Williams got out Haji's composition book and compared notes. Names and dates agreed. He had never doubted Haji's story for a moment, but now it was made doubly sure. The old scientist had died at about the same time as Haji had died, an ocean and a continent away. The possibility of collusion between two old men so separated by space and race, is remote indeed.

Later Williams wrote, "I kept the sheet with that newspaper story in the composition book with Haji's story for many years. In 1940, the school and sanitarium in which Mrs. Williams and I had worked for nine years, was destroyed by fire in 20 minutes by a butane explosion.

Everything we owned in the world was burned up, and my son Nathan, and I nearly burned to death. The composition book containing Haji's story and the newspaper sheet containing the atheist's confession on his deathbed were burned up in that fire, along with all that we owned on earth.

It is with deep regret that I am unable to submit these two testimonials as they were originally written. All I can offer is the vivid memory of the story as it was told to Mrs. Williams and me as I wrote it down, and the identical story as printed in the paper. At the time there were two daily papers in Brockton. I do not remember if it was one of these or a Boston paper in which we found the story, as I used to buy first one and then another. But this I feel sure of — Noah's ark is still on Mount Ararat, and when it pleases God, some expedition will give the news and facts to the world so that skeptics will have no excuse.

It has been stated and, we believe, correctly that if the momentous story just unfolded had come to light, and if it had been heeded 60 years earlier when it took place, the religious history of the entire civilized world would have been altered, and the conflict between creationism and Darwin's evolutionary theory would have been over before it had even been fairly begun. The Deluge story of Genesis 6 would have been verified.[39]

Mrs. Cummings has given us a very nice report on the life of Haji Yearam, particularly in his association with Harold and Mrs. Williams. I have a hard time understanding why Mr. Williams, the son of a pastor himself, and Mrs. Williams, would have kept this information to themselves for so many years without at least trying to get it out, by telling others who might have then been interested in organizing a search of their own.

It is difficult to understand the actions of the scientists, or their non-actions, as it were. How can a group of scientists, if in fact they were scientists, go on an expedition in the search for knowledge, if their minds are already made up to disprove any evidence contrary to their beliefs, as the situation demands? What could they prove?

With the action (or non-action) of those scientists in mind, in the past 140 years since that research expedition, has anything really changed?

EX-AIR FORCE PERSON

On January 14, 1985, I flew to Farmington, New Mexico, for the purpose of spending a couple of days with Eryl and Violet Cummings. While I was there, I studied the taped and written interviews of Mr. Guillford Officer and three others who, for personal reasons, prefer their names not to be used. One, an Armenian gentlemen, one an ex-Air Force person, and one an ex-navy photographer.

I can understand that not including the persons' names can put question to the credibility of their reports. So be it. I will not go against the wishes of these people who feel they have been questioned enough, and wish to retain a certain amount of privacy and anonymity. I hope you read this with that in mind.

The reports of Mr. Guillford Officer are included elsewhere in detail, and I'll not comment on them further. I will report briefly on the other three.

Mr. Ex-Air Force, stationed in Turkey in 1974, became friends with a Turkish soldier who was related to a shepherd who lived near Mount Ararat. To shorten what could turn out to be a long story, Mr. Air Force, a newly converted Christian, wanted to see the ark. He asked his Turkish friend, and a trip was arranged. Sounds simple, doesn't it?

They started their climb on a very cloudy day, and about all he remembers of the starting point is that there were ruins nearby. It could have been Karada on the west side of the mountain, although that is not certain. The town of Igdir is mentioned, and this does give us another clue as to where he might have started his climb, and that's on the northwest side of the mountain.

They walked on a plain, plateau, or pasture for a time and keeping the mountain summit to their right they walked up and across the face in a north and east direction. There are no landscapes given to identify the location of the climb. They were in the clouds and Air Force couldn't see where he was.

After the pasture, plain, or plateau, they walked on a lot of rocks which were partly covered in about a foot of packed snow. This all indicates to me they were not necessarily on any type of trail. However, the month was April, so a trail used by sheep in the summer, and known by the shepherd, could have still been covered by snow. Apparently, they followed the edge of the ice, and Mr. Air Force estimated his altitude to possibly be as high as 15,000 feet, but he wasn't sure. Keep in mind, it was cloudy and he couldn't see very far at all; except the summit was high and to his right.

After maybe 12 hours, they reached an area where there was a bunyon of rock (perhaps an outcropping). The shepherd, Turkish friend, and Air Force climbed around the rock, and after a short distance farther Air Force saw from a ledge as he looked down, the ark, mostly covered with snow. Unable to climb down to it, lacking the equipment to do so, they walked down and around the difficult area, and saw the ship above them. Again unable to reach it as they lacked the equipment, they spent the night, and descended the mountain the following day. Mr. Air Force never saw the gorge, but this doesn't necessarily mean he wasn't high above it. They were shrouded in the clouds. He has no real landmarks to help tell us where he was. In listening to his taped interview, and much later after a very brief phone conversation, I felt he could well have been there, but the question is, *where?*

THE OLD ARMENIAN

Next we have the old Armenian gentleman. The date of this discovery is not clear, but was sometime before 1930. The information given by this old gentleman leaves me confused, which seems to be the state of mind I am usually in while trying to determine the location of the ark.

The Armenian climbed from above a well near Ortulu, on the southwest side of the mountain. He started above a large grass plateau on a goat trail that turned right, and then left, winding around the mountain toward the summit.

He passed Lake Kop on his left, and went northeasterly around the summit. At one point, he said, "This will take you up into glacial land which is above the ark." The goat trail must have followed the edge of the ice. The path branched off many times, but the Armenian knew to stay on the one that eventually, after about three hours, led him through small valleys, along rock walls, and into the back end of an isolated canyon, which was alongside another canyon. The ark was there, surrounded by large rocks and small pointed peaks, on a ledge lying in a north-slightly-west direction, with about 40 feet exposed. The rest was encased in ice.

As the Armenian faced northeast, he tells us the large summit was on his right, Lake Kop on his left. He was in the area of 13,000 feet, and not by the Ahora Gorge.

The Armenian tells of another way to get there by passing Jacob's Well which is on the east side of the Ahora Gorge. From there a trail leads up to a cleft in the rocks, and ends above it. The ark can be seen just below him at this place.

As far as I can tell in listening to this taped interview, we have been given two separate locations. One, to the west of the Ahora Gorge, in a canyon area which could be close to the rim of the north canyon, and the other in a cleft of rocks above the Ahora Gorge. That cannot be.

In considering the northeast area, it would seem the ark would be above the Ahora Gorge, as it is reported not to be in the gorge. That, however, would put it well above the 13,000 to 14,000 foot elevation that is estimated for its location. Also, much ice may have to be crossed if the western trail from above the well at Ortulu was to join up with the Jacob's Well trail on the east side of the gorge.

I wondered if the two wells mentioned were the same well, and consequently the same trail, just confusion in translation; but the Holy Man's tomb is mentioned, which is near Jacob's Well in the Ahora Gorge, and also the village of Ortulu is mentioned, which is on the opposite side of the mountain.

The question comes up, could the trail from Jacob's Well actually cross to the west side of the gorge? Mr. Cummings thought this a possibility, and it would seem to give an answer to this problem.

I've wondered if Hagopian went this way when he passed by Jacob's Well. Then again, in studying his account, I couldn't see it. Also, what about the sightings which seem to put the ark above the gorge, and to the east of it? There is obviously some very important information that is not included in the Armenian's report, and that is basically — *How do you get there?*

NAVY PHOTOGRAPHER

Mr. Naval Photographer probably has the answer: you fly. On a mission that was at the time (approximately June of 1974) classified, a Navy aircraft flew on a quick reconnaissance mission up a wide gorge and around the mountain, then immediately left the area. I'm not sure of the type of aircraft, but it launched from an aircraft carrier. Probably it was a two-seat fighter equipped for reconnaissance. Neither am I sure whether the photographer was looking through a scope or a viewfinder which was used on the photo mission, or if he made his sighting from the aircraft's cockpit window. In this case, the tape I listened to was not clear, and not having personally located this photographer, whose actual Navy job as it turns out, was that of an electrical or photographic technician, the story has a couple of loose ends. This seems to be common ground to all reported sightings. The first question to be considered is whether or not he was so busy inside the aircraft with the cameras or the scope that he didn't have time to focus his eyes on what was outside the aircraft.

During the taped interview with Professor John Morris of the Institute for Creation Research in San Diego, Mr. Navy does give us a few clues. On the first pass, the Navy aircraft flew up a wide gorge on the north side of the mountain, and was looking for anything, such as a military installation, that could have been hidden there. In looking at photo slides of the mountain during the interview, the ex-Navy photographer recognized the Ahora Gorge as the gorge they flew up. The Ahora Gorge is on the northeast, the north canyon is on the north, but the gorge is the only really conceivable place an installation, or any large military construction could be concealed. It makes sense that the Ahora Gorge was the one. Also, on the flight they were down in the gorge with the rock walls even with the aircraft. This definitely describes the Ahora Gorge, as such a flight would be suicide in the north canyon.

Navy saw the ark on the first pass. At least he saw an object which was very foreign to the area. The object was right at the very top of a pie-shaped area, sitting on a vertical cut, a sharp face in the rock, high on the mountain in the ice cap or snow cover, 14,000 to 15,000 feet up.

It was to the left as they approached the summit, behind a rock formation that sticks up, or out, with a drop-off below, and the gorge is at the bottom of the drop-off.

When asked about the Cehennem Dere and the heart-shaped glacier on the west side of the gorge, Navy said it was not there, but it definitely was to the left of his flight path, which was up the middle of the gorge.

The object was very dark, long and rectangular, and he couldn't see it till he cleared the rough, jagged rock formation it was behind.

It was on the left side of a grayish rock area, on top of a ledge and well up into the ice, and above any strategic area. The ledge the object sits on is shaped like an upside down fishhook, and the object reminded him of a loaf of bread.

So, all we have to do is go to the top of the pie-shaped area and look for an object shaped like a loaf of bread, sitting on a ledge that looks like an upside down fishhook. Sounds simple enough! Now, let's consider the possibility of seeing all this on what must have been a quick trip (probably before breakfast), and quite possibly traveling nearly 300 miles an hour and at fairly low-level as they climbed up out of the gorge and past the summit.

It does seem to me, because of the visual clues, that Navy saw the object while looking out of the aircraft window. Let's consider the possibility of making the sighting while looking into a viewfinder. Errors in ground coverage, identification, size determination, displacement, or parallax could be possible due to the rugged terrain and the climbing flight path. Older equipment without certain optical elements could present a reversed image in the viewfinder. There is also the human error to be considered.

I would assume, since Navy's purpose, other than operating the cameras, was to see something that was to be concealed; that he had very good equipment, and probably a wide-angle lens to go with it. Also, he would have had to have been very observant with a quick eye, and the ability to identify what he was looking at. And it appears this individual has a pretty good memory.

Several years ago I was employed as an aerial photographer, and I spent many hours with my face stuck to a viewfinder. I did not have the experience of traveling at 300 miles an hour close to the ground while attempting to focus my eyes through that instrument, but I was able to get quite proficient at my job in a relatively short period of time. Most of the time I was mapping, so I was mainly concerned about the pictures being taken at the correct interval, and not so much what I was looking at on the ground. But when I wanted to pay attention to what we were flying over, I had no problem identifying objects on the ground by simply looking through the viewfinder.

When I was in the air force, my specialty was aerial cameras. I was classified as an Aerial Photographic Systems Technician. I became quite familiar with the workings of many types of these cameras. Rather than go into detail, I believe it is sufficient for me to say here that with the proper programming they operate fast enough, and cover sufficient area as to completely photograph the desired area several times, and continuously, with little more than the flip of a switch. Mr. Navy would not have been concerned about mapping or about the cameras tripping at certain intervals, as I would have been in my previous job. For him, that was already set into the system. He just made sure they worked, and then I would imagine he looked through the viewfinder, or if he were able he would have looked out of the window to see what he could see. I imagine this latter assumption to be the case, and he was probably paying a lot of attention, considering the nature of the mission.

Navy said the object was beneath a small ledge, on top of another one, and behind a jagged rock formation. This falls in line with other reports. I consider what Navy has told us to be, quite possibly, a true and accurate sighting, but he doesn't really tell us where the ark is, and that's the next question.

Taking all the sightings into account, the ark could either be above the Ahora Gorge, or near the north canyon. Maybe elsewhere, but I believe it is in one of those two places. At this time, I lean toward the area above the Ahora Gorge. Throughout this research, this northeastern part of the mountain becomes the most likely of all possible locations. The northeastern part of the mountain is a large and rugged area, with several potential hiding places.

We believe that on Mount Ararat, somewhere up there, is a small hidden valley, which can't be seen from anywhere in the Ahora Gorge or on its sides, except if you should happen to walk up to it or perhaps climb in such a difficult area that the only reason you would venture forth and attempt it is if you knew exactly where you were going. The only other method to find the small hidden valley would be by aircraft directly overhead and low, or at the precise level which would allow you to peer into its opening and unlock its secret. And then, as previously discussed, only if it is in God's time!

Do The Locals Know?

Over the years, it has bothered me some that an ancient artifact as important as Noah's ark could sit on a mountain in eastern Turkey and the local government either doesn't know of it or won't acknowledge it is there and divulge its whereabouts to let the world know.

It would seem to me that they certainly would search their own mountain — especially amongst such controversy over the subject. After all, the ark is mentioned in the Moslem Koran, also; since the majority of Turkey is Moslem, it really shouldn't make a difference whether a Christian or Moslem finds it.

Is it apathy? Is there so much disbelief not only in the existence of Noah's ark, but in God himself, that people just don't want to "waste" their time with it? Is it that the city folks don't care and the country folk are just trying to make a living and don't have time? I can't accept that. Some of the locals surely know, but they certainly are very closed-mouth about it. This, of course, assumes that the ark does, in fact exist.

This article, entitled "Noah's Ark Discovered," appeared in the *New York Herald* on August 9, 1883:

> A Constantinople Contemporary announces the discovery of Noah's ark. It appears that some Turkish commissioners appointed to investigate the question of avalanches on Mount Ararat suddenly came upon a gigantic structure of very dark wood protruding from a glacier. They made inquiries of the inhabitants. They had seen it for six years, but had been afraid to approach it because a spirit of fierce aspect has been seen looking out the upper window. The Turkish commissioners, however, are bold men, not deterred by such trifles, and they determined to reach it. Situated as it was amongst the fastnesses of one of the glens of Mount Ararat,

it was a work of enormous difficulty, and it was only after incredible hardship that they succeeded. The ark, one will be glad to hear, was in a good state of preservation, although the angles — observe, not the bow or stern — had been a good deal broken in its descent.

The article goes on to explain only three rooms within the structure could be entered, as the rest was encased in ice. Also, the article contains a certain element of what seems to be editorial hilarity poking fun at what was possibly a factual event.

They recognized it at once. There was an Englishman among them who had presumably read his Bible, and he saw it was made of the ancient gopher wood of the Scriptures, which as everyone knows, only grows on the plains of the Euphrates . . . needless to say, an American was soon on the spot, and negotiations have been entered into with the local police, for its (the ark's) speedy transfer to the United States.

The following day, August 10, 1883, the article "Ararat's Antique" was written in the *Herald* and the editor's humor continues: "An American is reported to have arranged to bring the old tub over here. If she is three hundred cubits long, according to contract, it may be quite a job to get her from the top of Mount Ararat to the Mediterranean; but a nation that has seriously thought of a ship railway across Central America cannot doubt that the ark can be brought to deep water. If no American engineers of sufficient ability are on the ground, the purchaser need only send to France for Jules Verne. All but three of her (the ark's) compartments are said to be full of ice, which at present prices, ought to pay the expense of bringing her over." It goes on and on.

Is there any doubt that with this world ridicule and laughter, the Turkish press would drop the whole thing?

On August 13, 1883, the *New York World* published the same story under the headline "Great Scientific Find."

The find was made by a party of Russian engineers who were surveying a glacier. An extraordinary spell of hot weather had melted away a great portion of the Araxes glacier, and they (engineers who were surveying the glacier) were surprised to see sticking out of the ice what at first appeared to be the rude facade of an ancient dwelling — on close examination it was found to be composed of longitudinal layers of gopher wood, supported by immense frames, still in remarkable state of preservation.

Assistance having been summoned from Nakhchevan, the work of uncovering the find was commenced under the most extraordinary difficulties, and in a week's time the indefatigable explorers had uncovered a section of what they claimed to be Noah's ark, as it bore indisputable evidence of having been used as a boat.

Reflecting back over these articles we read again, and excluding the editorial ridicule, "situated as it was among the fastnesses of one of the glens of Mount Ararat, it was a work of enormous difficulty and it was only after incredible hardships that they succeeded. The ark was in a good state of preservation, although the angles — observe not the bow or stern — had been a good deal broken in its descent."

This indicates to me that Noah didn't "park" it in this small place, but that it did descend from the peak down a ways.

Maybe as the mountain grew after the ark landed, or during an earthquake, such as the earthquake of 1840, which supposedly shattered the ice cap, the ark moved; and probably rather suddenly. I would guess that is a good possibility. I do not believe the ice moved it as in a slow-moving glacier. The ark would have surely been long since broken up if it was subject to a moving part of the glacier.

One source, in describing the earthquake of 1840, said the ice cap shattered and the ground undulated for many miles to the east of Ararat. However, the best description of this event comes from the pages of *The Ark on Ararat*, by LaHaye and Morris. This very fine report deals with the earthquake at length, and I recommend its reading. Just one quote to give the reader an idea of the destruction: "Towards sunset in the evening of the 20th of June 1840, the sudden shock of an earthquake, accompanied by a subterranean roar, and followed by a terrific blast of wind, threw down the houses of Arghuri, and at the same moment detached enormous masses of rock with their superjacent ice from the cliffs that surround the chasm. A shower of falling rocks overwhelmed in an instant, the village, the monastery, and a Kurdish encampment on the pastures above. Not a soul survived to tell the tale."[1]

With tons of rock and ice being broken and tossed off the mountain and destroying all in its path, it seems quite feasible the ark could have been dislodged from its secure mooring near the summit and moved rather abruptly farther down the mountain. As we indicated earlier, historical accounts seem to bear this out.

In relation to the wood of the ark, no one knows for sure, as I am led to understand, just exactly what gopher wood is. This presents a problem to the belief in this report. Maybe it was written by an overzealous newsman. I don't know. I guess it really doesn't matter at this point. "It bore indisputable evidence of having been used as a boat," and that is what we're looking for.

LaHaye and Morris mention a little more about the Turks' finding of 1883:

> While studying possible avalanche conditions on the upper slopes of the mountain, the team of experts accidentally stumbled onto the remains of Noah's ark protruding from the ice cap. Among the vastness of one of the glens of Mount Ararat, they came upon a gigantic structure of very dark wood, embedded at the foot of one of the glaciers, with one end protruding, and which they believe to be none other than the old Ark in which Noah and his family navigated the waters of the Deluge. The "mass" was protruding twenty or thirty feet from the glacier on the left side of the ravine. The place where the discovery was made is five days journey from Trebizand . . . and about four leagues from the Persian frontier. The villagers of Bayazit which was situated about a league away, had seen this strange object for nearly six years.[2] [Author: A league is a rough and variable measurement of approximately 3 to 4.6 miles. The longer measurement is more common in non-English speaking countries.]

Upon my inquiry, John Morris confirmed in a letter to me "The remains of Old Bayazit are still seen just beneath the pink mosque Isak Pasha." The pink mosque is easily seen on the hills above new Dogubeyazit. The Kurds in the area refer to the Turkish Dogubeyazit as "D. Beyazit"; hence the "old" and the "new." The *Ark on Ararat* indicates new Dogubeyazit is south of Mount Ararat. Having now been there since doing this research, I have seen the ruins of old Bayazit. It is located on the opposite side of the mountain from the Araxes glacier. The villagers would have had to travel quite a distance in order to see the object.

> The villagers positively refused to approach the glacier in which it was embedded. The way led through a dense forest, and the travelers were obliged to follow the course of

a stream, wading sometimes waist high in water from the melting glacier. The ark was a good deal broken at the angles from being subjected to somewhat rough usage by the moraine during the slow descent of the glacier from the lofty peaks towering away beyond the head of the valley to a height of over 17,000 feet.[3]

Now I'll try to add this up in order to attempt to make some sense of it all. According to what we've read, the ark is embedded in the foot of a glacier, on the left side of a glen or a ravine. The glacier that it is in is reported to be the Araxes, and it was a work of enormous difficulty and hardship to get there.

The ship's remains may possibly be close to an avalanche area, as the Turks were studying avalanche conditions at that time, much of which was caused by another earthquake. The Turkish report claims the ship to be located four leagues (I believe that's between 12 and 18.4 miles) from Iran, and one league (3 to 5 miles) from old Bayazit. A stream leads up to the glacier and the ark, after first going through a dense forest.

The problem here involves the distances mentioned. It appears to me any place on the mountain 12 miles from Iran and three miles from where old Bayazit must have been, barely touches the mountain and it would be far below ice cap or glacier. However, 18.4 miles could put us much closer to where we want to go. The question is, how long was the league used? To give this story added credibility I will assume the longer league of 4.6 miles was used. This is logical since Turkey is a non-English speaking country. Also, I don't understand the reference to a dense forest — it doesn't exist on Greater Ararat. The stream would be questionable, too, although that could be a possibility. However, I can't imagine why anyone would walk waist deep in a cold mountain stream with so much accessible dry land around them, unless they just had to cross it. This is a possibility if the villagers from Bayazit traveled around the mountain from south to west to north and then northeast of Ararat, with the stream flowing out of the Ahora Gorge.

Also, Mount Ararat is not over 17,000 feet tall (close —16,946), and as discussed before, I don't believe slow movement in a glacier could have kept the ark in any recognizable state as it simply would not have survived. So many of the facts are confusing. If this documented experience is based on a true sighting, then perhaps we have a few clues we can use. Still, a few just don't make sense.

Mr. C. Allen Roy, in his "Was It Hot or Not" article in the 1978

Bible Science Newsletter indicated in his weather-related research that "1883 was a cool and dry time." This is "not ideal" for a big snow and ice meltback, but he points out that the region had just been shaken by an earthquake, which caused the avalanches in the area, and possibly was responsible for the destruction of old Bayazit; and "1883 was the third year in a row with less than average precipitation."[4]

Also, remember that the local residents had seen the object for as many as six years. There is a very real possibility that this was a true sighting, with a few of the facts getting lost or confused in translating, or in the press.

RESIT

It had been sixty-five years, so far as is known, since a Turkish newsletter had announced a discovery of Noah's ark. On November 13, 1948, another announcement was released through the Istanbul press: "The petrified remains of an object which peasants insist resembles a ship has been found high on Mount Ararat, biblical landing place of Noah's ark.

While various persons from time to time have reported objects resembling a "house" or a "ship" on the mountain, Turks who have seen this new find profess it to be the only known object which could actually be taken as the remains of a ship.[5]

Before we go any further, let us consider the possibility of a wooded ship being petrified as Resit said. As far as the possibility of petrification taking place, the *World Book Encyclopedia* says this:

Petrified Forest: made up of tree trunks that were buried in mud, sand, or volcanic ash ages ago and have turned to stone. This action is caused by water that seeps through the mud and sand into the buried logs. There it fills the empty cells of the decaying wood with mineral matter until the structure has become solid stone. This stone still shows every detail of the original wood structure, even under a microscope.[6]

We will read in the chapters ahead of the likelihood of a tremendous amount of volcanic activity during the time of the Flood. Ararat is a volcanic mountain. In the aftermath of the Flood, is it not possible in the volcanism that may well have taken place, Ararat could have been active? On the sides of Ararat there are parasitic craters that could have filled the air with volcanic ash, covered the wooden ark, which was then covered by snow and ice, and the petrification process then could have begun to take place. It is, in fact, logical that this would have happened. To continue on:

> Early in September, a Kurdish farmer named Resit, was about two-thirds of the way up the 16,000-foot peak when he came upon an object he had never seen before, although he had been up the mountain many times. He moved around it and then climbed higher to examine it from above.
>
> "There," Resit said, "was the prow of a ship, protruding from a canyon down which tons of melting ice and snow had been rushing for more than two months. The prow was almost entirely revealed, but the rest of the object was still covered.
>
> "The contour of the earth," Resit said, "indicated the invisible part of the object was shaped like a ship. The prow," he added, "was the size of a house."
>
> Resit climbed down to it and with his dagger tried to break off a piece of a prow. It was so hard it would not break. It was blackened with age. Resit insisted it was not a simple rock formation.
>
> "I know a ship when I see one," he said. "This is a ship." He spread the word among little villages at the base of the mountain, and peasants began climbing up its northern slopes to see the weird thing he had found. Each who came said it was a ship.[7]

The year 1948 was hot and dry — good for the possibility of a great melt-back of snow and ice. "It could well have happened," according to C. Allen Roy, the weather data expert.[8]

We've skipped over a few years. I'm going to go back to 1905 and what Georgie Hagopian remembered.

HAGOPIAN

In 1905, a ten-year-old Armenian boy set out with his uncle on the long, seven-day journey from Azerbaijan in Old Persia to Mount Ararat to check on their flocks and herds, and to bring back a winter's supply of delicious butters and cheeses. Business attended to, the uncle packed supplies and brought around a sturdy little mountain esek (donkey) ready for a trip.

"Where are we going, Uncle?" asked the excited little boy.

"Georgie, we're going up to see the Holy ark. . . ."

For some distance the patient beast of burden plodded along the winding, upward trail, but at last they reached the place where he must be left behind. Here the stalwart uncle shouldered not only the supplies, but the boy, and started the steep ascent. Up, up, went the trail until the lad's excitement turned to bewilderment and then to fear, as the mist-shrouded valleys were left far behind. At last, when it seemed they must have reached the very top of the world, a gladsome sight appeared. There stood the old Ark "just as clear as you can see this car," as the old man was to describe it more than sixty years later. To the awestruck child it appeared to be "1,000 feet long and at least 600 feet wide," as he gazed upward at it from the ground.

The ship was sitting on a large rock, he recalled, and was surrounded by snow, on the edge of a cliff so deep and precipitous that is seemed to the child that it would have been well-nigh impossible to reach it from that side.

It seems there had been little precipitation that year, and the ark was visible from end to end. The uncle piled up rocks and hoisted the youngster to the top. He must have followed, at least part way, for Georgie vividly remembered watching his uncle brush the snow from the plain, flat roof with his hands. Under the light covering of snow, green moss was growing like grass.[9]

Before we go any further, I want to clear up this one point. "There is a legend (among the Turks) that the 'green ark' still stands on the summit of Mount Ararat, guarded by jinn. . . ."[10]

That lichens and moss can and do grow at an elevation between 14,000 to 17,000 feet was verified in 1978 by James Lee, who called the Smithsonian Institute to clarify Georgie's statement that "green moss was growing like grass" and that "the wood was dark brown but covered with a soft green mold."[11]

The ship was long, he remembered, "not square or round, and the sides tipped out." The part of the bottom that was visible was, like the roof, "as flat as can be." There was no door on the side they examined, only the window holes in the top under the overhanging roof, about eighteen inches high and perhaps thirty inches long; many of them, he remembered, perhaps fifty, he said — he couldn't count them all — ran along the side. [Note: The Scripture said in Genesis

6:16, "A window shalt thou make to the ark and in a cubit shall thou finish it above." This refers to a space "above" the ark, under the roof, I believe, "finished," or extending around the ark to a height of 1 cubit, or quite possibly, approximately 18 inches.]

The old man said the ship was definitely made from wood. "There was no two ways about it," he declared emphatically in his picturesque English. The grain was plainly visible but appeared almost "petrified," as hard as rock, so hard in fact that his uncle's muzzle-loading musket did not even make a dent in its sides. Georgie could not remember seeing any nails, but the sides were so smooth that the ship appeared as if it had been molded in one piece, and there was no place where one could put his fingers between the cracks. The wood was dark brown but covered with a soft green mold. Even his uncle's long, steel-bladed hunting knife failed to cut off a "good-luck" piece to take home.

Had Georgie ever seen anything like it since, he was asked? "Never," he replied, "except once a tunafish tanker that reminded him of the ark. It looked exactly like a barge," he said. "The nose was flat in front, with the underneath curve a little more pronounced." Did he know of anyone else who had seen the ship? "Oh yes," was the eager reply. "Many other boys had seen it, too." When he used to tell his friends about the thrilling trip with his uncle, they used to tell Georgie, "We saw the ark, too!"[12]

Georgie had seen the ark on many other occasions as he cared for his flocks on the slopes of Ararat.

To sum it up, Georgie's sightings were in the summer of a year that had had very little precipitation, and yet the ark was surrounded by snow. He says of the ark's location and his climb, they were at the top of the world, with the valleys left far behind. (He says nothing of the Ahora Gorge, but he may not have known the name. He mentions a cliff so deep and precipitous that it seems impossible to reach the ark from that side.) Evidently the donkey had to be left far behind as they climbed the steep ascent . . . on a rock by a precipice . . . it sits. Also, Georgie saw the ship while tending sheep.

LaHaye and Morris add this about Georgie:

It was a very hot year with little snowfall after a three-year drought. . . . The ark is on a large, bluish-green rock, but one side was on the edge of a steep cliff, impossible to climb from that side. A point later brought out is that "when he first saw the structure, it looked as if it were made of stone, he didn't realize that it was actually the ark." According to this, the ark may be hard to see or recognize, even when looking directly at it.

"A green moss covered the ark. It made the ark seem soft and moldy." This probably accounts for some reports indicating that it was very rotted or in a state of being "decayed"... besides if it was decayed or rotten, I don't think it would have lasted. "When he peeled the moss off, Hagopian exposed more of the dark brown petrified wood."[13]

Weather data from 1901–1904 suggests this was a time of drought and "less than average percipitation." This supports Hagopian's story.[14]

In considering the validity of Hagopian's report, I will point out that Elfred Lee, ark researcher and former head of the art department at Oakwood College, Huntsville, Alabama, interviewed Hagopian several times over a period of a year and a half before Hagopian's death in 1972. Through these interviews Elfred was able to draw a likeness of the ark from the memory of Georgie Hagopian. After spending time in discussion with Elfred, it is my opinion that this is one report which must be seriously considered as it is quite possibly a truthful account.

In the beginning of this chapter, I indicated how I couldn't accept that some of the locals didn't know of the ark's location. The reports that we've just read surely indicate that the ark could in fact exist, and at least some of the locals did at one time know its location. It's hard to understand why that information is now suppressed, unless there is something to an old Armenian tradition that says God himself is preserving Noah's great ship until the end of time, when it will again be revealed to prove to the world that the biblical story of his dealings with a wicked ancient world is true.[15] To add to this, I firmly believe that the governments of Turkey, Russia, and the United States know exactly where the ark sits. They suppress the information, but considering the Armenian tradition mentioned, God is in charge. The structure will be revealed in its time. We climb the mountain and search, hoping it is, in fact, God's time as we climb. Use us, O Lord, is our prayer.

WORLD WAR II
AND OTHER REPORTS

RUSSIA AGAIN

There were several reported sightings during the World War II time frame which should be considered for what importance they may have in contributing information helpful in a rediscovery.

During World War II it was reported in a newspaper clipping (exact date uncertain) from Albuquerque, New Mexico, that a Major Jasper Maskelyn, wartime Chief of Russian Camouflage had sent one of his fliers over Mount Ararat in a reconnaissance plane in an attempt to verify and check out the story of the aviator's sighting in World War I (the Roskovitsky account). According to this story, the second flier did discover a partly submerged vessel in an ice lake. Arctic climbers were again dispatched to the site. They reached the lake, which was partly thawed, and actually found the remains of the ark, which was reported to be more than 400 feet long. They said it was "very rotted" and composed of a fossilized wood looking almost like coal.[1]

As you recall, Hagopian's report said that the ship was covered with a soft, green mold and that lichens and moss can grow at altitudes of 14,000 to 17,000 feet.[2] This could explain the appearance of being "very rotted." Under the mold, Hagopian said it was "almost petrified, as hard as rock"[3] — compare to this report of a "fossilized wood-looking almost like coal."

This latter story seems to provide incontrovertible evidence that WWI "rumor" was true, that the photographs and other important data verifying the existence of Noah's ark did indeed reach Bolshevik hands, and that the material is still preserved in Russian government archives today — also, that this data contains detailed information as to how to reach the great ship either by ground or by air.

It is a mystery that such an electrifying news item as a rediscovery of Noah's ark should have caused so little stir in Christian communities of the day. As Viscount James Bryce once observed concerning another vital subject. "The public is extremely fitful . . . and soon ceases to note what does not fill the newspapers."[4]

An interesting sidelight to the Maskelyn report comes from a C. Allen Roy in a letter dated June 19, 1975: "One of my friends claims to have (somewhere) a small pamphlet with a photo of the Ark, and of the Russian airmen who took the picture, that his father gave him during WWII. It is printed on light blue paper and tells of the pilot taking the picture and of a group being sent up to it in 1942 (or so). He describes the picture with the Ark sticking out of the snow and ice into a small pond. There are supposed to be two of these pamphlets still around, the one my friend has and one his father has." To date, this pamphlet has not been located.

AUSSIE TAYLOR

Another strange but convincing story came to light in late June and early July of 1977.

Following a "Noah's Ark" presentation in the Fine Arts Building at Fort Lewis College in Durango, Colorado, Dale Nice, a businessman from Cortez, Colorado, announced that he had seen a picture of the ark in World War II. Not only that, but his wartime buddy Roy Tibbetts, who had served with him in the Seabees in New Guinea, also lived in the area, and he too had seen the picture.

In response to our request, and more than eager and willing to help, Nice immediately contacted his old friend. On July 4, the two men drove to Farmington, New Mexico, for a taped interview, from which the following story has been gleaned.

It seems that an Australian whom they remembered only as R. Taylor, had come to their tent to look up one of their platoon members, a Wes Taylor, to learn if there might possibly be any relation between them. It was during his brief visit that the Aussie, as they called him, had shown them several pictures that he carried in the breast pocket of his battle jacket, along with his can of Sir Walter Raleigh tobacco. Nice remembers looking at only one, but Roy

Tibbetts recalls seeing at least two pictures, not exactly identical, but very similar.

The photo was very clear, and the men recalled it distinctly, although they had not been particularly interested in hearing about the ark at the time. As they put it, they were more interested in passing around pictures of their wives and sweethearts than looking at snowfields and a purported ship on an icy mountain in a remote part of the world.

"What with war and Japs on their minds," said Tibbetts, "the average person wouldn't remember such things, but for some reason I've kept track of a lot of things."

Taylor, as they recalled, had been called back from Europe when the Australians had entered the war — around 1940–1941 — they believed. He had been sent to New Guinea to train convicted but rehabilitated headhunters as native police. It was probably during his European tour of duty that Taylor, described as an adventurous type, had made his journey to Ararat, where he told them he had climbed the mountain and photographed the ark.

It is not known what previous knowledge or curiosity had prompted him to climb Ararat's icy slopes to search for the ark, or if his discovery was accidental or planned.

The object, which Taylor had assured them was Noah's ark, appears to sit in a small basin which was situated in a larger basin, surrounded by snowfields. It looked to be slightly tilted to one side, also possibly slanting a bit downhill and grounded on the shore of a small pool of water at one end. Both ends were still buried in snow, and the object leaned against a dike, or hogback, or ridge, protruding some 30 to 40 feet above the snow.

Taylor had pointed out footprints, plainly visible in the snow, that led across the basin to the ship. They were his own footsteps, he declared, from boots specially made-to-fit in Turkey, from goatskin with the hair turned inside. It was obvious he had somehow managed to climb to a higher vantage point above the ship, and from there the pictures were taken.

The ark, the man said, was very dark, but not as black in color as the rocky ridge it was leaning against, and it seemed to be sitting at an angle, kind of on its side. Right at the end of it, recalled Nice, was what he took to be ice water. Neither

Dale Nice nor Roy Tibbetts recalled seeing a door. Perhaps it was still hidden under the snow. The top appeared to be slightly rounded but, perhaps because of the tilt, no catwalk or windows were visible in the photos. Said Nice, "The thing that impressed me was that there was a little pond of water there — I couldn't figure that out, at that altitude. . . . Was the ship quite close to the hogback?" "Yes," replied Tibbetts, "right at the base of it." Pointing to the sketch, Nice added, "It was lying right in here, and apparently right against it." "Actually," commented Tibbetts, "we don't know if the picture was taken from 100 feet or 100 yards."[5]

REFLECTION

We read many times of a pond of water associated with the sightings of the ark; glacial melt water very high up the mountain. Nice couldn't figure it out — he said "a pond of water at that altitude." The Rockies of Colorado, being about the same latitude as Ararat, could give us a clue here. I've noticed as I've flown over the Rockies several times all during the year, that only at the peak of the summer will all the little ponds on the mountain tops be seen without their frozen cover. Occasionally on the shady side, near 14,000 feet, a pond will still be partly covered with ice, even in early August. Since the reports of glacial melt water, a small lake, or a pond are so frequently reported with the sightings we have, I suggest the sun must shine on the area a good part of the day, perhaps the afternoon sun, as the day is then at its warmest.

Taylor's report mentions something additional. "The ark appears to sit in a small basin in a larger basin." Previously, we read of a "high mountain valley" as per Haji Yearam. An area where there was a "gem of a lake," as in the Roskovitsky report. "In the saddle of two peaks," Alexander Koors reports. A mountain "glen and ravine," in the Turkish reports. "A canyon," according to Resit. And the young boy who followed a stray goat up the mountain said he saw "a huge ship encased in ice and the object sat in a small lake on the mountainside, and rested on a sort of ledge or cliff which dropped off very rapidly on the front side. The valley was surrounded on the other three sides by walls of rock and small jagged peaks and terrain." Hagopian said it was "surrounded by snow." Taylor said it was "surrounded by snow fields." In Taylor's report, it "leaned against a hogback or ridge," and there was a "pool of water." There are many reports we've read of melted glacial water being present. The Turks reported it being on the "left side of a ravine." This gives the possibility of lying up against a ridge of rock or hogback. Being as it is, near or in a "wild and inaccessible area" as in the Turkish report, or "leaning on a big rock" in the Ayranci report, and "surrounded by small peaks" as in the Haji Yearam report, and considering again the report of the young boy who followed the goat up the mountain, to mention just a few, I do not believe Taylor's report to be any different from the others we've read.

As far as the ark being in such a place, and at an angle, I will assume this: the ark didn't land in that position or place; it moved; and I doubt by the slow glacial movement of the ice. Because of earthquake activity it could have moved rapidly to where it sits now. I will speculate that the ark was once buried in the ice on or very near the peak where it originally landed. The Bible says, "And the waters prevailed exceedingly upon the earth; and all the high hills that were under the whole Heaven, were covered. Fifteen cubits upward did the waters prevail, and the mountains were covered" (Gen. 7:19–20;KJV). "And the Ark rested in the seventh month on the seventeenth day of the month, upon the Mountains of Ararat. And the waters decreased continually until the tenth month: In the tenth month, on the first day of the month, were the tops of the mountains seen" (Gen. 8:4–5;KJV).

In the 73 days from the time the Ark landed to the time the tops of the mountains were seen with the water decreasing continually, I suggest the possibility that it landed very high on a tall mountain, at least taller than those which were surrounding it.

Many of you may find it difficult to believe there could ever have been water enough to land a huge ship high on a tall mountain. We will consider this later on in somewhat more detail. Perhaps you would rather believe that the mountain grew after the ark landed. This is something to consider, as the mountain is a volcano. There is evidence of some recent volcanic activity along the sides of Ararat, and the mountain shows evidence of much growth in an unusual way; also, it is in a highly active earthquake area. This area of eastern Turkey is an area of much uplift and block faulting. These avenues of thought, along with others, I will endeavor to bring out as you read on. My intention now is to continue along the line of thought that the ark did not land in such a rugged place as the reports indicate. I believe the ark landed near the summit, and the slope was gradual to its base below. The travel down the mountain then would have been easy. Since this is obviously not the case now, the ark must have moved. The explosion of 1840, which we have read about, could have jostled the hidden treasure around a bit (since it is reported that the ice cap near the Ahora Gorge shattered, and chunks of ice and rock were thrown quite a distance), and I believe the Lord saw that the ark was not destroyed, even though a few timbers may have gone here and there, but was safely tucked away in hiding until His time to reveal it.

Let us go on and explore this mystery further, first of all with a few more reported sightings.

STARS AND STRIPES, AND SUCH

This brings us directly to one of the most frustrating and elusive aspects of the search for photographic evidence of the existence of Noah's ark, and concerns that brief and, as some say, slightly facetious item that purportedly appeared in the armed force's publication, *Stars and Stripes*, late in the summer of 1943.[6]

One of the earliest confirmations of this story comes through two Southern California physicians, Dr. Chaunceford A. Mounce, and a Dr. Connor, both of whom served in Algeria during the first six months of 1943, and in Tunisia the last six months of 1943. "If you could get the *Stars and Stripes* of the 12th and 15th Air Force," suggests Dr. Mounce after these many years, "I am certain you would find the story about the ship on Ararat. . . . I saw the report on the front page of Stars and Stripes. . . . Mediterranean copy sometime during the summer of 1943."

Another gentleman, a Mr. Homer Wyman, a veteran of WWII who had also served in Tunisia during the summer of 1943, clearly remembered the article in *Stars and Stripes*. He said the story had created such a sensation at the Air Force base where he was stationed that the French chaplain had been moved to preach a sermon about Noah and the flood the very next day at church! Wyman had clipped the story and sent it home to his wife, and it was later included in a scrapbook with his other wartime souvenirs. One day while he was away on business, his wife decided to transfer all the mementos from the old scrapbook into a new one for a homecoming surprise. But the tattered, yellowed, old clippings in the original book — including the article about the aerial discovery of the ark in the *Stars and Stripes* — did not take kindly to the transplant, and they were thrown away. It was not until a few weeks later — in December 1969 — that Homer Wyman ruefully realized the importance of the loss, as he visited in the home of Eryl Cummings and discovered that this very item had been the object of intensive but unsuccessful research for so many years.[7]

A like story concerns a very exciting letter that arrived soon after the first edition of *Noah's Ark: Fact or Fable?* came off the press in 1972. The letter-writer was a Christian woman by the name of Mrs. Oscar Wild. Her letter was postmarked "Hoodsport, Washington." "My first husband," she wrote, "was an officer in World War II (with the 73 Station Hospital). He was a MAC officer — they were in Constantine and Claser according to various changes in the battle in Tunisia. He cut out and sent back the article and picture, which was printed in the *Stars and Stripes* in 1943. I remember the picture very well, but he died not too long after that. I'm remarried and, needless to say, the letters and many things he had sent were done away with in my new marriage. However, the picture I saw showed an air view of the Ark as seen through the ice — a plain, dark shadow, as it were, through the ice — the well-defined shape of a large ship."[8]

An interesting sidelight in connection with the *Stars and Stripes* came to our attention in the spring of 1976. A gentlemen by the name of Edward R. Babcock in the state of Washington wrote, "During World War II, I was in the Army as a radio operator. I was stationed at an air base in western Alaska. . . . while I was there (1943–1945), I saw a picture of Noah's Ark. I am nearly certain that it was in *Yank* magazine, which is a sister publication of *Stars and Stripes*." This gentleman had already verified that in the spring of 1943 no *Stars and Stripes* was published in Alaska.[9]

As our correspondent recalled it after thirty-two years, the picture he had seen was a large one, an air-photo and a large portion of the ark was exposed. "It appeared to have been taken," he said, "from a low level, and was very clear." The object was situated in a jumbled and broken ice field, and he remembered seeing no visible peaks. The end . . . was higher than the center, which disappeared downward into the ice at a fairly shallow angle.[10]

Notice in this report the ship is also at an angle, as in previous reports. This report does seem a bit contradictory, however, in that it was in a "jumbled and broken ice field," and he remembered "seeing no visible peaks." Therefore, I have a difficult time with this particular report. I don't think the ark would survive in a jumbled and broken ice field, as that would indicate ice movement, unless it appeared to be a broken ice field with chunks of ice that had fallen on it from above, and the aforementioned peaks are not in his memory. This fact may actually give us another clue; the picture was taken from low-level, the peaks are not seen because they are higher up or farther back, and out of the picture. Consider also that his recollection comes 32 years after he had seen the photo.

Since there was greater air activity over Ararat during the second World War than during any other period of aviation history; since the mountain was on the direct flight route between the Allied Air Base in Tunisia and the Russian base in Erivan (Yerevan) in Soviet Armenia; and since hundreds of flights were made to airlift supplies from the United States' base to our allies in Russia, such stories involving the *Stars and Stripes*, and possibly the *Yank* magazine, at least have a strong ring of credibility.

Even though countless volunteer man (and woman) hours, have been spent trying to "run down" and verify this important link with the rumors, no trace of the story has been found. Private collections of the *Stars and Stripes*, government archives, and military libraries and files — for some mysterious reason — have not turned up entirely complete editions. [Author comment: In my own intensive library search, neither could I locate this story.]

Nevertheless, one cannot entirely ignore the statements of the reliable individuals who have offered their personal testimonies of either having read the news item themselves, or at one time actually having the clipping in their possession. . . .

Ever since 1945 persistent rumors had drifted in of fliers, sometimes said to be Australians, who had appeared briefly in an English pub where they showed aerial pictures of an object they said was Noah's ark, and which they had photographed in a cleft of Mount Ararat. In another story, a Florida veteran reported seeing motion pictures of Mount

Ararat, purported to have been taken from a U.S. Air Force plane, in which a large portion of the ship could be seen.[11]

Now let's add this up. Remember what Hagopian said, "The ship was sitting on a large rock surrounded by snow on the edge of a cliff, so deep and precipitous that it seemed well nigh impossible to reach it from that side." Also recall the young boy who followed the goat up the mountain; he came to the end of the trail, there he was astonished to see below him a huge ship encased in ice. "The object sat in a small lake on the mountainside, and rested on a sort of ledge or cliff, which dropped off very rapidly on the front side. The valley was surrounded on the other three sides by walls of rock and small jagged peaks and terrain."

Australians in an English pub showed pictures of Noah's ark in a cleft of Mount Ararat. This falls in line with reports previously discussed of the ark in a little valley, small basin, saddle of two peaks, glen, canyon, ravine, and the like.

The picture in the *Stars and Stripes*, according to at least one report, showed an air view of the ark through the ice — "a plain, dark shadow, as it were, through the ice — the well-defined shape of a large ship." Here I theorize the ice must have been fairly clear; I believe this could indicate a non-moving area of ice as previously discussed. There is something I must consider at this point. The *Stars and Stripes* and the *Yank* were sister publications. The same photo could have been printed in both papers, yet reports of what was seen, do not necessarily agree. More information is needed to comment accurately here. The march of time between actually seeing the picture and telling about it may be contributing to this possible inaccuracy.

Two things I get from this information which are important: The ark can be seen from the air, particularly if someone is looking for it over the right area of the mountain, and it is probably very high up and near the edge of ice and snow on a cliff, in a secluded and rugged area of the mountain.

THE BARGE

There is one more report to back up and add to what we've already read. This report concerns a Gregor Schwinghammer, an F-100 pilot of the 428th Tactical Fighter Squadron, based in Adana, Turkey.

One day a Turkish liaison officer and C-47 pilot, whom Schwinghammer and another American pilot used to play poker with, asked them if they had ever seen Noah's Ark. Their shocked reaction was immediate. No, but they would like to. A few days later, the two American pilots and the Turk were in the air to make a hasty, counterclockwise circle around the peak. They were a bit nervous being so close to the Russian border, and only made one pass around the peak. Suddenly, there it was, lying in the snow in a sort of "saddle in the mountain." From the air it "looked like an enormous boxcar or a rectangular barge lying in a gully." Schwinghammer's first thought was, *Who would make a wooden building like a boat so high up on the mountain?* When we made a quick pass over it, I was able to see that it was banked, not as if it were a building, but like something that was moveable but just stuck there. The section "protruding from the snow and ice was about thirty to forty feet wide," and about 100 feet of the structure was exposed. "It was blackish in color."

When asked if he believed that what he saw on Mount Ararat was really Noah's ark, Col. Schwinghammer replied, "All I know is that it was a great rectangular barge-type construction alone in the ice on a big, desolate mountain. That is why it dazzled me."[12]

From this report we have the ark or "a great rectangular barge-type construction" in a sort of saddle on the mountain, lying in a gully protruding from the snow and ice about 100 feet exposed, and 30 to 40 feet wide. The ark actually should measure in the area of 80 feet wide (depending on the size of cubit used in measurement), so it is possible that their guess of 40 feet was only about half of the actual width, therefore, the exposed length of 100 feet could have been in the area of 200 feet — supposing, of course, that they did see the ark. They flew around the peak and the flight was hurried.

From this report, if it is an accurate sighting, then we can believe that the ark must lie on the Russian side of the mountain . . . otherwise, there would have been no reason to fly in a hurried circle around the peak. In this sighting we can only determine it is on the Russian side and near the peak — so it makes no difference, as far as I can tell, in which direction around the peak they went. However, they chose to go counterclockwise.

A recent report of an interview of Schwinghammer by Bill Crouse, formerly of Probe Ministries, and now of Christian Information Service of Richardson, Texas, tells us that Schwinghammer was flying an F-100, and the year was 1959.

In the interview, Schwinghammer remembered that he was flying very fast, and got a quick look at some non-descript rectangular object partially buried in the ice. It was down a ways from the summit, and located in some type of a gully. The gully had a horseshoe shape to it.

Before we go on, there is one observation I want to make as to the shape of the ark, Hagopian told us it had a flat nose — he allowed Elfred Lee to draw what his memory recalled of the shape and design of the vessel. The report we've just read gives us "a great rectangular barge-type construction." This falls in line, and is contrary to the apparent design of the ship-like bow seen of the "boat-shaped object" at the Tendurek site, which some seem to believe, is Noah's ark.

There were no photographs with the last report; however, in recalling the WWII reports, we have a different story. This brings about the obvious question. Where are they? Certainly all of them were not destroyed, and what about the people who took them — where are they? Why hasn't the ark and its location been made known to the people of the world?

Whatever the reasons, here is another account where photographs were supposedly taken and seen by several people only to disappear.

GREENE, AND HOW CLOSE?

The following is an excerpt from *Has Anybody Really Seen Noah's Ark?* by Violet Cummings:

> George Jefferson Greene was employed by an American oil company hired by the Turkish government for a dual role: To discover, if possible, new sources of oil on their eastern frontier, and at the same time, to keep a "weather" eye out for any unusual developments across the Araxes River on their Soviet neighbor's bordering frontier. Whether Greene was also keeping a weather eye out for Noah's ark, is not known.
>
> Late one summer afternoon in 1952, while reconnoitering Ararat's northeastern flank, Greene found himself staring incredulously down from his helicopter at a most startling sight. In the slanting rays of the western sun, the prow of a great ship protruded from a rubble of brush, mud, stone, and large chunks of ice.
>
> The joints and parallel horizontal timber of a great wooden structure could be seen plainly. It lay on an imbricate

fault or ledge, its prow pointing northward and slightly west. Only one side of the ship could be seen, but Greene knew instinctively that he was gazing at the Ark.[13]

In the book *In Search of Noah's Ark*, by Charles E. Sellier Jr. and Dave Balsiger, it says Greene's discovery is "on the northeast face, or north and northeastern side."[14] In John Montgomery's *Quest For Noah's Ark,* Greene was "on the northeastern flank of Mount Ararat in the late summer, and about one-third of the prow was visible from the air, and sticking out of a partly melted glacier."[15]

In *The Ark on Ararat,* by LaHaye and Morris, Greene "detoured from his major area of interest on the northern flank of the mountain to the high elevations above Ahora Gorge."[16] Friends of the late geologist say that in the late summer of 1953, Greene did indeed spot the ark in an almost inaccessible region at the 13,000-14,000 foot level on Mount Ararat. (This date conflicts with the Cummings' report by one year.) Greene described the ark as "lying generally in a north-south direction, situated seemingly on a large bench or shelf on the side of a vertical rock cliff. Protruding from the end of a melting snow field or glacier, only about one-third was visible." The friends of George Greene mentioned in Cummings' book are Frank Neff of Corpus Christi, Texas, and Fred Drake of Benson, Arizona. There is also a Mr. Fred Kelly of Columbus, Kansas. He sent a drawing of what he remembers of the photograph to Violet Cummings.

Violet Cummings' book goes on to report:

> Directing his pilot to maneuver the craft as close as possible, Greene reached for his camera to record the sight. From as close as they could fly, the shutter snapped again and again, photographing priceless views, both from the side and front. The quick-thinking engineer also sketched a map of the area, with landmarks that would be useful later when he returned to make a ground investigation of the object, as he knew immediately he must do someday.

> Back in civilization once more, his startling story of discovery was strongly reinforced by half a dozen clear, 8 x 10 black-and-white- photos of the ship. Greene confidently expected to interest financial sponsors for an immediate return to the site. Unbelievable as it now seems, neither family nor friends responded to his pleas. They were simply not interested in Noah's Ark, located on a strange mountain in a strange land halfway around the world! Many people

saw and remembered the photos and heard the story; at least 30 persons still clearly recalled them in 1967, some 15 years later.

For several years, Greene apparently pursued his dream, showing his pictures and telling his story in the various places where his engineering profession took him to work. At last, possibly disheartened at this failure, to realize what seemed to him an important undertaking, he left for British Guyana to engage in placer mining for gold. Here on December 17, 1962, Greene met a violent death, under mysterious circumstances that have never been completely clarified.

He was found floating in the pool of his hotel. From a reliable source, it seemed an impossibility that Greene could have "fallen" into the pool, for, according to memory after many years, the pool was not under the balcony. It seems much more likely that Greene was murdered in his room, thrown from the balcony, then dragged to the pool and dumped in. A member of Greene's family who personally investigated his death, reports that many of Greene's bones were broken.

There was considerable newspaper publicity about the strange case at the time, with rumors of foul play drifting through the town. It has been supposed that Greene was murdered for his gold. However, his briefcase was found still under the bed, but all its contents, including his personal papers, were gone. Had the criminals also been after the priceless photos of the Ark, or Had Greene left them in the States in some bank vault, known only to himself? To date, we do not know.[17]

In review of this report, the first thing we will consider is whether or not a helicopter could reach an altitude of 14,000 feet at that time — the year was 1952 or 1953.

We don't know which helicopter Greene had in his possession at the time. I obtained from an ex-Marine pilot, an Aircraft Recognition Manual dated 1962, and issued by direction of Chief of Bureau of Naval Weapons. This document tells us that in 1962, (which is nine or ten years later, but it was the best I could come up with to that point), Turkey was using the Sikorsky made by Chickasaw HD-19 helicopter. This military document does not tell me the service ceiling of the HD-19 helicopter.

Keep in mind, I do not know if the HD-19 was the chopper Greene had, or not. It may have been a helicopter owned by the oil company he worked for, and not in the Turkish registry. My ex-Marine pilot friend, now an airline captain, used to fly the HD-19, and he felt the chopper would have had a tough time reaching an altitude of 14,000 feet, unless it was a planned operation and the aircraft had a very light load. So far, this information has not been very helpful in our making a determination as to whether attaining an altitude of 14,000 feet was possible in 1952 in a helicopter.

I wrote to Sikorsky. I also wrote to the air force and requested information pertaining to what helicopter could have been there during 1952–1953, and also information as to the service ceiling of the aircraft. Sikorsky sent their reply, dated 5 December, 1984: "In response to your letter of 14 November, 1984, we are unable to provide the exact information you request based on variables involved; density, altitude, ambient temperatures, aircraft gross weight, etc. But we would conjecture that a ceiling of 10,000 to 11,000 feet above sea level would be realistic." Not exactly the information I had hoped for.

I sent an inquiry to the Air Force. I received a reply from the Air University Library, Maxwell Air Force Base, Alabama, dated March 7, 1985. It said in part, "The Air University interlibrary does not have the staff to do the in-depth research required by your request. We did check our collection for easily obtained information. Several items are enclosed; maybe they will be of some value." The material later sent to me by the Air Force, listed the service ceiling of the HD-19 as 10,500 feet, which is in line with Sikorsky's reply.

All in all, the information I received did not really help, and referred me to the Smithsonian Aerospace Museum Library in Washington, D.C. I appreciate their reply and their attempt to help. I then contacted the Smithsonian.

While awaiting their reply, I considered the Soviet Union and their helicopter technology of the time. One all-purpose helicopter that was used in the USSR, Turkey's neighbor, and possibly could have been used by the Turkish government, was the "Hound." The aircraft had a single piston engine and a service ceiling of 18,000 feet. On April 26, 1956, it set an altitude record of 19,843 feet.[18]

The "Horse" was another Soviet helicopter. This one, with two-piston engines, also had a service ceiling of 18,000 feet, and on December 17, 1955, the horse was able to carry a load of 4,000 lbs. to 16,673 feet.[19] So there definitely were helicopters in the Soviet registry that could do the job two to three years after Greene's sighting.

The helicopters discussed so far have been powered by piston engines. Possibly the oil company had its own chopper and, if so, it could have been the top of the line at that time. Oil companies usually go first class. If a turbine-powered chopper was used, attaining 14,000 feet would have not been an obstacle. Helicopter news coverage does that and more, everyday. Whether or not a turbine-powered helicopter was available for commercial use in 1952, I don't know for sure. However, I am inclined to believe that this was not the case. From an article entitled "The Turbine Revolution":

> It was also in the mid-1950s that the next major break-through gave the fledgling helicopter industry an unexpected impetus. This was the application of the turboshaft engine to helicopter use. All the early helicopters, like their fixed-wing counterparts, had been powered by conventional piston engines.[20]

One of the very first turbine-powered helicopters was the French-made Alouette, Jet Powered DJINN. This Alouette helicopter appeared on the scene in 1953.[21]

Even though the chances are that Greene was not in a turbine-powered helicopter, this does not necessarily mean he would have been in a helicopter that lacked the performance to reach the altitude at which Greene reportedly saw the ark.

I received a reply to the letter I wrote to the Smithsonian. It reads, in part:

> The standing altitude record for helicopters in 1952 and 1953 was 21,215 feet, set in May 1949 by a Sikorsky S-52-1 helicopter. During the 1952–53 time frame there were at least five piston engine helicopters, the Sikorsky S-51 and S-55, Piasecki PO-22, Breguet Type III and the Bristol 171, which advertised service ceilings above 13,000 feet, and at least another six or eight helicopters being manufactured which could probably fly at or above that level at a reduced weight.

It was signed, R.F. Dreesen, Library Assistant, and dated August 28, 1985.

We now can believe it possible for Greene to have had access to a helicopter that had that capability. The photographs of the ark (which mysteriously disappeared) of which more than 30 people claim to have seen, which had been taken by Greene from the air, lend credence to the story.

Now, let's look at what Greene is supposed to have seen. First of all, he was on the north or northeastern side of the mountain. It was late on a summer afternoon, and "in the slanting rays of the western sun."

"It lay on an imbricate fault or ledge" or on a large bench or shelf on the side of a vertical rock cliff. There are many reports we've read of a ledge or cliff, including Hagopian, Nouri, and the young boy who followed the goat.

Greene's report indicated that the ark's prow points north and slightly west. We read earlier that Duran Ayranci wrote, "It was resting on a rock. It extended from north to south." The illustrations of the Australian's picture that Nice and Tibbetts drew indicates the ark lies in a north-south direction.

Again, the ship is seen from the air, sticking out of a glacier and it's at an elevation of approximately 14,000 feet. Greene says the ark is in an almost inaccessible region. Remember the Turks' description of their climb, "It was a work of enormous difficulty, and it was only after incredible hardship that they succeeded," and, "they traversed a wild and inaccessible terrain." Haji Yearam said, "After an extremely perilous and difficult climb, perhaps three-fourths of the way up, the small party came to a little valley on Greater Ararat surrounded by small peaks. Here, they found the prow of a mighty ship protruding from a glacier whose melt waters formed a lake, then spilled them over in a little river that tumbled down the mountainside."

One very important statement about Greene recorded in *The Ark on Ararat* by LaHaye and Morris was, "He detoured from his major area of interest on the northern flank of the mountain to the high elevation above the Ahora Gorge." This may give us a clue. The ark may not be down in the Ahora Gorge, but in the upper reaches of, or above the gorge, and accessible to someone by a different route than the wild, inaccessible, and perilous route as described by the Russians, the Turks, and Haji Yearam.

The ark may be located two-thirds to three-quarters of the way up the 16,000-foot peak which would put it above, at the very top, or very near the top, of the rugged Ahora Gorge.

Pieces of Wood
on a Treeless Mountain

NAVARRA

Quite a lot of publicity was made in the mid-1950s about the Navarra find. Navarra claimed to have seen a great shadow under the ice and recovered a piece of hand-hewn timber from a crevasse in 1955. Photographs show him and his son pulling a piece of wood from the ice. Questions linger over the entire episode. Did he discover the remains of the ark? There is rumor that he hired a native to carry pieces of wood up the mountain, which had been previously purchased from an old fortress in Spain. There is controversy in the dates put on the wood. For example, Navarra's book says the wood tested to an age of 4,484 years, and the age of the tree at the time of the cutting was 57. This would date the cutting of the tree 4,427 years before Navarra had it tested, 4,459 years prior to 1987,[1] or 2472 B.C. If the wood is from the ark, and if the date is accurate, then the Flood would have been sometime after this date; possibly as late as 2352 B.C. assuming the ark may have taken as long as 120 years to construct.

I personally have some trouble with Navarra coming up with such an exact date on the wood he tested.

Radiocarbon dating is a method of estimating the age of carbon-containing materials by measuring the radioactivity of the carbon in them. The validity of this method rests upon certain observations and assumptions, of which the following statement is a brief summary.

An assumption is that there has been a relatively constant rate of cosmic-ray formation of C-14 in the earth's atmosphere over the most recent several thousands of years. This consideration leads to the conclusion that the proportion of C-14 in the carbon reservoir of the earth is constant, the addition by cosmic-ray production being balanced with the loss by radioactive decay.

In the use of radioactive dating or age-determining processes, a basic assumption is, in general, that the concentration of the radioactive element is changed during the life of the sample only by its natural decay process, and that the accuracy of the determination depends primarily, therefore, upon the accuracy with which the half-life of that radionuclide is known. This assumes no contamination.

If we wish to determine how long ago a tree was cut down to build an ancient fire, all we need to do is to determine the relative C-14 content of the carbon in the charcoal remaining, using the value we have determined for the half-life of C-14. If the carbon from the charcoal in an ancient cave has only one-half as much C-14 radioactivity as does carbon on earth today, then we can conclude that the tree which furnished the firewood grew 5,730 ± 30 years ago.[2]

So you can see, in this example an accuracy of plus or minus 30 years can be concluded. Is it probable that Navarra's test could determine an age, exact to the very year?

A sample given by Navarra to Jim Irwin tested out in the area of only 1,500 years old. The accuracy, or not, of carbon dating will be discussed again later in this book.

After his find, Navarra led other parties up the mountain, particularly the Archaeological Research Foundation (ARF), an outgrowth of that foundation known as SEARCH. Navarra seemed to lead the parties in different directions and different areas each time they went. At least in one case, when Navarra couldn't make the trip, his maps were followed, but proved to be too vague, and again, nothing was found.

Navarra had originally said the site of his 1955 find was on the northeastern peak, but he led the SEARCH Foundation in 1969 to the northwestern side in the area of the Parrot Glacier.

Mr. Pat Frost, an elementary school principal of Kingfisher, Oklahoma, visited the site in 1979. In a personal letter to Cummings on September 12, Frost wrote:

> Navarra's glaciers is also not the resting place of the ark. In 1969, this glacier or ice pack extending back in the mountain, might have looked like a good place for the Ark to be hidden. Today, this ice peak is melted, filled with very deep crevasses, and is only about 150 feet long. It is not large enough to be the resting place of the ark. Also, the mountain has caved in on a lot of the ice pack. The glacier that runs beside the ice

pack has melted down 50 to 75 feet since 1969. The water is rushing down this glacier and disappears into big holes in the mountain, making a loud noise as it goes into the mountain.

My guide and I were eating our lunch on a big flat rock overlooking the mill pond at Navarra's glacier the other day, when the whole side of the area starting sliding into the water. We grabbed our cameras, food, and equipment, and got out of the way as fast as we could. By the time I finally got my movie camera going, everything had disappeared into the water. The water was still boiling from the rock slide.[3]

It is interesting to note that the "Navarra site" on the Parrot Glacier is not in an area of the mountain described as rugged, with small peaks and small valleys, such as the other reported discoveries we have read about. The Parrot Glacier is not a stationary glacier; neither is it located in an area of imbricate faults as the sighting reported by George Greene. The Parrot Glacier is not in a wild, inaccessible locality, it is not large enough to conceal a great wooden structure the size of a city block, it is not on the northeast side of the mountain on the 16,000-foot peak, it is not necessary to carve steps in the rocks in order to reach it from below, neither does the Parrot Glacier overlook the Great Chasm of the Ahora Gorge, and it is not at the division of the glaciers that feed the Ahora valley below and the northwest glacier on the 17,000-foot peak. All these descriptions were detailed not only by Navarra, but in various other accounts.[4] (Navarra's own account of the climb is outlined later in this chapter.)

William Farrand, a geologist on a survey of the Parrot Glacier said, on March 8, 1973, to James Lee, the former secretary-treasurer of the SEARCH Foundation, "Considering that the artifact area is part of a moving glacier, and that glacier was bigger and, therefore, more vigorous in the recent past (200 years), I would say that it is extremely unlikely that a wooden construction of the dimensions that you cite, could have remained intact under the moving ice. Fragments and splinters of wood may well have remained, however, and to my knowledge, this is all that has ever been reported."[5]

Apparently, during the 1969 expedition some small fragments of wood were found. Although it is fair to say Navarra may have done his best to lead the team to the site of the ark, and maybe the wood found was actually from the ship, some believe they were planted there. Navarra had apparently become lost for a day, and shortly after his return, a few pieces of wood suddenly appeared. Bud Crawford, a member of the expedition, put it this way, "It was strange that only a day or so after Navarra had become lost, we found the wood."[6] Elfred Lee, the photographer, had another question. "Why such 'shingles' when Navarra had reported 150-foot beams in 1955?"[7] Navarra's theory apparently is that the ark was broken up in the glacier and most of the wood lies in a lake under the ice. This broken-ark theory does not fit well with the other reports of sightings, and is contested by at least one, in the person of Georgie Hagopian.

When told of the find of pieces of wood during the 1969 expedition, Hagopian, then an old man, was questioned.

> The old man refused to believe that the pieces of Navarra's wood he was shown, could possibly be a part of Noah's ark. "Almighty God," he insisted, "would never permit the ark to be cut and broken up. When I saw Noah's ark," he reminisced, "it was absolutely petrified. It was pure stone. It would be impossible to break it piece by piece. I would not believe it if I saw it with my own eyes."[8]

Mr. Navarra may well have found wood on the mountain, however it does sound as though there is room for doubt in Ferdinand Navarra's finding of wood from Noah's ark; at least on that expedition. I prefer to believe that, than to doubt Hagopian, for I, too, cannot accept a broken-ark theory. I believe the ark will be found essentially intact. Prehaps there is another source for the wood found on the 1969 expedition.

Now let's backtrack a bit to 1952–1955, and look at what Navarra said then about the route to the area of his find. Cummings is of this opinion concerning Navarra's journey:

> Navarra seemed sure of his route, as he began his expedition in the summer of 1952. His most important objective, after scaling the 17,000-foot peak, was to explore the gorge of the Ahora Valley on the northeastern face, and to penetrate as far as possible into the Great Chasm so mutilated by the explosion of 1840. But like many explorers before and since, Navarra received scant encouragement from the villagers he met as he passed through. The Moslem Kurds who, with the Armenians, had claimed Ararat as their ancestral home since the beginning of recorded history, also shared their superstitious beliefs about the Ark. "Yes," said the old men of Bayazid, the ark was "indeed on the mountain," but "it would never be found."

As the party progressed up the gorge, their shepherd

guides tantalized them with tales of former "pious pilgrimages" by devout monks who had formerly actually visited the ark. "Which way did they go?" asked Navarra, curiously. A shepherd pointed out a breach on the right-hand wall ahead on the other slope, toward the southwest, but assured the explorers that they could never negotiate the steep cliffs ahead. "You can't go that way," warned a young shepherd, "because there's magic there." Then at 10,000 feet, their native escorts abandoned them with significant glances, refusing to go a step further into the forbidden zone."[9]

Navarra explains the "magic" this way:

> Men had become this far in former times, mountain-sickness had taken hold of them, and in their simple minds, they had ascribed this phenomenon to the diety.[10]

I disagree with this assessment. The Kurds are mountain men. They don't get mountain-sickness.

Nevertheless, in 1952, in spite of the dire warnings and the desertion of their guides, Navarra and his party proceeded to the head of the gorge, then turned and made their way across the treacherously crevassed Black Glacier. Here they were stopped by the forbidding canyon wall. It was almost dark.[11]

It seems profitable at this point to remind the reader that prior to the 1840 disaster, the "steep cliffs" at the head of the gorge, and the "forbidding canyon wall," did not exist.

The report says that Navarra and his team had "brought no suitable equipment to attempt a climb." I assume by this that they either were referrring to a technical climb, for which they were not prepared, or they were just on a hike to investigate that particular area of the Ahora Gorge, with no intention of a complete search at that particular time. Navarra said of his plans:

> First we wished to penetrate as far as possible into the valley of Ahora, the village destroyed in the 1840 earthquake. Next, we wanted to climb Mount Ararat, and finally we hoped to discover the lake in which, according to many witnesses, the ark is partly submerged.[12]

The party contented themselves with climbing up into a "rock chimney" where they came out upon a platform from which they could survey that face of the mountainside from a height of 11,500 feet. From this vantage point, they could see the "breach," or opening on the southwest wall which the shepherds had pointed out as the route the monks had used to climb to the ark. "We would not mind going that way ourselves," wrote Navarra later, "in spite of the stiff climb (1,500 feet higher) to 13,000 feet, but we had made no preparations to camp at night. Evening was coming, it was time to go back."[13]

They apparently had made no preparations to camp at night, because they had no intention of climbing from the Ahora Gorge. They must have simply been on an information-gathering hike. Navarra said he "wished first to penetrate into the valley of the Ahora."

Had the explorers climbed the gorge on that day and managed to reach the little valley they had at first sought from below, the ark, if it is up there, would still have been buried deep in its protective ice blanket in the ice pack at the end of the secondary glacier that had not yet melted back. However, despite the cover of ice, and according to Navarra, a ship may have been found. The events of the next few days seem to indicate this. "The outlines of the great ship were plainly visible when certain circumstances of light and shadow at a particular time of day, revealed it when it was approached from above."[14]

From Navarra's own account, they climbed to a point above the Ahora breach—the division of the glaciers. It might be assumed then that the Navarra party reached the north-northeastern side of Ararat and the 16,000-foot peak above the Ahora Gorge. This was the area above where they had previously investigated just a few days prior. Navarra does not tell us his entire route of travel, but by studying certain film footage which was taken on the Navarra expedition, Eryl Cummings believed that Navarra climbed from the west, past the area of Lake Kop, crossed the Abich I Glacier above the Cehennem Dere, (which has a vertical drop to nearly twice that of the Grand Canyon), crossed moraines which mark a division in glaciers, and descended on the Abich II Glacier in an attempt to reach the valley high above the rugged area of the Ahora Gorge, which was described by shepherds just a few days earlier.[15]

Besides not divulging the route of travel, neither does Navarra state the distance they had covered. Their persistence was eventually rewarded, for as they advanced slowly over deep, transparent ice, their attention was suddenly arrested about 2 p.m. by an astonishing patch of blackness within the ice, its "outlines sharply defined."

> I crossed an arm of the glacier and climbed to the top of the moraine. On one side I could see a mountain of ice lined with crevasses, on the other a sheer wall. At the bottom, I saw a dark mass. This mass was clearly outlined, its lines straight

and curved, and approximately 120 yards long. The general shape, I thought, resembled that of a ship.[16]

Navarra comments further:

Fascinated and intrigued, we began straightway to trace out its shape, mapping out its limits foot by foot: two progressively incurving lines were revealed which were clearly defined for a distance of three hundred cubits before meeting in the heart of the glacier. The shape was unmistakably that of a ship's hull: On either side the edges of the patch curved like the gunwales of a great boat. As for the central part, it merged into a black mass, the details of which were not discernible.

Conviction burned in our eyes: No more than a few yards of ice separated us from the extraordinary discovery which the world no longer believed possible. We had just found the ark.[17]

To comment on this discovery, I think back to the barge-like structure reported in previous sightings, and to the canyon, or rough terrain, in which the ark is reported to rest. I wonder how Navarra and his team could simply advance over deep transparent ice and see the outline of the incurving lines, and a ship's hull? It almost sounds too easy. Also, there seems to be some question in the shape of the ship. Other reports tell of a barge, not incurving lines to a ship's hull. Also, I would be interested to know how Navarra determined the length of a cubit.

As his story goes, Navarra was unable to actually get to the ark that year (1952) as it was under the ice, and in the next year his attempt was short because of mountain sickness. In 1955, he and his son Raphael made the trip and this time descended into a crevasse, and recovered a large piece of wood; wood that he claimed to be part of Noah's ark.

The wood and the controversial dates recorded in the laboratories, along with his leading of subsequent expeditions to other areas, leave his entire experience in question.

As a sidenote, C. Allen Roy, in his study of the Ararat weather history, says 1952 would not have been a good year to see the ark, as it was "the wettest year since 1896." Navarra said he saw the shadow under the ice. In 1955 the weather conditions were good for something to have been seen.[18] This is when Navarra and Raphael reportedly brought the wood out of the crevasse.

To put this short study of Navarra into perspective, Violet Cummings writes:

In a letter dated January 29, 1960, from Bordeaux, France, the French explorer explained to Eryl Cummings that Resit's discovery in 1948, on the northeastern face of the 16,000-foot peak, was very close to his own discovery in 1955. [Author — It seems to me it should have been not just "close," but the same place.]

It is over this very point that the mystery of Navarra really begins. It has become painfully apparent, for reasons known only to himself, that Navarra has led other hopeful explorers-for-the-ark, in an opposite direction on the north-western slopes to the Parrot Glacier, and each such guided expedition is now known to have been a hoax.[19]

The unanswered question is, why?

MORE WOOD

There are other reports of wood being sighted, or found high on Ararat. A Turkish-born gentlemen I have had the privilege to meet, tells a story of a piece of wood being seen by two Turkish climbers, who laughed when they saw it, thinking the Russians had carried it up there. The wood was seen on the northeast side, high up above the Ahora Gorge. This Turkish gentleman prefers to remain nameless because of this next added bit of information. He told a story of the ark being photographed by Turkish pilots as they flew over the mountain in the 1933 Kurdish uprising. There was almost no snow on the mountain that year, and the ship was seen. The Turkish gentleman has a friend working in the Turkish National Archives storehouse, and the friend "thinks" the photos are in a top secret file.

There are at least two additional sightings of wood recorded in the following two reports.

BRYCE

A devout Christian English statesman, Viscount James Bryce, climbed Ararat in 1878 and reportedly found a piece of wood high on a treeless mountain. Mrs. Cummings' book gives the elevation of the find at 13,500 feet.[20] Two other sources give the elevations of 13,000 feet and 13,900 feet.

KNIGHT

In 1936 a young archaeologist by the name of Hardwick Knight "made an accidental discovery of a framework of huge timbers extending out of the glacial ice and moraine at the 14,000-foot level on the northern slopes." Knight was within a few hundred yards of the western face of the Ahora Gorge. At the time, Knight did not associate his find with the possibility of it being part of Noah's ark, but years later (1967), after an in-depth study, Knight became convinced that the find may well have had something to do with the ark.

A return trip found the area covered with an unusual amount of heavy snow. Knight writes, "What I feel is more significant than the area of my previous find, is the area directly above the area which would feed the glacial flow. This we found to be a most inaccessible part of the mountain."[21]

We've read in previous chapters that the ark was reported to have been seen with one end damaged, with a hole in the "front" end, and part of it missing. Yet, the superstructure was essentially still intact. Could the framework of timbers found by Knight be part of, or most of, the missing timbers? Could the explosion of 1840, which I believe moved the ark, have damaged it and actually "tossed" the timbers along with large chunks of ice and rock to the place where Knight found them, and from a place not directly over the find? Possibly so. Could the ark be at the very top of the gorge, or on the northeast side, where Bryce found his piece of timber? Possibly so. Could Navarra's original report of his find on the northeastern part of the mountain be accurate, or are his subsequent climbs to the northwestern side closer to the area of his find? Personally, I tend to lean toward the northeast.

Taking into account that most of the clues seem to point to the north or northeast side of the mountain, and east and west of, and/or above the Ahora Gorge (as large an area as it is), do we then have a fairly good idea of a general area of search? Yes! Yes, if we can accept the information quoted and entered into this report, then we can assume this much. Now the question is, will the Lord God Almighty and the Turkish government allow us to find it?

Akki Usta, an old Turkish gentlemen, known as the historian of Igdir, said to Navarra and his companions on August 11, 1952, "Young men of France, you have come to explore Noah's mountain, and you think to find the ark there. Well, this is what I have to say to you: You know the legend, the beautiful legend of the vessel which God the Father brought to land on Ararat with its cargo of men and animals. And it was as a result of that loving kindness of God that the earth was repeopled after the Flood had satisfied his wrath. While Noah, his family, and the animals were able to descend from Ararat, and to go in the direction of Ahora and Erivan, the ark stayed on the mountain. You know that.

"And now listen to what I am going to say. The ark is still there! This I was told by the greybeards, and they were told it equally by those who were old during their youth. And all of us here believe it. All the people of Igdir, of Bayazid, of Erivan, to the last shepherd on the twin mountains, all believe it. And we shall hand on that belief to our children, with the bounden duty of passing it on to their descendants."

"What are your grounds for stating this with so much conviction?" Navarra asked him. The old gentleman replied, "Are there not enough signs? Do you believe that the monasteries of Ahora, of Koran and of Etchmaidzian could [have] arisen if these historic facts were not true? Know ye that to reach it [the ark] one must be as pure as a newborn child. Presumptuous is he who has known life and who yet wishes to go and seek it. The ark cannot be submitted to the outrage and sacrilege of the eyes of men."[22]

I suggest what the old man may have meant is that a close walk with God would be, no doubt, a first consideration. The motives for such a discovery must be right. By this I mean if any thought of financial or personal gain is motivating the would-be explorer, then he may just as well stay home. Also, another point that could be considered, is that if there was an ark which landed on the "mountains of Ararat," as the Bible says, if Mount Ararat is the mountain it landed upon, and if the ark has been preserved and quite well hidden until now, then is it not possible that the publicizing of such a find will be in God's own timing, and not necessarily that of the explorers?

The accidental sightings and the expeditions of the Russians before World War I, and also of Prince Nouri, who claims to have found the ship, could tell us the ark is there for anyone to find, as long as they go to the right spot. How the world perceives such a discovery may be where God's timing comes in.

By rights, the Turkish government should know where the ark is right now; that is, if it's on the mountain. Perhaps if the government of Turkey would give substantial proof of the discovery of a massive wooden ship found in the ice high on Ararat, then maybe many more people in this world would take the story of Noah, the Flood, and the written Scriptures a little more seriously. If this is to be, then perhaps it would serve as a reminder of what did happen, and possibly a warning of what may lie ahead. Perhaps this is yet to take place.

WHAT IS ARARAT?

Dr. Clifford Burdick, a structural geologist from Tucson, Arizona, carried out extensive research of Mount Ararat in eastern Turkey in the summers of 1966, 1967, and 1973. Some of what he concludes is as follows:

> Evidence gathered at Mount Ararat indicates that the original mountain was much lower than the present one, and was of a different composition, or at least of a different texture and different color. . . . The original Mount Ararat apparently was not more than 10,000 to 12,000 feet in height. The present peak is about 17,000 feet and at its greatest height, perhaps measured nearer 20,000 feet.[1]

John Morris, who holds a Ph.D. in geology, goes further to explain, in *The Ark on Ararat*, the possibility of the mountain being 20,000 feet tall at one time.

> During the Flood period, Mount Ararat grew to its greatest height, estimated at 20,000 feet. A shield-type volcano, it repeatedly erupted, not only adding to its height with the addition of the lava above, but also the pressures below simply shoving the mountain up. Since that time, erosion has worn the mountain down. As the subterranean pressures were relieved, the massive mountain sank, forming a moat around its base. This is a poorly drained area, especially on the south side, where today remains an uninhabitable, snake-infested swamp, and the rivers run toward the mountain.[2]

An observation by geologists as they visit Ararat is that of pillow lava on the mountain. Pillow lava forms under water during volcanic activity. The water has an extremely rapid cooling effect on the molten lava, and the outer 5 cm of a stagnate pillow solidifies in about

20 minutes. A pillow sack can form when lava flowing from a crack in the earth's surface is pinched off on a steep hill, and it tumbles a meter or more down a slope — such as on a mountain, under water, or even beneath the ice.[3] The possibility of pillow lava forming under the ice, as stated in this article, must be taken into consideration when realizing pillow lava exists on Ararat which is covered by an icecap.

For a professional point of view, LaHaye and Morris tell us: "Evidence that Mount Ararat was once underwater was revealed when a certain type of lava was discovered on Mount Ararat as high up as rocks are exposed, at least to the 15,000-foot level. This lava is known as "pillow" lava, because of its pillow-like appearance, and is formed only when the lava is spewed out under great depths of water. The heat sink of the water "freezes" the lava almost immediately, so quickly that only very small crystals are formed. Because of the intense water pressure, gases in the lava are trapped inside, having no time to bubble out. Consequently, the resulting rock is very dense and hard, and has a high glass content. The quick cooling also causes the rock to take on a smooth, rounded shape resembling a pillow."[4]

During some cataclysmic time in the past, the original mountain might have been 10,000 to 12,000 feet tall, as Burdick says. It erupted, and grew through the various mountain-building mechanisms involved by faulting and uplift, by underthrusting and upwelling, and the doming of the rocks from inside. The weight of this mass might well have settled the mountain as it was growing, forming what is now known as a caldera, but ultimately, I think Ararat itself grew in the area of 5,000 feet to its present height of 17,000 feet during and after the time of the Flood.

To come up with this 5,000-foot number is to assume Burdick's 10,000 to 12,000 feet as the original elevation, and add what Richard Flint, the author of *Glacial Geology and the Pleistocene Epoch*, has said:

> In North America late Pliocene or Pleistocene movements involving elevations of thousands of feet are recorded in Alaska and in the coast ranges of Southern California. — Conspicuous uplifts of what had been lowlands in Labrador and eastern Quebec occurred between middle and late Pliocene. — Iceland underwent great faulting movements, with vertical components of more than 6,000 feet, as late as the Pleistocene.
>
> The Alps were conspicuously uplifted in Pleistocene and late pre-Pleistocene time. In Asia there was great Pleistocene uplift in Turkestan, the Pamirs, the Caucasus, and Central

Asia generally. Most of the vast uplift of the Himalayas is ascribed to the latest Tertiary and Pleistocene. In South America the Peruvian Andes rose at least 5,000 feet in post Pliocene times. In Australia, the great Kosciusko Plateau uplift occurred at the close of the Pliocene, and in New Zealand there was strong late Pliocene and early Pleistocene uplift. In addition to these tectonic movements, many of the high volcanic cones around the pacific border in western and central Asia and in eastern Africa, are believed to have been built up to their present great heights during the Pliocene and Pleistocene.[5]

Now we've introduced something else into the picture. Suppose the Ice Age — that period of time known as the Pleistocene — was a result of climatic change after a global flood. If the mountains grew to great heights during this Pleistocene time, which then followed the flood, could this be an argument for improving the feasibility of "all the hills under the entire heavens" being covered with water; especially if they were not then elevated to the heights we see them now?

This chart is included along with two different points of view, on this subject of the Ice Age.

ERAS	PERIODS	ESTIMATED YEARS AGO
Cenozoic	Quaternary:	
	Recent Epoch	25,000
	Pleistocene Epoch	975,000
	Tertiary:	
	Pliocene Epoch	12,000,000

Geologic Ages according to Standard Geologic Column,
published in *What is Creation Science?*[6]

Kummel, in *History of the Earth* on page 555, suggests the glacial epoch began about 2 million years ago.[7] Morris, in the *Genesis Flood*, believes that glaciation is a result of climatic change and the Flood.[8] The Ice Age may have ended as little as five thousand years ago.

It is obvious by the vast differences in age estimations, that no one really knows when the Ice Age was present, nor when the mountains experienced a rather sudden worldwide uplift.

The growing of the mountains in the pre-Pleistocene or later Pliocene or in the Pleistocene period, was then as a result of the cataclysmic events, including the time of the Flood, and afterwards.

Dating of these periods of time will be discussed in later chapters.

Dr. Burdick explains the growth of the mountain: "The Ahora Gulch exposes the inner core of the original mountain which is distinct in color and texture from the volcanic rock. It is course-grained porphyry with a light buff color and much pyrite. This indicates a deepseated intrusive that cooled slowly, permitting the coarse phenocrysts to form first. Then the whole mass was uplifted through the cover rock, allowing the remainder of the magma to cool more quickly and form fine-grained crystals and glass. This inner core may represent the original mountain dating from creation."[9]

Apparently the Paleozoic-Mesozoic (135-600 million years ago, according to Kummel)[10] limestone complex which covered parts of the region was severely deformed, compressed, folded, and in places like the Ararat area, domed up when the rising magma burst through. This doming effect is most evident when one views the same lime-stone formations on all sides of Mount Ararat. The beds dip away from the mountain on the Turkish, the Russian, and the Persian (Iranian) sides.

Burdick points out that limestone is precipitated under water. "Therefore, such sedimentary rock must have been laid down during the inundation of the earth by the flood waters — the early part, perhaps — since Mount Ararat was apparently elevated to its full height during the latter period of the flood, to provide a haven for the Ark. There are small peaks on the top of Greater Ararat, which might well have provided that haven."[11] Obviously, Burdick disagrees with Kummel as to when the limestone was formed.

"During the Flood period — in the broad sense — at least three blankets of basaltic or andesitic lava were extruded over the first Ararat. Volcanic eruptions have taken place periodically ever since, but with subsiding activity. More recent flows have been extruded from cracks lower down on the mountain as each succeeding extru-sion had less force than the preceding one."[12]

Dr. John Morris says:

> A great deal of evidence exists indicating that not only was Mount Ararat once covered by water, but it even erupted while submerged under great depths of water. In common with many mountains around the world, Mount Ararat exhibits fossil-bearing strata. Sedimentary rock (by definition, laid down by flood waters) containing the fossil-ized remains of ocean creatures has been found as high as the snow line, approximately a 14,000-foot elevation. Further-

more, on the exposed northeastern face, layers of lava are intermingled with layers of sediments.[13]

The ice cap of Ararat is still covering the mountain to 14,000 feet in late summer . . . the approximate elevation of where the ship reportedly rests. I would imagine the ship rests at the terminal end of a glacier in non-moving, stagnate ice, in a crag, or along the side of a hidden valley above or near the upper portions of the Ahora Gorge. The ice cap itself may be up to 400 feet thick with much activity and movement in the Parrot and Abich Glaciers — not a good place for what may have once been a wooden ocean-going vessel to survive. The mountain consists of various zones, and one of importance is the pastures which are as high as 11,500 feet. Shepherds have, on occasion, reported seeing the ship. (We have already read of a couple of these sightings.) Because of the highest elevations of the pastures, at 11,500 feet, we can assume they climbed somewhat higher, in order to see the remains of the huge wooden ship which, if it is there, could in fact be Noah's ark.

In 1840, an earthquake, which has been referred to as an explosion because of the results, opened up the Ahora Gorge and scattered rocks for miles.

The cause of this explosion is controversial to some extent. One source said an earthquake could have opened one of the many faults (most lie in a southwest-northeast direction — the direction of the gorge) under a huge subterranean lake. The water mixed with the hot magmas down in the depths of the earth, and a tremendous pressure built up. Something had to give — the weak spot blew away and the gorge, as we see it now, was formed. There was no reported lava flow with the event. One possible answer is that the water put the fire out. Reports say "the ground was shaken by undulating waves from Great Ararat to the east, and the ice cap was shattered" with the blast.[14] Then again, the blast might just have been caused by a tremendous pressure build-up along the fault, and the movement of the earth along that fault releasing that pressure with one sudden movement — no water or magma involved.

Whatever the cause, it did happen, and perhaps it was then the ark moved from the area near the peak (a stationary part of the ice cap on a plateau between the peaks) or next to a peak, to the hidden valley lower down. Reports of the ark being seen have filtered down through the years, and seem to tell us that before 1840 the ark was just below the summit, and apparently in good condition. After 1840, the ark has been seen lower down, and with one end damaged.

So, what is Ararat? It's a volcano that shows evidence of growing while under water. It's a mountain with a permanent ice cap, and is located in an earthquake-active area. And, quite possibly, it is the hiding place for a great historical treasure — Noah's ark.

Was There a Flood?

A PRELUDE:
WHAT HAVE WE LEARNED?

When Charles W. Elliot retired in 1908, after nearly 40 years as president of Harvard University, he was asked to give the outstanding impression from his many years as an educator. He is reported to have replied:

> The astounding capacity of the human mind to resist the impact of a new idea. (Quoted from a Southern Baptist Sunday school quarterly in 1980).

It's ironic that a new idea can actually be the original.

I find it impossible to attempt to fully discuss the possibility of Noah's ark without discussing the extent of the Great Flood.

I find it impossible to attempt to fully discuss the extent of the Great Flood without discussing the Bible as the Word of God.

I find it impossible to discuss the Bible as the Word of God without believing in a creation.

I find it difficult, when considering the vast impact of evolution and uniformitarianism as taught to us in our schools and universities, to expect the student who has been influenced by such teachings and accepted curriculum, to believe by his own will and power of reasoning, in anything other than what he has been taught; because I once was there.

Yet, at this time in my life, I find it impossible to believe in any other answer than creationism.

I find that in order for me to write on the subject of Noah's ark, I must also attempt to deal with what I believe to be complex inaccuracies in what is taught, and accepted, as scientific theory and doctrine.

I trust you will open your minds, and find these next few chapters interesting.

WAS THERE A FLOOD?

The Doctrine of Uniformitarianism says that existing processes acting in the same manner as at present, are sufficient to account for all geological changes.

> The essential uniformity of the world in its physical aspects, is, and has always been the same with conditions unchanged, and, that the activities of the past were essentially similar to those now prevailing.[1]

This is, of course, without the possibility of a cataclysm disrupting the processes.

Charles Lyell, in *Principles of Geology*, says, "The forces now operating upon and beneath the earth's surface, may be the same both in kind and degree, as those which at remote epochs have worked out geological changes."[2] To understand this is important to the understanding of this chapter.

James Hutton, a Scottish geologist (who was first an agriculturalist), said the key to the present is in the past, in the geologic column given to us by a history of uniformity, shown by records in sedimentation and fossil data. The assumption, of course, is that the oldest rock is on the bottom and the newest is on top in a vertical column, divided into geological ages, based on the fossils found in them, correlating with the age of the rocks. This is the basis and idea of the column.

The column is interpreted on the basis of uniformitarianism. We observe and measure today how long it takes the sedimentary process to occur, and assume this has always been the case in the past. We apply this rate to the sedimentation evidence of the past, and thereby derive a concept of great ages.

The question of how thick is the geologic column, is dealt with taking the geologic column from Cambrian to Ordovician, Silurian, Permian, Triassic, Tertiary, and Pleistocene. It is estimated that the column would be at least 100 miles high, and it is impossible to have even a considerable fraction of the column in any one place. The college textbook is the only place where you will find the geologic column in its entirety. If uniformitarianism was, in fact, earth's complete history, it seems to me one would be able to find the complete column everywhere.

By the application of the principle of super position of beds, lithologic identification, recognition of unconformities, and reference to fossil successions, both thick and thin masses are correlated with other beds at other sites. So, you find one here and there, and use these principles to pile them on top of one another; then we get a stratographic succession of geologic ages. Charles Lyell developed this theory in 1830 after adapting earlier theories advocated by James Hutton and William Smith, "the father of stratigraphic geology," who believed rock layers always occur in the same sequence, and can be traced over vast areas by noting the type of fossils (index fossils). Today, Lyell's uniformitarianism model is still used as a geologic standard. In this model there is no room for cataclysm, only uniformity over vast periods of time. Consequently, we get one very old planet Earth.[3]

Dr. Gary Parker, once an evolutionist and now head of the Biology Department Graduate School at the Institute for Creation Research in San Diego, says in the Grand Canyon it is indeed true that fossils are not found at random. "They are found in certain groups known as 'geologic systems,' and these geologic systems do have a tendency to be found in a certain vertical order. That order is represented in an idea called the geologic column." The reason for this, says Parker, is not because of a sequence of evolution, but rather "because they live in different ecological zones." For instance, dinosaurs are land animals, and trilobites are bottom-dwelling sea creatures. "According to creationists, the geological systems represent different ecological zones, the buried remains of plants and animals that once lived together in the same environment." Dr. Parker also tells us there is a place in the Grand Canyon where Mississippi rock rests on top of Cambrian rock. This is difficult to explain for the evolutionist because it represents a gap in "hypothetical evolutionary time of 125 million years."[4]

It is also interesting to know that within the Grand Canyon, there is a certain water-laid sediment present in areas 600 vertical feet apart. This sediment gives evidence of having been transported and laid down by turbidity currents (a turbulent current, dense in slurries of mud and sediment moving at remarkably high speeds)[5] which could have traveled at 50 to 60 miles per hour, and rapidly eroded an area of soft rock into what we now know as the Grand Canyon. The water would have been more than 600 feet deep, and moving quite fast. This is in obvious conflict with the uniformitarianism and evolutionary theories, yet there is substantial evidence of this rapid water erosion all over the western United States.[6]

I encourage you to read *The Genesis Flood* by John Whitcomb and Henry Morris or *The Modern Creation Trilogy* by father and son Henry M. and John D. Morris.[7] These classic writings should, in my opinion, be required for each person who goes to school, or even entertains the thought of an evolutionary and uniform past. The information presented in argumentative form as to the evidence for the worldwide cataclysmic event, is shown clearly from a scientific view, in light of geologic discoveries, and it gives the biblical record to support those scientific findings and its implications. The book points out the inadequacies of uniformitarianism and evolutionism as unifying principles. The authors propose a biblically based system of creationism and cataclysm.

Let's take a look at some of what is written by these authors.

"The hostility of modern uniformitarians toward geological cataclysm, in general, and the concept of a universal deluge, in particular, is a striking phenomenon of contemporary scientific thought. In spite of the fact that actual observation of geologic processes is strictly limited to those now in operation, uniformitarians have assumed that these, and only these, acted in the past and, therefore, must be applied to the study of origins. Geologic evidences for the Great Flood are ignored and even the possibility of such a catastrophe in the past is ruled out on the basis of a prior philosophical reasoning."[8]

I have a college text book that says: "The doctrine of uniformitarianism has been a strong guiding principle in the reconstruction of the earth history, and the doctrine of uniformitarianism provides the framework within which the historical geologist operates."[9] The possibility of a Genesis flood is, of course, not even mentioned to the extent of being seriously considered as a factual event in that textbook, nor any of the others that I have. Again, the doctrine of uniformitarianism leaves no room for any biblical flood, nor any cataclysmic event of any kind. Yet, look at a mountain and wonder how it grew, or a volcano as it erupts (remember Mount St. Helens), or a tidal wave (Bangladesh, India), an earthquake (too numerous to single out), or any of the many other earth-related events that changed the landscape in a rather dramatic manner. I believe these fall into an area of definition of cataclysmic and catastrophic events.

This observation should then put a question in the minds of any thinking person to the validity of the doctrine of uniformitarianism as an absolute history of the earth through all geologic processes; the exception to this statement could possibly be in interpretation of sedimentary data.

Charles Lyell, "the high priest of uniformitarianism," and author of a famous textbook, *Principles of Geology*, was a young English attorney who had enthusiastically accepted the doctrine of gradual geological changes which had been advocated at the end of the 18th century by a Scottish geologist, James Hutton (1726–1797). Lyell insisted that all geologic processes had been very gradual in the past, and had utter abhorrence for anything suggestive of sudden catastrophes.[10]

In reading through the pages of Lyell's *Principles of Geology*, I found he challenged theories of sudden catalysms, and he referred to them as the "doctrine of alternate periods of repose and disorder." This simply means, according to Lyell, that some writers have speculated the planet Earth has had alternate periods of tranquility and convulsion — the former enduring for ages, and resembling the state of things now experienced by man; the other brief, transient, and paroxysmal, giving rise to new mountains, seas, and valleys, annihilating one set of organic beings, and ushering in the creation of another. It will be the object of the present chapter to demonstrate that these theoretical views are not borne out by a fair interpretation of geological movements.[11]

In the chapter Lyell refers to, he discusses sedimentary deposition, and volcanism as part of the uniformity of change. He speaks of living creation in a continued state of flux, and subterranean movements as gradual, and says, "There has been no universal disruption of the earth's crust or desolation of the surface since times the most remote." In other words, nothing sudden. In the summation of this chapter, Lyell concludes: "All theories are rejected which involve the assumption of sudden and violent catastrophes and revolutions of the whole earth and its inhabitants."[12] This is not in agreement at all with the biblical viewpoint of the Flood, as told to us in the Book of Genesis.

I would imagine that Lyell's doctrine of uniformitarianism is still accepted and taught today because it's somewhat easy to explain since there is no mention of the Flood, and the question of God doesn't have to be dealt with. Also, the period of time since the Flood actually has been quite uniform, except as I mentioned before for perhaps an occasional volcano, an earthquake or tidal wave, and any other related event, which many don't qualify as a uniform change. (Then there's the matter of glaciation, an interesting idea.)

An article in *Sea Frontiers* magazine, a scientific journal of the

International Oceanographic Foundation, reports on a study using oxygen-isotope analysis and radiocarbon dating methods in the Gulf of Mexico. The article says, "The study of marine sediments from the Gulf of Mexico using these methods, now suggests that there was indeed a universal flood, and that this flood came from the sea rather than from the sky." It also says the "major period of flooding was from 12,000 to 10,000 years ago, with a peak about 11,600 years ago."[13]

The study was on recent environmental evolution, and focused mainly on glaciation and interglacial environments, and sea levels of the past. Oxygen isotopic analysis and radiocarbon dating are tools used in this exercise. In the scientific article, the term "universal flood" was used, as was simply, "a major period of flooding." This had been determined because the Gulf of Mexico, where the study took place, is in open communication with the world ocean.

There is a problem with the date attributed to the universal flood in this article. It does not agree with the general time of the biblical flood according to interpretation of the biblical record. But, excluding for a moment the date, if the data from the Gulf of Mexico indicates that there was indeed a universal flood, then does this data in itself support the biblical record?

It seems to me that if the Flood of the past as reported by scientists is the same Flood of the biblical record, then some scientists or theologians are incorrectly interpreting the data necessary to date the Flood.

Now, consider the possibility of the year-long Noachin flood of the Bible being the same flood of 2,000 year's duration, as reported in the study in *Sea Frontiers*. If this was the case, then perhaps there are areas on the earth where the waters of the Flood stood over what is dry land now for a considerable length of time. That stands to reason, and maybe in those areas 2,000 years is not out of line, and not contradictory at all. I have no trouble with a 2,000-year flood, except possibly in the dating of its peak, 400 years after it began. In order to support the biblical record, I must believe that happened in the first few months. The earth was probably undergoing a lot of physical changes during the period of the Flood, and for some time afterward; all while the human race, animals, and birdlife were rebuilding again, in another part of the globe.

Here in this article we have at least some scientific evidence in the findings of this study, for a universal flood. It is notable to read that the flood came from the sea — remember what the Bible says about the fountains of the deep opening up? "The same day were all the fountains of the great deep broken up, and the windows of heaven were opened" (Gen. 7:11). The flood came from the sea and the sky.

Harold T. Wilkins writes that the earth's greatest disaster was the Noachin flood. It was not a local event, but a worldwide disaster. Wilkins tells of the ruins of many dead cities found in the jungles of South America; he believes they were inhabited before the Flood.

Old men in villages of the Sertao of Bahia had told traditions about an ancient city, under a mountain, that had been overwhelmed by an earthquake and a flood. He who went there never returned. It was a long and perilous journey, beset with serpents and jaguars.

Concerning the city of Tiahuanaca, which is now 12,000 feet up in the Andes, Wilkins quotes an explorer by the name of Colonel Fawcett. "These megalithic ruins of Tiahuanaca were never built on the Andes at all. They are part of a great city submerged ages ago in the Pacific Ocean. When the crust of the earth upheaved and created the great Andean Cordilleras, these ruins were elevated from the bed of the ocean to where you now see them." What appears to have been a seaport has been found nearby, and marine fossils and images of flying fish and seahorses are found among the prehistoric ornaments of the structures. Also in the area, bones have been found of human giants which would have been over eight feet tall.[14] Of the time before the Flood, the Scripture says, "There were giants in the earth in those days" (Gen. 6:4).

I think at this point we should consider some other evidence for water-related cataclysm found in the strata of the earth.

The great deposits of fossils all over the world — especially in the coal and oil beds of the world, are difficult to explain on the basis of uniformity. For instance, "a rock slab taken from a well-known bone bed at Agate Springs, Nebraska, is a stratum in which thousands of bones and fossil mammals have been found. The bone layers run horizontally for a large distance in the limestone hill, and have evidently been water laid. Fossils of the rhinoceros, camel, giant boar, and numerous other exotic animals are found jumbled together in this stratum."[15]

The fossils in this example could hardly have been formed in various positions of entanglement had the animals died and been gradually covered by sediment over a long period of time, as the doctrine of uniformitarianism demands. It seems to me a sudden event would more likely be reasonable, and would be a more logical answer.

Many rich fossil deposits have been found in caves, one of the outstanding being the Cumberland bone cave in Maryland. Remains of dozens of species of mammals ranging from bats to mastodons are found together in the cave, together with some reptiles and birds from different types of climates and habitats.

In this one cave, there has been found such types as the wolverine, grizzly bear, and mustelidae, which are native to Arctic regions. Peccaries, the most numerous type represented, tapirs, and an antelope, possibly related to the present day eland, are indigenous to tropical regions. Ground hog, rabbit, coyote, and hare remains are indicative of dry prairies, but on the other hand, such water-loving animals as beaver and muskrat suggest a more humid condition.[16]

The organisms could have been transported a great distance by a violent cataclysm.

This same picture is seen in a certain fossil-carrying strata of lignite in Geiseltal, Germany:

Here too, there is a complete mixture of plants and insects from all climate zones and all recognized regions of the geography of plants or animals. It is further astonishing that in certain cases the leaves have been deposited and preserved in a fully fresh condition. The chlorophyll is so well preserved that it has been possible to recognize the alpha and beta types. . . . An extravagant fact, comparable to the preservation of the chlorophyll, was the occurrence of preserved soft parts of the insects: Muscles, corium, epidermis, keratin, colour stuffs as melanin and lipochrome, glands and the contents of the intestines. Just as in the case of the chlorophyll, we are dealing with things that are easily destroyed, disintegrating in but a few days or hours. The incrustation must, therefore, have been very rapid.[17]

There are many more examples of fossils in strata which are apparently water-laid and many of these fossils indicate a rather sudden cataclysmic event. For those readers who wish other examples, I would refer you to *The Genesis Flood:* "Yet, in these very fossils beds, the organic fossils, some which are known as 'index fossils,' have been made the basis for the standard geologic time-scale, and this in turn has been the pillar of the structure of evolutionary theory!"[18] This is to say that the fossilized conglomeration of various types of animals in any one place, in water-laid strata, evidence of a water cataclysm, is apparently ignored.

It is my opinion that evolution and uniformitarianism are intricately woven together and the theories are taught in colleges and high schools without presentation of all the known data pertaining to the earth's history. I've taken some of those courses. Keep in mind that this book is not only on my own observations and experiences, but also on the writings of some who profess to be experts in their fields.

In order to best utilize these resources, along with discussing the possibility of a universal flood, we're attempting to separate the two theories, and deal with uniformitarianism and evolution in separate chapters. However, considering the nature of the subjects, they are often mentioned together as one unified idea. Let's now review the writing of the most qualified of all, and find out what He has to say about the Great Flood; this is in order to get a background and basis for discussion pertaining to the extent of this event, as related to us in Scripture. Then we'll continue with commentaries and on into the complexities in these chapters.

> And the Lord said, I will destroy man whom I have created from the face of the earth; both man, and beast, and the creeping thing, and the fowls of the air; for it repenteth me that I have made them (Gen. 6:7).

> And God looked upon the earth, and, behold, it was corrupt; for all flesh had corrupted his way upon the earth And God said unto Noah, The end of all flesh is come before me; for the earth is filled with violence through them; and, behold, I will destroy them with the earth (Gen. 6:12–13).

> And behold, I, even I, do bring a flood of waters upon the earth, to destroy all flesh, wherein is breath of life, from under heaven; and every thing that is in the earth shall die (Gen. 6:17).

> In the six hundredth year of Noah's life, in the second month, the seventeenth day of the month, the same day were all the fountains of the great deep broken up, and the windows of heaven were opened (Gen. 7:11).

> And the rain was upon the earth forty days and forty nights (Gen. 7:12).

And the waters prevailed exceedingly upon the earth; and all the high hills, that were under the whole heaven, were covered. Fifteen cubits upward did the waters prevail; and the mountains were covered. And all flesh died that moved upon the earth, both of fowl, and of cattle, and of beast, and of every creeping thing that creepeth upon the earth, and every man. All in whose nostrils was the breath of life, of all that was in the dry land, died (Gen. 7:19–22).

And God remembered Noah, and every living thing, and all the cattle that was with him in the ark: and God made a wind to pass over the earth, and the waters assuaged. The fountains also of the deep and the windows of heaven were stopped, and the rain from heaven was restrained. And the waters returned from off the earth continually: and after the end of the hundred and fifty days the waters were abated. And the ark rested in the seventh month, on the seventeenth day of the month, upon the mountains of Ararat. And the waters decreased continually until the tenth month: in the tenth month, on the first day of the month, were the tops of the mountains seen (Gen. 8:1–5).

And it came to pass in the six hundredth and first year, in the first month, the first day of the month, the waters were dried up from the off the earth: and Noah removed the covering of the ark, and looked, and, behold, the face of the ground was dry. And in the second month, on the seven and twentieth day of the month, was the earth dried. And God spake unto Noah, saying, Go forth of the ark, thou, and thy wife, and thy sons, and thy sons' wives with thee. Bring forth with thee every living thing that is with thee, of all flesh, both of fowl, and of cattle and of every creeping thing that creepeth upon the earth; that they may breed abundantly in the earth, and be fruitful, and multiply upon the earth (Gen. 8:13–17).

WAS THE FLOOD LOCAL OR UNIVERSAL?

What about a local flood? I came upon this line of thought in a most surprising place — Bible commentaries. I think for the sake of this possibility it's worthwhile to take a look at a couple of them.

Let's consider first the commentaries edited by Ellicott and his interpretation of biblical Scripture as it relates to Noah and the Flood. Ellicott, in proposal of a local flood says, "The earth, is limited to the earth as known by Noah and his contemporaries."[1]

In contrast, the Bible says in Genesis 7:19, "And the waters prevailed exceedingly upon the earth; and *all* the high hills that *were* under the *whole* heaven were covered." Take note of the words in italics. We will study these meanings throughout this chapter. Ellicott says, "The Bible word 'all' means much less than with us, and the "whole heaven" simply means the whole sky bounded by the line of the spectator's vision!"[2]

Genesis 8:4 and 5 tells us that on the 17th day of the seventh month, the ark came to rest on the mountains of Ararat. The waters continued to recede until the tenth month, and on the first day of the tenth month, the tops of the mountains became visible. This is from the New International Version. The King James Version in Genesis 8:5 reads, "And the waters decreased continually until the tenth month; in the tenth month, on the first day of the month, were the tops of the mountains seen." Consider what could be meant by "visible" versus "seen." Here we may have a problem in understanding the two different translations. I personally think we ought to stick with the King James Version.

Ellicott says, "Upon the mountains of Ararat, upon some chain of hills there, and seventy-three days afterwards, Noah found himself surrounded by an amphitheater of mountains, the word used in verse 5 being emphatic, and signifying, "The tops of the mountains became distinctly visible," and not that they had just begun to emerge. For, doubtless, after so vast a flood, mists and vapors would for a long time prevail, and shut out the surrounding world from Noah's view."[3]

I found it interesting also that Ellicott has the mist shutting out Noah's view of the mountains here, and earlier during the Deluge, Ellicott says, "Far and wide, in every direction, to the utmost reach of the beholder's gaze, no mountain was in sight."[4] Here it seems to me that he indicates Noah could see, and his vision was not obstructed.

I must wonder if Noah was even looking, or if he was able to. First of all, as I understand the Bible, Noah didn't open the window until 40 days after he landed, and I don't think he was able to see out until the window was opened, as I find no indication anywhere of there being glass in those days, so he couldn't have seen through it. I can assume the window was but a small door made of wood, large enough to let birds in and out, and kept closed in the storm. When he did open the window, he apparently wasn't able to see out of it enough to make a determination of what he was seeing. On the other hand, I imagine if Noah did look out of the window in the days before he sent the raven and the dove, that the same was true; he couldn't conclude much from what he could see. If this was not the case, why did he send the birds?

It was not until after the dove was sent out and didn't return, and the water was dried up from the earth, that Noah took a look.

> And he stayed yet other seven days; and sent forth the dove; which returned not again unto him any more. And it came to pass in the six hundredth and first year, in the first month, the first day of the month, the waters were dried-up from off the earth; and Noah removed the covering of the ark, and looked, and behold, the face of the ground was dry (Gen. 8:12–13).

It seems to me that the Bible tells us here that Noah did not look out from the covering of the ark until this time. He had to remove it first. This was probably quite a process in itself, considering that the covering must have been well secured to withstand the violent downpour and wave action for such a long period. When he did remove the covering, it was then that he looked and saw the ground was dry.

When we look at the construction of the ark in Genesis 6:16 it tells us there was a space of one cubit from the top, probably all around the ark (for air circulation, no doubt), besides a window. "A window shalt thou make to the ark and in a cubit shalt thou finish it above, and the door of the ark shalt thou set in the side thereof; with lower, second, and third stories shalt thou make in it." I believe in the verse, "it" refers to the ark. "In a cubit shalt thou finish it above," indicates to me that this space of one cubit was all around the top. The third story, or at least part of it, I will assume, is where Noah and his family lived while the heavier animals were mainly on the decks of the lower two stories. This would stand to reason, not only because of the stability of the ship, but also because from the third story he could remove the covering and look out.

One of the reasons for belief on the part of some authors for the ark to have landed on another mountain or lower level, seems to stem from a bit of confusion over the olive leaf and the travels of the dove.

Ellicott says this:

> But as this species of bird (dove) does not fly far from its home, except when assembled in vast numbers, it quickly returned, finding water all around. This proves that the ark had not settled upon a lofty eminence; for as it had been already aground 120 days, and as within another fortnight the waters had 'abated from off the earth,' it could only have been in some valley or plain among the mountains of Ararat that the waters were thus 'on the face of the whole earth' the larger word, yet which certainly does not mean here the whole world, but only a very small region in the immediate neighborhood of the ark — it is thus plain that the olive tree had had plenty of time on some of the higher lands while the flood was subsiding, to put forth new leaves.[5]

I have a tough time following Ellicott's reasoning.

Gill's Bible Commentary says, "The olive tree which grows abundantly in Armenia, can vegetate under water."[6]

The Preachers' Homeletic Commentary believes the Flood was universal, but it in part bases that belief on the dove. "If the flood was not universal, the dove with its immense rapidity of wing . . . would soon have reached that part of the 'globe' that was not covered by the Flood, but she found no rest."[7] This seems to be a contradiction to what Ellicott indicates about the dove.

Regardless of their point, it is interesting that two biblical commentaries have a contrary explanation on what appears to be for the birds. It was interesting to find opposing views on the flying habits of the dove from these commentaries.

With this disagreement, I found it necessary to attempt to pin down the flying habits of a dove. The Bible doesn't tell us what species of dove Noah sent forth. In researching the flying habits of a dove, I found it interesting that ornithologically there is no distinction between doves and pigeons. The term pigeon is usually applied to the larger species, and dove to the smaller species. Interbreeding has produced various races, and ultimately different species within a given geographical range. For instance, the stock dove is a member of a group thought of as pigeon, but the ancestor of the domestic pigeon is often called the rock dove.

Some species, such as the flocked pigeon and masked dove, have larger wings and can fly far and fast. The extinct passenger pigeon was known for this. Also, the homing pigeon can find its home from 500 miles distance. Other species such as the Barbary dove, domesticated diamond dove, or the Old World doves in the "Geopelia" classification, have rather short, rounded wings and fly only short distances.[8]

Now the question is, what kind of dove did Noah use? Was it one with the ability to fly far in search of land, or just short distances? The Bible doesn't tell us, but I could only guess that an olive leaf plucked from somewhere reasonably close to the ark, indicating dry land in the immediate area, by a dove who liked to stay close to home makes logical sense to me. Therefore, I would tend to agree with Ellicott in the flying habits of the bird Noah used, but I still can't follow his logic in claiming proof that "the Ark had not settled on a lofty eminence." The question here is — how far away did the dove fly to find the olive leaf?

I go now to the book *The Genesis Flood*: "Olive trees are not on the heights of Ararat, but lower down in the valleys to the south."[9] I know firsthand there are no olive trees now on the heights of Ararat — just rocks, dirt, and ice. I do not know if there were olive trees on Ararat at the time of the Flood.

Whitcomb and Morris, the authors of *The Genesis Flood*, go on to say, "Even if every olive tree in Armenia had been up-rooted and covered with diluvian, it is evident that sufficient time had elapsed to allow for the germination of the seed on the rising grounds, although the plains were still lying under water. Just as much of modern horticulture is carried on by the use of cuttings from older plants . . . so also much of the past diluvian plant life probably began from broken branches near the surface. It is significant that the olive leaf is mentioned since it is well known that this is one of the hardiest of all plants, and would be one of the first to sprout again from such a cutting after the Flood. Neither does the tree have to grow in the plains; it could have sprouted high on the barren hillsides long before the floodwaters retreated to the lowlands."[10]

To help answer our question of how far the dove flew in order to find the olive leaf, let us also ask at what rate did the water recede?

I don't know how fast the waters of a universal flood would recede, I can only guess that there must have been vast numbers of variables involved. The wind God sent and its effect on evaporation, the porous landscape, the change in land structure and the earth's crust are among the many, I'm sure.

Whatever the rate may have been of the subsiding waters, or however tall the mountain was at that time, the area around the mountain (possibly 221 days after the landing, according to Scripture) certainly was dry. "In the second month, on the seven and twentieth day of the month, was the earth dried" (Gen. 8:14).

To conclude our discussion on the flight of the dove, we will assume for the reasons given, and for the following reasons, that it could have been quite short. Arnad Krochmal, in *Olive Growing in Greece*, says: "The adaptable nature of the trees permits them to be grown in soils of high lime content and rocky hills unsuited for other crops."[11] Morris and Whitcomb add: "It must be kept in mind that even mountain peaks would have been only a few hundred feet above sea level during the weeks immediately following the grounding of the ark. Consequently, climatic conditions could have been most favorable at the time for rapid sprouting of leaves from an olive tree cutting even on the highest mountain."[12]

Contrary to Ellicott, this information tells us the ark could have settled on a lofty eminence and the dove could have found the olive leaf on the highest mountain. The argument for a lower mountain because of the birds just does not fly.

Was the Flood story written from Noah's point of view, or from God's? From what we've read in the first part of this chapter, Ellicott seems to indicate Noah's viewpoint.

Henrietta C. Mears, author of *What the Bible Is All About*, says, "The age-long Hebrew and Christian position is that Moses, guided by the spirit of God, wrote Genesis. This includes the Flood story.

"The book closes something like 300 years before Moses was born. Moses could have received his information only by direct revelation from God, or from historical records . . . to which he had access, that had been handed down from his forefathers."

Henrietta Mears goes on to say, in reference to the creation story, which seems to be her opinion about the entire Book of Genesis, "No doubt . . . it was written long before, maybe by Abraham, or Noah, or Enoch, who knows?"[13]

No doubt, there is more than one viewpoint as to who wrote the Book of Genesis in its entirety. Henrietta Mears certainly indicates this with her statements of "Who knows?"

Henry Morris writes in *The Genesis Record*:

> Probably most conservative scholars in the past have accepted the view that Genesis was written by Moses. This has been the uniform tradition of both the Jewish scribes and the Christian fathers. . . . Assuming that Moses was responsible for the Book of Genesis as it has come down to us, there still remains the question as to the method by which he received and transmitted it. There are three possibilities:
>
> 1) He received it all by direct revelation from God, either in audible words, or by visions given him of great events in the past.
>
> 2) He received it by oral traditions, passed down from father to son over the centuries.
>
> 3) He took actual written records of the past, collected them, and wrote them in a final form.
>
> In all, or any of the three ways, he was guided by the Holy Spirit.
>
> Since Genesis is a collection of historical events, it is suggested that Moses took written records handed down over the centuries and recorded them.
>
> For instance, "This is the book of the generations of Adam," in Genesis 5:1 could have been written by Adam, or a descendant.
>
> "These are the generations of Noah" (Gen. 6:9) could have been written by Noah, or one of his descendants.
>
> "These are the generations of the heavens and of the earth" (Gen. 2:4) must have been written by God, or transmitted from God to Adam, who then wrote them, or were transmitted by God directly to Moses.[14]

There is more than one opinion also on the creation of the earth and the extent of the Great Flood, or even if they happened at all.

I'm addressing these questions from the perspective of one who not only has been searching for Noah's ark, but of one who is searching for the answers himself. I am attempting to find the answers to these questions through my own personal research. The model I am using is the Holy Bible.

Again, in regard to this question of "who knows," let's look at the Scriptures: "All scripture is given by inspiration of God, and is profitable for doctrine, for reproof, for correction, for instruction in righteousness: That the man of God may be perfect, throughly furnished unto all good works" (2 Tim. 3:16–17). This verse of Scripture seems to tell us the Bible is written from God's point of view, regardless of who held the writing instrument.

Many advocates of a local flood (a category Ellicott seems to fall into) maintain that "the Deluge may have been universal insofar as the area and observation, and information of the narrator extended."[15] This is assuming again for the sake of argument, that Genesis chapters 6 and 9 depict the Flood from Noah's standpoint and not from God's.

Let's continue to reflect on what Ellicott has said: "Upon the mountains of Ararat, upon some chain of hills there, and seventy-three days afterwards, Noah found himself surrounded by an amphitheater of mountains, the word used in verse 5 being emphatic, and signifying 'the tops of the mountains became visible and not that they had just begun to emerge.' "[16]

Genesis 8:5, in the New International Version, says the tops of the mountains were seen. Ellicott goes on again, "For doubtless after so vast a flood, mists and vapors would for a long time prevail and shut out the surrounding world from Noah's view."[17] I have repeated what Ellicott said in order to make another point — that he has the ark landing on lower hills. When Ellicott stated, as we read earlier, "The Bible word 'all' means much less than with us, and the 'whole' heaven simply means the whole sky bounded by the line of the spectator's vision,"[18] he then put himself in the position of believing and perpetuating the theory of a local flood. The ark landing on lower hills is the result of his belief and "all" the high hills . . . under the "whole" heaven are not considered as absolute terms. We have already discussed the probability that Noah was unable to see with the ark covered and the window shut. Now let's consider the word "all."

Ellicott said in his commentary of the Bible that the word "all" means much less than it does to us — we must take a look into Scripture to accurately consider this point. Please stay with me.

> For the prophecy came not in old time by the will of man: but holy men of God spake as they were moved by the Holy Ghost (2 Pet. 1:21).

Now a word of prophecy from the Scriptures (author's emphasis):

> But as the days of Noah were, so shall also the coming of the Son of man be. For as in the days that were before the flood they were eating and drinking, marrying and giving in marriage, until the day that Noah entered into the Ark. And knew not until the flood came, and took them *all* away; so shall also the coming of the Son of man be (Matt. 24:37–39).

> They did eat, they drank, they married wives, they were given in marriage, until the day that Noah entered into the ark, and the flood came, and destroyed them *all* (Luke 17:27).

> Likewise also as it was in the days of Lot; they did eat, they drank, they bought, they sold, they planted, they builded [business as usual] (Luke 17:28).

> But the same day that Lot went out of Sodom it rained fire and brimstone from heaven, and destroyed them *all* (Luke 17:29). ["All" in this passage of Scripture refers to all who were left in Sodom obviously, not all who were on the earth.]

Whitcomb and Morris say this:

> Now it is very important that we observe the context into which our Lord places the Flood destruction. It is placed alongside the destruction of Sodom and the destruction of the ungodly at the time of Christ's second coming. This fact is of tremendous significance in helping us to determine the sense in which the word "all" is used in reference to those who were destroyed by the Flood.
>
> Our argument proceeds in the following manner: the force of Christ's warning to the ungodly concerning the doom which awaits them at the time of His second coming, by reminding them of the destruction of the Sodomites, would be immeasurably weakened if we knew that some of the Sodomites, after all, had escaped. This would allow hope for the ungodly that some might escape the wrath of God in that Day of Judgment. But we have, indeed, no reason for thinking that any Sodomites did escape destruction when the fire fell from heaven.

In exactly the same manner, Christ's warning to future generations, on the basis of what happened to the ungodly in the days of Noah, would have been pointless if part of the human race had escaped the judgment waters . . . therefore, we are persuaded that Christ's use of the word "all" in Luke 17:27, must be understood in the absolute sense. Otherwise, the analogies would collapse and the warnings would lose their force.[19]

I agree with Morris and Whitcomb, and I believe Genesis was written from God's point of view; this is in opposition to Ellicott. It is also my contention, that if "all" is in the absolute sense in Luke 17:27, then "all" is in the absolute sense in Genesis 7:19.

It is my impression that Ellicott is adding to what is written as biblical truth and that he is attempting to compromise with the geological theories of uniformitarianism, which became so popular in his day, and are still taught in colleges today. In his commentary on the six days of creation, Ellicott refers several times to what the geologists say.

Ellicott supplies geological explanation with each day of creation as it is recorded in Genesis. He briefly describes a long process in the creation of the earth by introducing the example of "an eon, or period of indefinite duration" in the first day. An agreement is seen between geology and Ellicott's interpretation of the Scriptures in reference to the creation, and includes stages of evolution up the hierarchy of life until the fifth day, when God created "after their kind." At this point Ellicott says, " 'After their kind' suggests the belief that the various genera and species of birds, fishes, and insects were from the very beginning distinct, and will continue so, even if there be some amount of free play in the improvement and development of existing species."[20] From this point on Ellicott does not refer to what geology says of the days of creation.

In the previous example, Ellicott put the Bible on trial. Geology was the truth, and the biblical record stood the test of comparison. Ellicott compares the biblical record of the Flood to what geologists say. Geology promotes the doctrine of uniformitarianism as the guiding principle, not only to present earth processes, but as assumed always to have been the case. In this uniformitarian doctrine, there is no room for cataclysm. The Bible does not at all agree with that principle.

One cannot cover "all the high hills under all the whole heaven" with a flood, which is definitely a cataclysmic event, and at the same time promote a doctrine of uniformitarianism, which leaves no room for cataclysm of any kind.

In other words, a biblical viewpoint, as it is written in the Scriptures, cannot be combined with the doctrine of uniformitarianism, which is an opposite view, and come up with a local flood. It appears that Ellicott, and as we shall see, some of his contemporaries, have tried to do just that.

> The local flood theory, which thousands of Christians have accepted in order to be in step with some modern geologists, is altogether incompatible with the uniformitarian presuppositions of modern geologists! [Also incompatible with the Bible.] The only kind of harmonization of Genesis and geology that can satisfy a consistent uniformitarianism geologist, is one which eliminates entirely any flood that even faintly resembles the one described in Genesis. There can be no concord between Moses and Lyell [Charles Lyell, "High Priest of Uniformitarianism"], in spite of the wishful thinking of all too many Christians today. The biblical doctrine of the Flood cannot be harmonized with the uniformitarian theories of geology.[21]

In reviewing a few pages of *Ellicott's Commentary*, he said:

> Forty days and nights are not enough to supply the water required for the vast Flood. Fountains of the deep, that is, a subterranean ocean burst upward, or water from the equator rushed toward the poles, or a great cosmic catastrophe caused the 40 days and nights of rain, plus a vast displacement of water added to enough water to produce the deluge this vast, and caused the ark to float against the currents of the watershed of Ararat and the Tigres and Euphrates Rivers; and was high enough to cover the hills and mountains by 22 feet at least in the site of the horizon.[22]

In my opinion, here Ellicott sounds as though he is right on track, till the very end of his statement. He seems to assume the ark didn't move very far on the floodwaters in the five months it survived what was probably the wildest storm the earth has ever known.

For example, from *A Dictionary of the Bible*, edited by William Smith: "We shall see more clearly when we come to consider the language used with regard to the Flood itself, that even that language, strong as it undoubtedly is, does not oblige us to suppose that the Deluge was universal. It was universal, so far as man was concerned; we mean that it extended to all the then-known world."[23]

The language: "And the waters prevailed exceedingly upon the earth: and all the high hills that were under the whole heaven were covered" (Gen. 7:19). "All in whose nostrils was the breath of life, all that was in dry land died" (Gen. 7:22). From my point of view, the language is not only strong, but absolute in its meaning. I do not agree with the commentary by Smith. Neither do I agree with the following commentary:

Peloubet's Bible Dictionary teaches: "The language of the Book of Genesis does not compel us to suppose that the whole surface of the globe was actually covered with water. It is natural to suppose that the writer, when he speaks of 'all flesh,' 'all in whose nostrils have the breath of life,' refers only to its own locality. This sort of language is common in the Bible when only a small part of the globe is intended. Thus, for instance, 'A decree went out from Caesar Augustus that all the world should be taxed.' The language must be understood in the sense it would bear to the authors. The world, as then known, was very small. The truth of the Bible would not be shaken were the Flood to be limited to a comparatively small area in Asia."[24]

I am not convinced that the "world," in the verse "all the 'world' should be taxed" (Luke 2:1), from Peloubet's example, and the "earth" are synonymous in meaning. The verses of Scripture Peloubet is referring to reads: "And all flesh died that moved upon the earth, both of fowl, and of cattle, and of beast, and of every creeping thing that creepeth upon the *earth*, and every man: All in whose nostrils was the breath of life, all that was in the dry *land*, died. And every living substance was destroyed which was upon the face of the *ground*, both man, and cattle, and the creeping things, and the fowl of the heaven; and they were destroyed from the *earth*: and Noah only remained alive, and they that were with him in the ark (Gen. 7:21–23, author's emphasis).

The physical planet, that is, "the ground, the country, land, portion of the earth's surface" we walk on, and the "surface" we observe does not necessarily mean the "world."

The process of tracing out and describing the elements of a word with their modifications of form and sense is known as etymology. The etymological meaning of "world" is "being the age or life of man — the earthly state of human existence; this present life: state of human affairs, state of things; season or time as marked by the state of affairs."[25] "All the 'world' should be taxed," doesn't mean that all the "earth" should be taxed. It means that the human existence which is on the earth should be taxed. "And all went to be taxed, every one in his own city" (Luke 2:3). This tells me "all the world" was that in existence and under the influence of Caesar Augustus.

"The waters prevailed exceedingly upon the *earth*; and *all* the high hills, that were under the *whole* heaven, were covered . . . every creeping thing that creepeth upon the *earth*, and every man . . . *all* that was in the dry *land*, died. And every living substance was destroyed which was upon the face of the *ground*" Gen 7:19–23, emphasis added). Genesis does not tell us the *world* was destroyed. Genesis does not tell us that just the area of human existence was covered by water. Genesis tells us that everything on the ground was destroyed, everything on dry land died. Genesis tells us the earth was completely covered by water. I don't think Peloubet has a valid point.

Clark's Commentary, paraphrased, says, "God ordered the strata to sink to fill in a void left by the large quantity of water that was forced upward. It sounds like a major cataclysmic event, and the waters above and below the firmament which had been separated since the second day of creation, again came together."[26] I do think Clark has a valid point: "It sounds like a major cataclysmic event." Certainly Clark is commenting on what is actually written.

From the pages of *Archaeology and Bible History* we read:

> There are two main views among fundamentalists as to the area covered by the Flood: (1) It covered the inhabited earth, that is Mesopotamia and perhaps some of the surrounding lands, but not the whole world. According to this view, there was no need for a worldwide deluge, because a flood over the inhabited earth would have been sufficient to bring life to an end. (2) The Flood covered the entire earth. The writer recognizes the possibility of the first view, but he sees no reason why the second view of a universal flood should not be adhered to. Scriptural evidence supports the universality of the flood: (1) The fact that every living creature was to be destroyed would indicate that the whole earth was subject to the Flood (Gen. 7:4). Probably the animals had scattered over much of the earth; a universal flood would have been needed to destroy them. (2) All the high hills were to be covered (Gen. 7:9). After the Flood was over God referred to having smitten "every living thing" (Gen. 8:21). It would seem that a universal flood would be required to bring about this result. There is also a physical

reason for positing a universal Flood: since water seeks its own level, it is difficult to imagine water being at a great depth in Asia Minor, and not elsewhere over the earth.[27]

With this statement in mind, it seems to me that it is logical to assume that if Noah's ark rested high on a mountain, then it took a great depth of water to get it there. Since there are reported sightings of the ark hidden on Ararat, it stands to reason then that if they are factual sightings then a universal Flood must be considered as having actually happened. That possibility gives pertinence to this direction of research and the report you are reading.

Karl Fredrick Keil, author of *The Bible Commentary on the Old Testament*, and advocate of a universal Flood, says:

> The verses of Genesis 7:17–24 contain a description of the flood: how the water increased more and more, till it was 15 cubits above all the lofty mountains of the earth, and how, on the other hand, it raised the ark above the earth and above the mountains, and, on the other, destroyed every living being upon the dry land, from man to cattle, creeping things, and birds. — If the water covered "all the high hills under the whole heaven," this clearly indicates the universality of the flood. The statement, indeed, that it rose 15 cubits above the mountains, is probably founded upon the fact that the ark drew 15 cubits of water, and that when the water subsided, it rested upon the top of Ararat, from which the conclusion would very naturally be drawn as to the greatest height attained. Mount Ararat is only 16,946 feet high, whereas the loftiest peaks of the Himalayas and Cordilleras are as much as 26,843 feet, with Everest reading 29,028 feet. The submersion of these mountains has been thought impossible. Even if the peaks, which are higher than Ararat, were not covered by water, we cannot therefore pronounce the Flood merely partial in its extent, but must regard it as universal, as extending over every part of the earth, since the few peaks uncovered would not only sink into vanishing points in comparison with the surface covered, but would form an exception not worth mentioning, for the simple reason that no living beings could exist upon these mountains covered with perpetual snow and ice; so that "everything that lived upon the dry land, in whose nostrils there was a breath of life" would inevitably die, and, with the exception of these

shut up in the ark, neither man nor beast would be able to rescue itself, and escape destruction.

A flood which rose 15 cubits above the top of Ararat could not remain partial, if it only continued a few days, to say nothing of the fact that the water was rising for 40 days and remained at the highest elevation for 110 days. To speak of such a Flood as partial is absurd, even if it broke out at only one spot, it would spread over the earth from one end to the other, and reach everywhere to the same elevation.[28]

In this commentary, we have a universal Flood which could put the ark on the top of Ararat, destroy every living thing on dry land, yet leave the higher mountain peaks of the globe rising above the flood waters. If the higher mountain peaks were at their present heights or nearly so, before the flood, then this is certainly easier to accept than "all the high hills that were under the whole heaven" being covered. A key word in this verse may be "were." It could tell us that the hills that "were" are not the hills that "are" now, after a change in the surface of the earth. This assumes that there was a change. If the surface of the earth has not experienced a tremendous change in appearance due to the shifting strata, with mountains attaining great heights as the result of the cataclysm, then I would tend to agree with Keil, and possibly even lean more toward those who favor a local or partial Flood theory.

My position at this point is to believe in the Bible and the word "all" being in the absolute sense, with the Scripture being the inspired Word of God, and written from God's point of view, as the Spirit of God moved the author of Genesis to write it.

Dr. Bernard Ramm, an evangelical writer who believes only part of the human race was destroyed by the Flood, says:

There is the problem of the amount of water required by a universal Flood. "All the waters of the heavens, poured all over the earth," would amount to a sheath seven inches thick. If the earth were a perfect sphere, so that all the waters of the ocean covered it, the depth of the ocean would be two and one-half to three miles. To cover the highest mountains would require eight times more water than we have now. It would have involved a great creation of water to have covered the entire globe but no such creative act is hinted at in the Scriptures.[29]

Now for another opinion on the question of a universal Flood covering the earth with tall mountains, Morris and Whitcomb say this:

> For Ramm's objection to be valid we would have to assume that there were no waters "above the firmament" before the Flood, and that the earth's topography was unaltered by the Flood. In other words, we would be assuming the truth of uniformitarianism in order to prove the impossibility of catastrophism! But if we accept the biblical testimony concerning an antediluvian canopy of water (Gen. 1:6–8, 7:11, 8:2; 2 Pet. 3:5–7), we have an adequate source for the waters of a universal Flood. Furthermore, such passages as Genesis 8:3 and Psalm 104:6–9 suggest that ocean basins were deepened after the Flood to provide adequate storage space for the additional waters that had been "above the firmament" from the second day of creation to the time of the Flood, while the mountain ranges rose to heights never attained during the antediluvian era.[30]

To reflect on information provided by Dr. Ramm: "If the earth were a perfect sphere so that all the waters of the ocean covered it, the depth of the ocean would be two and one-half to three miles." If we take a statute mile of 5,280 feet, and multiply it by two and one-half, just to be conservative, then we have 13,200 feet of ocean above a spherical earth.

Consider this: Peter Stoner and Robert Newman said in their book *Science Speaks*, "It is generally agreed 'in its earliest stages, the surface of the earth was quite smooth and of nearly uniform height.'"[31]

In a report written by Dr. Clifford Burdick he says, "The original Mount Ararat apparently was not more than 10,000 to 12,000 feet in height."[32]

Dr. Bernard Ramm, in his book titled *The Christian View of Science and Scripture*, is quoted as saying, "If the earth were a perfect sphere so that all the waters of the ocean covered it, the depth of the ocean would be two and one-half to three miles."[33] Theoretically, if the timing were right, that could put the level of the ocean, and the ark, above the top of Mount Ararat during a cataclysm so designed. Our study does tell us there's a lot of water which is stored in the great valleys and trenches of the ocean floor, and in the existing ice caps, as well as ground water and the atmosphere. We can believe the ark could have landed on a tall mountaintop, if we also believe in the evidence of these scientific findings of earth's history. We then should also agree that the cataclysmic event must have continued on a scale of global wide proportion to put the mountains at their present heights and the ocean trenches at their present depths. The timing of these events to the Noachian flood may be crucial for acceptence on our part of the evidence presented in this book as factual. To accept this as fact, and assume the timing, allows us a fresh look at the possibility of an ark on a mountaintop, as it is presented to us in the scriptural truth of the Book of Genesis. This is a reflection of my opinion, based on the results of research which is provided in this report.

The ark sat for 73 days on a mountaintop before the waters receded to the point where the *tops of the mountains could be seen.* It was over seven months after the landing that the waters receded to the place where Noah and his company were allowed by God to leave the safety of the ark. If we can believe, as evidenced by paleontology, that at least wildlife was worldwide at a time before the cataclysm, then a universal flood was required to reach and destroy *all in whose nostrils was the breath of life, of all that was in the dry land.* If we can believe in the properties of liquid water, then a universal flood or a flood of a great magnitude was required to put the ark on top of Mount Ararat, or on any other of the tall mountains.

Whitcomb and Morris comment, "Besides, for Noah to have built the ark of such size and magnitude, it is inconceivable that there was just a local flood; there would have been no need for an ark at all, he could have just moved."[34]

Another issue we can touch on in order to possibly shed some light on and deal with the question of a universal or local Flood, is that of world population before the Flood. To consider this, we must deal with the question of how long has man been around, and was all of the world populated? Morris and Whitcomb tell us: The fact that the *entire* earth could have been populated by the time of the Flood . . . stems from longevity and large families; each family had sons and daughters and lived a long time. In possibly 1,656 years from Adam to the Flood, according to biblical genealogy, the population could have been 774 million."[35] They compare a 1.5 percent growth rate per year in antediluvian times, to a 2 percent growth rate per year now. So 774 million may be conservative, it could have been 1,030 million. This large population would surely have spread out far beyond the Mesopotamian plains — for all practical purposes they may have filled the earth.

Paleontology gives us another reason for believing man traveled far before the time of the Flood: human fossils in Africa, Europe, Asia, and America — in fact all over the northern hemisphere.[36] Bernard Ramm, author of *The Christian View of Science and Scripture*, and one who favors a local Flood theory says: "In Africa, India, China, and America, there is fossil evidence for the existence of man many thousands of years before the Flood. Dates assigned to some fossils are 10,000 to 15,000 years old." This doesn't mean that man in those areas was destroyed by the Flood according to this point of view. Ramm believes the emphasis in Genesis is upon that group of cultures from which Abraham eventually came. In other words, as I understand Ramm, he advocates that man's destruction in the Genesis record does not include those who lived on another part of the earth. Ramm quotes J.W. Dawson, author of *The Meeting Place of Geology and History*, and adapts the view that the Flood was universal insofar as the area and observation and information of the narrator extended.[37]

However, the opposite point of view, as held by Morris and Whitcomb, that of a universal Flood which covered all the earth, such as given to us in Genesis, demands that peoples on other parts of the globe were also destroyed.

Far from the Mesopotamian Valley, on the American continent, "A female clay doll, known as the 'Nampa Image,' was found in a flood-laid sedimentary deposit, at a depth of 300 feet, while boring for an artesian well in Nampa, Idaho, in 1889. Whoever made the doll had lived there, or it was washed there by flood action."[38] I think it is quite possible the Deluge buried the pre-flood civilizations, encasing fossils and artifacts alike in what are now the sedimentary layers of the earth's crust.

Some Old Testament scholars believe that there is much more time than 1,656 years between Adam and the Flood; they look to possible gaps in genealogy in chapter 5 of Genesis. If so, chances are there were even more dispersions.

Also, something we must not forget in this discussion of population dispersion is the dispersion of the animals and birds. Remember the scriptural reason for the flood: "And God said unto Noah, The end of all flesh is come before me; for the earth is filled with violence through them; and, behold, I will destroy them with the earth" (Gen. 6:13).

In the mud and permafrost of the Arctic regions, there are the remains of millions of animals which were suddenly "quick-frozen" during a relatively recent geological period. It is as if millions of animals were swept together by a huge tidal wave, which extended from Siberia to Canada and Alaska.

Dr. Frank Gibbons, professor of archaeology at the University of New Mexico, visited the area and writes:

> Within the mass, frozen solid, lie the twisted parts of animals and trees intermingled with lenses of ice and layers of peat and mosses. It looks as though in the middle of some catastrophe of ten thousand years ago, the whole Alaskan world of living animals and plants was suddenly frozen in mid-motion...dumped in all attitudes of death....Legs and torsos and heads and fragments were found together in piles, or scattered separately — animals torn apart and scattered over the landscape even though they may have weighed several tons.[39]

Charles H. Hapgood writes in "The Mystery of the Frozen Mammoths," published in *Coronet Magazine*:

> Locked in the eternally frozen mud of northern Siberia is an unsolved mystery that has intrigued scientists for more than a century. The arctic wasteland is a burial ground for hundreds of thousands of mammoths, a hairy species of elephant, now extinct, that seem to have died about 10,000 years ago and [were] quickly deep-frozen, some in midsummer. Frozen mammoth bodies have been found so perfectly preserved that their flesh is almost as delicious today as fresh beefsteak.
>
> In 1901, a complete mammoth body was found near Siberia's Beresovka River. [Another mammoth was recently found in the same area of Siberia.] This animal had apparently frozen to death very suddenly in the middle of the summer. His stomach contents were so well-preserved that the plants he had been eating could be identified. They included buttercups and wild beans in full bloom, a stage they reach only in late July or early August. Death had been so sudden that his last mouthful of grasses and flowers were found in his mouth. He had been caught up by some terrific force and carried some miles away from his feeding ground. He suffered a broken leg and pelvic bones, and then, in kneeling position, froze to death — at the hottest time of the year.[40]

Consider for a moment the animals in the ark. "They went in two and two unto Noah into the ark, the male and the female, as God had commanded Noah" (Gen. 7:9).

> The animals were not searched for, hunted out, and driven by Noah into the ark; they repaired to it spontane-ously: and perhaps their movements may be explained in part, by some sensible impression and uneasiness on their bodies, like what is supposed to be the monitor of birds of passage, or by that natural instinct which prompts animals, under a secret presentment of danger, to seek refuge with man; but, over and above any such physical impulse, they must have been prompted by an overruling Divine direction, as it is impossible, on any other principle, to account for their going in pairs.[41]

Male and female of every species or "everything that creepeth upon the earth" (Gen. 7:8) which was necessary for the multiplication of their respective kinds, and food to sustain them, was loaded on the ark. "And take thou unto thee of all food that is eaten, and thou shalt gather it to thee; and it shall be for food for thee, and for them. Thus did Noah; according to all that God commanded him, so did he (Gen. 6:21–22).

If, in fact, God did in some fashion command the pairs of animals to enter the ark, why would He go to all that trouble if the Flood was just local, or less than what would cover all the hills under the whole heaven and destroy all the creatures on dry land, as the Bible says?

We discussed earlier how long the cubit was that Noah used in his building of the ark. We did not determine for sure how long that cubit was, but it probably was between 17.5 and 20.6 inches in length. It could also have been much larger. For the purpose of this example, let us use what has been determined to be the length of a cubit, at least during one period of history.

In the late 19th century, an inscription at the entrance of a tunnel in Jerusalem gave the length of the tunnel, which was built in 700 B.C., as 1,200 cubits long. The tunnel was measured to a length of 1,800 feet. By this discovery we can assume this particular cubit to measure about 18 inches.

According to the Bible, the size of the ark is specifically given as 300 cubits long, 50 cubits wide, and 30 cubits high. Using this 18-inch cubit gives the ark a length of 450 feet, a width of 75 feet and a height of 45 feet. "The ark, if rather 'squarely' built, with three floors, would give a displacement of about 43,000 tons. This would be just a little smaller than the largest of the pre-War (WWII) Italian liners, the 'Rex,' which had a displacement of about 50,000 tons. Many of our large ocean-going ships have a displacement of about 25,000 tons, a much smaller capacity than the ark would have, according to the above computations."[42] Why would such a large ocean-going vessel as the ark be built for the purpose it was designed for, if the Flood was only local?

For the ship to be practical and necessary as a logical means of escape for man and all the species of animals, the Flood must have been extensive to the point of covering, at the least, a sizeable portion of the earth's surface.

Perhaps it covered a continent as the waters of the Deluge rose. Perhaps during the cataclysm of the Deluge, lands subsided to fill the voids in strata which were left as the fountains of the deep opened up and the water rose to cover the land. Perhaps elevations of the continents so drastically changed during the subsiding and sinking of landmasses, that there was a tremendous influx of water from the oceans that actually covered the entire earth, as the Bible says; and only an ocean-going ship the size and shape of the ark, could possibly survive it.

The antediluvian canopy, the waters "above the firmament" as read in the Scriptures, and a great source of water from within the earth coming to surface in a great cataclysm, and receding again into the earth after some change in the earth's surface, can be seen in aforementioned Scriptures.

Now to review:

> And God said, Let there be a firmament in the midst of the waters, and let it divide the waters from the waters. And God made the firmament, and divided the waters which were under the firmament from the waters which were above the firmament: and it was so. And God called the firmament Heaven. And the evening and the morning were the second day (Gen. 1:6-8).

> In the six hundredth year of Noah's life, in the second month, the seventeenth day of the month, the same day were all the fountains of the great deep broken up, and the windows of heaven were opened (Gen. 7:11).

> The foundations also of the deep and the windows of heaven were stopped, and the rain from heaven was re-

strained; And the waters returned from off the earth continually and after the end of the hundred and fifty days the waters were abated (Gen. 8:2–3).

For this they willingly are ignorant of that by the word of God the heavens were of old, and the earth standing out of the water and in the water: Whereby the world *that then was*, being overflowed with water, perished: But the heavens and the earth *which are now*, by the same word are kept in store, reserved unto fire against the day of judgment and perdition of ungodly men (2 Pet. 3:5–7, author's emphasis).

Thou coverest it with the deep as with a garment: the waters stood above the mountains. At thy rebuke they fled; at the voice of thy thunder they hasted away. They go up by the mountains; they go down by the valleys unto the place which thou hast founded for them. Thou hast set a bound that they may not pass over; that they turn not again to cover the earth (Ps. 104:6–9).

The following is from the International Standard Bible Encyclopedia:

The spread of the water floating the ark is represented to have been occasioned, not so much by the rain which fell, as by the breaking up of "all the fountains of the great deep" (Gen. 7:11), which very naturally describes phenomenon connected with one of the extensive downward movements of the earth's crust with which geology has made us familiar. The sinking of the land below the level of the ocean is equivalent, in its effects, to the rising of the water above it, and is accurately expressed by the phrases used in the sacred narrative. This appears, not only in the language concerning the breaking-up of the great deep which describes the coming-on of the Flood, but also in the description of its termination, in which it is said, that the "fountains also of the great deep . . . were stopped . . . and the waters returned from off the earth continually (Gen. 8:2–3).[43]

The ark landed on the mountains of Ararat, however tall they were then. It must have landed on the tallest one. The Bible indicates this by the 73 days which passed before the tops of the other mountains were seen. During this 73-day period of time the water was subsiding; going back into the earth where upheaval of the lands and openings in the ocean floor made the space. "And the waters returned from off the earth continually" (Gen. 8:3).

Perhaps the tall mountain of the mountains of Ararat that the ark landed on was indeed Mount Ararat, where the reported sightings and local legends support that possibility.

WHERE IS THE WATER?

We've talked about a universal Flood, now let's deal with another aspect: Where is the water? Where did it come from and where did it go?

To attempt to answer these complicated questions, I will deal with what might have started the Flood in the first place, that is, what physical trigger, if any, did God use to set off the cataclysmic chain of events and then, where did the water go?

First of all, to set this up, I will make two brief assumptions — one, that God exists. To the skeptic, we will further discuss this later. Second, that Genesis 1:7 is true: "And God made the firmament, and divided the waters which were under the firmament from the waters which were above the firmament." I will further believe that although there was water above the firmament (the space in which the birds flew or space in which we live), that it did not rain. "For the Lord God had not caused it to rain upon the earth. But there went up a mist from the earth, and watered the whole face of the ground" (Gen. 2:5–6).

I will, for the purpose of this possible explanation, assume there was a water canopy above the earth (above the firmament) and that canopy helped to provide a warm and uniform climate on the earth before the time of the Flood. This agrees with science, as in the formation of a planet there is a canopy over the planet characteristic of that planet. The earth is a water planet — the earth had a water canopy.[1]

So what upset this condition? What broke the canopy and started the deluge? We know who did it, and why he did it. "And God said unto Noah, the end of all flesh is come before me; for the earth is filled with violence through them; and behold, I will destroy them with the earth" (Gen. 6:13). But how? A cosmic catastrophe? There are different theories. One possible explanation is a reversal, or a change, in the magnetic poles. There obviously could be a conflict with this. Although geologists know there have been reversals of polarity in the earth's magnetic field in the past, they also say, "The earth's field has had its present, or normal, polarity for the last 700,000 years."[2]

One book I read, entitled *We Are the Earthquake Generation*, gave sudden polar shift as explanation for mountain building, volcanic activity, continental drift, animal extinction, and erratic occurrence of glaciers. Could something similar happen again?

> And there shall be signs in the sun, and in the moon, and in the stars; and upon the earth distress of nations, with perplexity; the sea and the waves roaring. Men's hearts failing them for fear, and for looking after those things which are coming on the earth; for the powers of heaven shall be shaken (Luke 21:25–26).

> Immediately after the tribulation of those days shall the sun be darkened, and the moon shall not give her light, and the stars fall from heaven, and the powers of the heaven shall be shaken (Matt. 24:29).

> And every island fled away, and the mountains were not found (Rev. 16:20).

> The earth is utterly broken down, the earth is clean dissolved, the earth is moved exceedingly. The earth shall reel to and fro like a drunkard (Isa. 24:19–20).

> Therefore I will shake the heavens, and the earth shall remove out of her place, in the wrath of the Lord of hosts, and in the day of his fierce anger (Isa. 13:13).

Could a reversal in magnetic polarity of the earth's surface cause "perplexity and the roaring of the waves of the sea," could it cause the sea to roar and toss, and maybe even jump its shores? Will the stars fall from the sky and will the powers of the heavens be shaken in this period of end-time prophecy . . . the coming of our Lord; or will they just appear that way to those of us on earth as the earth reels like a drunkard, and is shaken from its place at the wrath of the Lord Almighty? Will a reversal of the magnetic poles cause the earth to be removed from its place?

"But as the days of Noah were, so shall also the coming of the Son of man be" (Matt. 24:37). Did a magnetic polar shift break the canopy and start the deluge? An historical astronomer of south

In the foreground is a 1,000-year-old mosque (formerly a church). Behind it in the limestone and sandstone rocks are ruins of the Urartu civilization which dates back to around 800 B.C. Out of this civilization came the Armenians.

Studying photographs of Ararat with a man who saw
the ship in 1944, the Reverend Vincent Will (1995).

The northeast side of Ararat and the upper part
of the Ahora Gorge.

The author's first climb of Ararat, in 1984, standing beside Jim Irwin and John Christiansen.

The author, John Christiansen, Redvan Karpoes, and Jim Irwin, on the 16,946-foot summit of Mount Ararat (1984).

Ole Honnungdalanes, Bob Stuplich, Jim Irwin, and the author in Ankara, Turkey (1985).

A market in Degukeyaret.

A market in Degulsey.

This is the garden where the author sometimes gathers his
thoughts. The garden wall, new restaurant under construction,
and Isak Pasa Palace are in the background (2000).

The author, keeping up with his writing, in eastern Turkey. Some
of the ruins of old Bayazid are seen in the background (1999).

Here is a view of the upper Abreh glacier.
The ark may be under that ice.

A crevasse
on the
Vostney.

The 16,000-foot peak of Mount Ararat.

The author.

Paul Thomson climbing the rocks of Ararat (2000).

The author near a
shepherd's camp (1999).

Eating with
the Kurds.

Lake
Kop.

This is close to the 14,000-foot campsite, near the edge of Ararat's glacial ice (2000).

Horses were a big help on the lower portions of the climbs.

The author, on the ice between crevasses above the Cehennem Dere. The elevation is above 15,000 feet (1999).

At approximately 15,500 feet, Paul Thomson sits by a crevasse near the Ray Anderson site. The team looked into the opening and was only able to see more ice. The author, at the end of the rope, photographed Thompson (2000).

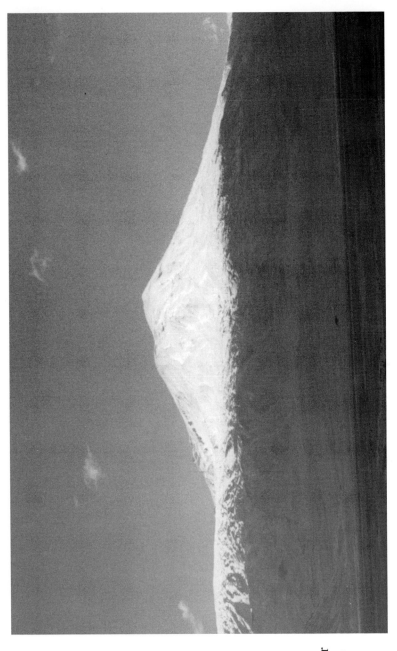

Mount
Ararat after
a snowfall.

John McIntosh, a long-time ark researcher, in Turkey (2000).

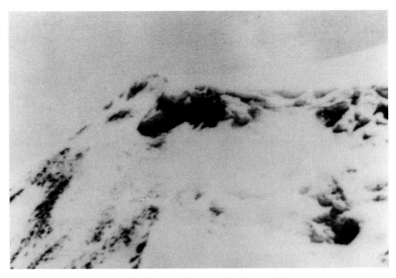

A 1949 air force photo of Mount Ararat.

Artist's depiction of
the ark on Mount
Ararat, based on
eyewitness sightings.

Australia, George F. Dodwell, places a date of the change in the earth's axis as 2345 B.C. — approximately the same date the Flood is assumed to have happened, according to biblical genealogy. Dodwell says, "The earth went from vertical to 26-1/2 degrees suddenly, then to 23-1/2 degrees over a period of 3,194 years."[3]

Could a collision with a meteor have caused this sudden tilt? There is what appears to be a crater 100 miles wide on the ocean floor near Cancun, Mexico. There is what appears to be another crater 28 miles wide off the coast of Nova Scotia, to name just two. Could meteors be the key? Scientists have been claiming for years that meteors killed the dinosaurs. Maybe they made a greater impact than that.

Now we have considered a device in which God may have triggered the events. Let us continue to deal with the questions of "Where did the water go" after the flood, and "Where did it come from in the first place?" To begin with, realize that the oceans cover 71 percent of the earth's surface as it is seen today.

"The waters above the firmament seem to imply more than our present clouds and atmospheric water vapor, especially since Genesis 2:5 implies that during this time (before the Flood, even before Adam) rainfall was not experienced on the earth."[3]

> And every plant of the field before it was in the earth, and every herb of the field before it grew: For the Lord God had not caused it to rain upon the earth, and there was not a man to till the ground. But there went up a mist from the earth, and watered the whole face of the ground (Gen.2:5–6).

This tells us that there was water under the surface — perhaps a lot — as the whole surface of the ground was watered, and there was no rain. If such was the case, the atmosphere before the breaking of the canopy was characteristically different from the atmosphere of today. This explains why there was no rainbow until after the Flood. How do we know that? After the Flood, God said in Genesis 9:13, "I do put my bow in the cloud and it shall be a token of a covenant between me and the earth." (A promise not to destroy the earth again by water.)

> Morris and Whitcomb comment: "These upper waters were therefore placed in that position by divine creativity, not by the normal processes of the hydrologic cycle of the present day. The upper waters did not, however, obscure the light from the heavenly bodies, and so must have been in the form of invisible water vapor.

Such a vast expanse of water vapor would necessarily have had a profound effect on terrestrial climates, and therefore on geological activity."[5]

This leads us into a brief discussion of the greenhouse effect, and how the climate of the earth could well have been, for the most part, more constant and warmer. Harold Blum, author of *Times Arrow and Evolution*, says this about the greenhouse effect: "The principle atmospheric absorber for the entrant sunlight is water vapor, with CO_2 and ozone playing lesser roles . . . the part absorbed tends to warm the atmosphere and just as the warm glass of the greenhouse tends to raise the temperature of the interior, the water vapor tends to raise that of the earth's surface below it."[6] Losing this canopy, and its greenhouse effect, would certainly have a cooling effect on the earth.

As previously discussed, subterranean waters were very much included in the Flood. More than that, Morris and Whitcomb say:

> Great volcanic explosions are clearly implied in the statement that, "the same day all the fountains of the great deep were broken up" (Gen. 7:11). This must mean that great quantities of liquids, perhaps liquid rocks or magmas, as well as water (probably steam), had been confined under great pressure below the surface of the rock structure of the earth since the time of its formation, and that this mass now burst forth through great fountains, probably both on the lands and under the seas.
>
> The Bible makes it abundantly plain that the events associated with the Deluge were of immense geologic potency, and must have caused profound geologic changes.[7]

Continents themselves could have submerged as oceans swept over them, while other submerged land masses could have been displaced to rise through the ocean surface — all part of the profound geological changes of a universal Flood.

I think we pretty much have dealt with where the water came from. Is it not also quite possible during this probable time of geologic change, along with perhaps the liquid magmas from the "great deep," that there was a period of mountain building?

Most supporters of a local flood theory believe that the mountains were at their present heights before the Flood. The Bible says, "Let the waters under the heavens be gathered together unto one place, and let the dry land appear: And it was so" (Gen. 1:9). This verse tells us that before the dry land appeared, the earth was in flood stage from the creation. It also tells us that mountain building took place after the creation.

Bernard Kummel, in *History of the Earth,* says, "Beginning in the late Cretaceous and continuing into the Eocene (somewhere between 60 and 135 million years ago), widespread diastrophism, the bending, folding, and breaking of the earth's crust, caused mountain building and general emergence of the continents; and regression of the continental and geosynclinal seas (seas within a large depression or trough in the earth's surface)."[8]

Whitcomb and Morris again: "It is extremely interesting, in light of the biblical suggestion of uplift of the lands at the conclusion of the deluge period, to note that most of the present mountain ranges of the world are believed to have been uplifted (on the basis of fossil evidence), during the Pleistocene or late Pliocene."[9] (A million years ago or less.) This is in contrast to what Kummel's book says,[10] but I trust this is an accurate statement for reasons we'll soon see.

It is necessary to also understand that as the displacement of surface of the earth gave rise to mountains, basins and deep trenches were created by the displacement.

> Thou coveredst it with the deep as with a garment: The waters stood above the mountains. At thy rebuke they fled; at the voice of thy thunder they hasted away. They go up by the mountains; they go down by the valleys unto the place which thou hast founded for them. Thou hast set a bound that they may not pass over; that they turn not again to cover the earth (Ps. 104:6–9).

Consider for a moment "the valleys" spoken of in this psalm. Where are they?

Joseph Weisberg and Howard Parish in their book *Introduction to Oceanography*, give us the following information: "The great depressions found in the ocean floor are called trenches, and they are found in every major ocean in the world." For example, "The Mariana trench in the western North Pacific, is over 36,000 feet deep."[11] That's 2,000 feet more than twice the height of Mount Ararat, and the trench goes on for many, many miles. Could this trench be one of the valleys spoken of in Psalm 104?

Let's look, for a moment, at the ocean floor, the obvious place for valleys filled with a tremendous amount of water, to be located. "The topography and the structure of the oceans may be divided into three major units: the continental margins, the deep ocean basin floor, and the mid-ocean ridges."[12] I will not go into any detail concerning the deep ocean basin floor, nor the mid-ocean ridges, other than simply to mention them. "Extending throughout the world's oceans, this continuous mountain range circles the earth for 40,000 miles or more. Reaching into every ocean basin, the ridges are between 600 and 2,500 miles wide, with a relief of 6,500 to 13,000 feet above the ocean floor."[13]

The continental margins and the continental shelves are transition zones between the continents and ocean basins. "The width of the shelf varies from a few miles to several hundred, and is relatively shallow, in the area of 600 feet, but around these shelves are deep sea trenches and slopes, which represent one of the most marked relief features of the earth. This slope is scarred by submarine canyons which resemble gullies, and sometimes rival the Grand Canyon in size."[14] The "trenches along the continental shelves also circle the earth, for over 40,000 miles."[15] It is these deep sea trenches which bring reason to this part of our discussion.

Need I go on? There are many, many "valleys" in the ocean floor that store an incalculable amount of water. The oceans cover nearly 3/4 (71 percent) of the earth's surface.[16] This leaves only 25 to 29 percent of the earth's surface as dry land (excluding inland concentrations of water). If the valleys in the ocean floor were not there, at least to such a great extent, where do you suppose the water would go?

For the purpose of attempting to partially theorize what the heights of the mountains may have been before the Flood, and along with the ocean trenches, their effect on displacing the waters at the end of the Flood, let's look again at the writings of Richard Flint, author of *Glacial Geology and the Pleistocene Epoch*. "In North America late Pliocene or Pleistocene movements, involving elevations of thousands of feet, are recorded in Alaska and in the coast ranges of Southern California. . . . The Alps were conspicuously uplifted in Pleistocene and late pre-Pleistocene time. In Asia, there was great early Pleistocene uplift in Turkestan, the Pamirs, the Caucasus, and central Asia, generally. Most of the vast uplift of the Himalayas is ascribed to the latest Tertiary and Pleistocene. In South America, the Peruvian Andes rose at least 5,000 feet in Post Pliocene times. . . . In addition to these tectonic movements, many of the high volcanic cones around the Pacific border, in western and central Asia, and in eastern Africa, are believed to have been built up to their present great heights during the Pliocene and Pleistocene."[17]

The Pleistocene is shown as ending fairly recently on the geologic column. However, the age attributed to the Pleistocene will be a subject of argument in this book.

Morris and Whitcomb say, "Since the Pliocene and Pleistocene are supposed to represent the most recent geological epochs, except that of the present, and since nearly all the great mountain areas of the world have been found to have fossils from these times near their summits, there is no conclusion possible other than that the mountains (and therefore the continents of which they form the backbones), have all been uplifted essentially simultaneously and quite recently. Surely this fact accords well with the biblical statements."[18]

Another variable has entered into the realm of possibility. Mount Ararat could have grown since the ark landed. (If you recall, in chapter 7, "What is Ararat?" geologist Clifford Burdick believes the original Ararat was 10,000 to 12,000 feet tall.)

Geologist Clifford L. Burdick writes in his report from a personal investigation:

> Greater Ararat is a compound volcano, comprising two strato-volcanos. Greater Ararat ejected much more lava than Little Ararat. Lava was ejected from the central cone as well as two notable cones on the flanks at 3,300 and 3,800 meters elevation. (Greater Ararat is 5,165 meters high.) The mountain has no typical crater, although there is a crater lake on the northwest side at Kop Gol. The flank volcanos are known as parasitic and are aligned along radial fissures in the sides of the mountain. Also, instead of Ararat forming a drainage pattern radiating from the mountain, the watershed drainage flows to the Aras (Araxes) and Tigres and Euphrater Rivers, apparently as if it did not know that Ararat existed, this suggesting a more recent birthday for Ararat. The original drainage system may have been established from the days of creation. Everything about Ararat suggests youth.
>
> It has been brought out before, that the bursting forth of Ararat domed the surrounding rocks such as in the Ahora Gulch and the limestones surrounding Ararat, but our investigations on the shoulders of Ararat near the Ahora Gulch, showed a strange tectonic phenomenon — underthrusting — that is, the upwelling magma pushed the deeper rocks aside as it made room for the rising magma, while the surface rock was stationary.[19]

As Ararat grew, it domed the surrounding rock strata to make room for the rising magma. This tells us the mountain grew from within. Another source, which is given to us in the next paragraph, tells us the entire block of East Anatolia, where Ararat sits, was uplifted by as much as 6,600 feet, and this would be in addition to any growth due to underthrusting, or upwelling of magma on Ararat.

It's also interesting to note, as mentioned previously, that pillow lava has been found at 15,000 feet on Ararat. In 1984, while climbing the south side of Ararat, Jim Irwin and I observed what appeared to us as vast amounts of lava which had been compressed to a smooth texture; very fine-grained in its external composition. We thought this could well be pillow lava. In a later discussion with geologist Dr. John Morris, I described what Jim and I had seen. Dr. Morris did not say we had seen pillow lava, but that the fine-grained lava rock we did see could very well have had an underwater origin. Pillow lava has been identified on Ararat by geologists who have climbed on the mountain. Pillow lava is formed "under great depths of water."[20]

If the ark landed on Ararat, and did so during a time of eruption, and was not destroyed, then it certainly must have landed on an area of the mountain that was not being covered by lava. According to John Morris, the older, northern side of the mountain is such an area. Also, according to what we've just read, the ark could have landed at 10,000 or 12,000 feet, probably somewhere on the north side, and the mountain could have grown to nearly 17,000 feet by underthrusting and uplifting, after the landing.

We researched where at least some of the water went after the Flood, into ocean basins and displaced by rising mountains. What about the rest of the water?

From *The Genesis Flood*:

> And now begins another aftermath of the Deluge, of tremendous significance. As the modern cycle of evaporation, atmosphere turbulence, vapor transportation, condensation, and precipitation became established, snow began to fall, quite possibly for the first time in the earth's history. As we have already seen, there is strong evidence that the climate of the entire world prior to the Flood was uniformly mild and pleasant. [Canopy and greenhouse effect.] This snow, falling primarily in the Arctic and Antarctic regions, was, of course, derived via the hydrologic cycle from the waters which only recently were covering the earth. Great

amounts of snow also accumulated in the mountains which had just been uplifted. In this way, large amounts of water were removed from the oceans and stored in the Polar regions in the form of great ice caps, which in some instances are believed by glacial geologists to have attained the immense size of continental ice sheets thousands of feet thick, and thousands of square miles in area. The great accumulation of water stored in the continental ice sheets, combined with the agency of orogeny (mountain building), to cause the retreat of the globe-encircling waters off the continents.[21]

Bernhard Kummel, in *History of the Earth,* says: "The deterioration of the Cenozoic climate culminated in the Pleistocene, when the temperatures in the higher latitudes were lowered sufficiently to allow the accumulation spread of immense ice sheets. *The ultimate cause* of this (or any other) glacial episode *is not known*, though many theories have been proposed"[22] [author's emphasis].

As was indicated by Morris and Whitcomb, the breaking of the canopy and loss of the great extent of the greenhouse effect, saw the temperatures of the earth dramatically cooled. The results of this cooling is quite possibly the ice of the Pleistocene. "*The biblical deluge* offers an eminently satisfactory explanation" to the Ice Age [author's emphasis].

Morris and Whitcomb also comment:

It may be objected that a flood-induced glaciation does not account for the four glacial stages which are quite generally accepted as composing the entire Pleistocene glacial epoch. Glacial geologists believe that each of the four stages was separated by a warmer period comparable to that of the present, or perhaps even warmer. A glaciation such as we have envisioned as brought on by the deluge, would more likely be one event, not four separate events.

It is admitted that it is difficult to account for the four stages on the basis of our present explanation. But it is also true that it is equally difficult to account for the four stages on the basis of any of the other glacial theories that have been devised.

As a matter of fact, the reason that it is so difficult to account theoretically for the four glacial stages may simply be that they never existed.

It should not be thought that the evidence for the three earlier stages is the same as that for the last. The latter is found in nearly all the present surface features of the topography in the glaciated regions — the moraines, the drumlins, eskers, striations and grooves, etc. But these are found only in connection with the supposed last glacial maximum and its retreat, the so-called Wisconsin stage.

The earlier stages — in retrograde order, the Illinoian, Kansan, and Nebraskan — are evidenced mainly by a deposit of "gumbotil," supposedly a very mature and weathered clay soil containing small stones. It is explained that these gumbotils are the weathered remnants of former till deposits. (A till is an unstratified deposit of gravel, sand and clay, which is considered evidence of glacial origin.)

The evidence for the several glacial stages has been primarily those of the supposed weathered tills underlying fresh tills, that is, soil deposits. If this is the case, then it would seem reasonable for the observer to be able to determine an approximate age of the weathered tills.

The length of time required to weather fresh material and develop a soil profile is unknown.[23]

Richard Flint, author of *Glacial and Pleistocene Geology*, says, "It has not been possible to estimate the time required for the development of any given soil. Indirect evidence suggests that some kinds of soils can develop to maturity within periods of a few hundred years, and possibly even within much shorter periods."[24]

In other words, no one knows how old the soil is. It seems then, if this is the case, that the observer is making a calculated guess based on and biased by previous learning of information known to be inaccurate.

Some German geologists, for example Geinitz, are of the opinion that there is no proof of the existence of several glacial periods. "They have held the opinion that the withdrawals separating two successive stages were very unimportant and there was no proof of the existence of several glacial periods. These Monoglaciologists believe the glacial periods had one maximum advance and was stationary with small oscillations in detail, then began to retreat spasmodically, and the climate did not become similar to the present until after this retreat, in post glacial times."[25]

Morris and Whitcomb go into great detail on the subject of glaciation, just as they do so thoroughly cover every other area of investigation, which refers to questions surrounding the Genesis flood. We will go only so far as to say that according to the information presented there appears to be solid evidence for only one period of glaciation, with perhaps some oscillations in its retreat; still it was fairly abrupt when it stopped its advance.

It is clear that a major fluctuation in climate occurred at some time in the past. The primary observation that both surface ocean temperatures and deep sea sedimentation rates were abruptly altered at this time is supplemented by evidence from more local systems. For instance, the level of the Great Basin lakes fell from the highest terraces to a position close to that observed at present. An example of this statement is seen in the history of the Great Salt Lake of Utah.

> The Great Salt Lake is but a small remnant of its ancient predecessor, Lake Bonneville. The ancient lake was named in honor of an army captain, B.L.E. Bonneville, who on a trapping expedition in 1833, proved the remaining Great Salt Lake was truly an inland sea. The Great Salt Lake lies in the "Great Basin" with interior drainage only. The surface of the present Salt Lake is at an elevation of 4,200 feet. This is higher than the average elevation of the Allegheny Mountains, but it only averages 13 to 15 feet deep. The surface of the ancient Bonneville was one thousand feet higher and covered an area of 19,750 square miles; (according to Grove Karl Gilbert, geologist of the Wheeler survey 1869–70), this equals ten times the size of the present lake.[26]

Geologists tell us that Bonneville was formed during excessive periods of precipitation during the period of tremendous climatic change in the glacial epoch, 20,000 years ago or more. Except for the date, I believe this falls in line with what Morris and Whitcomb have been telling us. That is, just before the glacial period, during a time of climatic change, there was a period of excessive precipitation. It is called the "Genesis flood."

An article in the *American Journal of Science* entitled "Evidence for an Abrupt Change in Climate Close to 11,000 Years Ago" reports, "A rapid ice retreat opened the northern drainage systems of the Great Lakes and terrestrial temperatures rose to nearly interglacial levels in northwestern Europe. In each case the transition is the most obvious feature of the entire record."[27]

Morris and Whitcomb do not agree with the date. They feel it is too high. Radio carbon dating was used and it may be inaccurate. They do agree that the change was abrupt. This statement comes from the same article: "There is evidence for an abrupt worldwide change in climate close to 11,000 years ago which marks the end of the Wisconsin glacial period. This evidence is largely correlated on the basis of radiocarbon measurements."[28]

I'll not go into the many variables that may have caused the Ice Age to come to its abrupt end. However, I will include this one possible explanation that is given to us in *The Genesis Flood:*

> As plants and animals began to grow again and gradually to multiply, their life processes would gradually restore carbon dioxide to the atmosphere (lost when the canopy broke), approaching the balance that has, in general, characterized present times. Along with this, carbon dioxide equilibrium between ocean and atmosphere required gradual discharge of the gas from the ocean into the air, further volcanic sources undoubtedly yielded a certain amount to the atmosphere. And all of this (and other variables such as bogs, which produce CO_2 in large amounts, re-establishing in part the pre-flood carbon dioxide back into the atmosphere) in turn would have caused a gradual rise in terrestrial temperatures, probably at an accelerating rate.
>
> A substantial increase in CO_2 content in the air would trap more of the earth's radiated heat and cause a warming of temperatures. This increase in CO_2 did not lead to the greenhouse effect the earth had once experienced, still it was enough to cause an increase in temperatures, etc., to the end of the Ice Age.[29]

It has been calculated that 97.6 percent of all water is in the oceans. Three-quarters of all the remaining water is in the glaciers and ice caps. Beyond this, what remains consists mainly of ground water, water stored in the voids of rocks beneath the surface, moisture in the soil, the lakes, rivers, and the atmosphere.[30]

One vast storehouse of water that we have neglected to focus on is the present day ice pack; the ice that did not melt with the end of the Ice Age. It is this water which is locked up in the ice caps, which is fairly significant. "The Antarctic ice cap covers about 5 million square miles, which is an area larger than the United States, Mexico, and Central America put together." The thickness of the ice varies from about 1,000 feet (or 300 meters) thick near the coast, and 6,000 feet (or 1,800 meters) in the interior. The area in east Antarctica near the pole resembles a high deserted plateau buried under nearly 9,000 feet (2,700 meters) of ice. In west Antarctica, the ice cap is 14,000 feet thick (4,200 meters) in some places.[31]

The Arctic Ocean remains frozen much of the year with as much as 90 percent covered with ice, and all of the year with at least 70 percent covered with ice.[32] Estimates in the thickness of the ice cover vary from 10 feet for the oceans,[33] to ice islands with thicknesses of as much as 200 feet in some areas. Also, most of Greenland is covered by ice.[34]

Along with the various estimates of the thickness of the ice pack, (and there are many more than we have mentioned), estimates also vary as to how much the sea level would rise should all the ice melt. I'll mention only one. "Complete melting of the polar ice packs would result in the sea level rising 160 meters (or approximately 540 feet) above its present level."[35] If this would prove to be a fairly accurate figure, think of all the land which is now above the surface of the oceans that would be covered by water with the rise in sea level, just due to the melting of the ice pack.

Now we quite possibly know a little more about the water, where it came from, and where it went. So much for the doctrine of uniformitarianism as it pertains to earth's history over the long haul. Morris and Whitcomb make this statement: "The essential differences between biblical catastrophism and evolutionary uniformitarianism are not over factual data of geology, but over interpretation of that data."[36]

WHEN WAS THE FLOOD?

Looking through the work by Kummel which was referenced in the last chapter and in comparing that information to what Whitcomb and Morris have to say, I find little accord between them. Perhaps the information on the results of the various dating methods is recorded differently in different publications. This assumes there is a question in the agreement of the results from methods used to determine age. An exception to this assumption could possibly be in the counting of tree rings, which should give accurate data agreeable to scientists on all sides of the basic question, and that question being, "How old is it?"

One day in June 1985 my family and I were visiting Central City, Colorado, and I noticed a fossilized rock slab in the window of the Baby Doe Mining Company. A gentleman inside the store informed me the fossils were of a fish they labeled "Knightia Eocenia." The fossils were found near Green River, Wyoming, and they showed evidence of a mass mortality, a quick encrustation. The rock slab itself was said to be compressed volcanic ash. I asked how old the rock slab was. This very considerate gentleman, not a geologist, told me he had been informed that the rock slab was dated 47 to 49 million years old, and he thought by the carbon dating method, but in all fairness he was not sure. If it was carbon dated, would the results be accurate? Absolutely not, as you will understand in this chapter, but this example is one public perception, according to their interpretation of scientific truth.

Whitcomb and Morris say the following: "Dr. Stuart Piggott, a British archaeologist, reports that two radiocarbon tests on a sample of charcoal indicated a date of 2620-2630 B.C. for an ancient structure at Durrington Walls in England. But absolutely compelling archaeological evidences called for a date approximately 1,000 years later! Dr. Piggott concludes that the radiocarbon date is archaeologically unacceptable."[1]

In his book *The Turin Shroud Is Genuine*, Rodney Hoare cites the following information on radioactive carbon dating:

In the upper atmosphere, nitrogen atoms are hit by cosmic rays and become radioactive carbon atoms, and at the same rate radiocarbon atoms down below are decaying back into nitrogen atoms, so the proportion of radioactive carbon atoms in the atmosphere is almost constant. An extremely small portion of the atoms are radioactive, about one in every trillion.

The newly created radioactive carbon atoms in the upper atmosphere combine with oxygen atoms to become carbon dioxide, which sinks down to the earth and is breathed in by plants. That is why living creatures have, while alive, the same proportion of stable and unstable carbon atoms as the air has.

But they die. Absorption of carbon dioxide stops. The proportions of the carbon atoms are fixed at the moment of death. Then the radioactive carbon atoms slowly decay into nitrogen.

In practice, there is another complication, for the radioactive carbon does not decrease at a regular rate, but at a rate depending on how many radioactive atoms are left. So the rate of decay decreases from the moment the plant dies. The formula for the change is known.

It follows that since scientists know the rate at which radioactive carbon atoms have decayed since the plant died, and can calculate from the stable carbon atoms how many radioactive atoms were in the first place, they can work out the age of the sample.

In the "old" gas counting method, the amount of carbon atoms is found by weighing to calculate the radioactive carbon atoms. At only one part in a trillion, the accuracy of the method could be questioned. With a "new" method, the Accelerator Mass Spectrometry or AMS method, molecules are fired through a mass spectrograph, and by the resulting circles created by the atoms, the age can be determined by counting the different circles according to their mass. This could work only if the specimen to be dated is not contaminated.

Whichever method is used, pretreatment — getting rid of all accretions on the specimen so that only the original carbon remains — is essential, and in many ways this is the most important part of the experiment and the way mistakes most often arise. If some extra carbon has gotten into the specimen, the result is bound to be wrong.

It should be obvious from the minute proportion of radioactive carbon in the sample that the experiment has to be extremely exact. Those who deal with carbon-dating results, the archaeologists, do not have much faith in it.

In archaeology, if there are ten lines of evidence, carbon dating being one of them, and it conflicts with the other nine, there is little hesitation to throw out the carbon date as inaccurate due to unforeseen contamination.[2]

This is a view other archaeologists share. A specific case is reported by the highly respected Greek archaeologist Spyros Iakovvidis:

In relation to the reliability of carbon dating, I would like to mention something which happened to me during my excavation at Gla (Boeotia, Greece). I sent two different laboratories in two different parts of the world a certain amount of the same burnt grain. I got two readings differing by 2,000 years, the archaeological date being right in the middle. I feel that this method is not exactly to be trusted.[3]

There are many examples of carbon dates proven to be wrong by a considerable amount. The Shroud of Turin is another example. Dated between 1260 and 1390, there is speculation that the three laboratories, who were to do their work independent of the others, actually collaborated at some level.

An article in the *Tampa Tribune*, dated May 22, 1996, says, "Shroud May Have Been Woven around Time of Jesus' Death." The article says, in part:

A microscopic layer of bacteria and fungi may have thrown off carbon dating of the shroud and all other ancient fabrics by hundreds, even thousands of years, a team from the University of Texas Health Science Center in San Antonio reported Tuesday. "This means that at the present time, the radiocarbon dating of ancient textiles is not a reliable test," said one of the researchers, Leonio Gasrza-Valdes, a pediatrician and archaeologist.

Returning again to the book *The Turin Shroud Is Genuine*, the author says this: "The laboratories concerned in experiments do not publish their wrong results. They would be unlikely to cooperate if asked what mistakes they had made."

You may recall at the end of the previous chapter I referred to carbon dioxide increasing to a balance as a casual effect on the end of the Ice Age. If this theory is correct, and if the Ice Age is a result of the Flood, then before the Flood, and before what must have been a tremendous downpour of rain, there must have been a high concentration of carbon dioxide in the earth's vapor canopy. This canopy would have been made up of water vapor, ozone, and carbon dioxide.[4] The canopy's greenhouse effect would have helped to provide the mild climate thought to have existed on earth before the Genesis flood.

After the 40 days and nights of downpour, it is then possible that the amount of carbon dioxide content in the atmosphere may have changed. It may have decreased significantly.

Gilbert N. Plass says in an article in the *American Scientist*: "All calculations of radiocarbon dates have been made on the assumption that the amount of atmospheric carbon dioxide variations in the atmosphere is correct, then the reduced carbon dioxide amount at the time of the last glaciation means that all radiocarbon dates for events before the recession of the glaciers are in question."[5] In other words, if the proposed theory is accurate, then radiocarbon dates assigned to periods before the end of the Ice Age may not be correct.

Bernhard Kummel also discusses the dating process in his *History of Earth*. "The half-life of carbon is about 5,570 years; theoretically this limits the use for dating to about eight half-lives, or a maximum of about 50,000 years. The technique has been checked on archaeologically dated woods, and the dates derived demonstrate the approximate validity of the method for at least the last 5,000 years. No accurate checks are available on the older dates; there appears to be fair agreement, however, among several determinations on the same or comparable samples, from set horizons. The method has to be used with great caution, since there are numerous factors that can lead to contamination of the sample, and thus give erroneous dates."[6]

As long as we're talking about how old we are, let's look at the whole thing for just a minute, and see if we can decide how old planet Earth is, from a scientific viewpoint, of course.

One day in June of 1984, I was visiting the docks in Seattle. I had gone there for the purpose of trying to determine for myself how a ship the size of Noah's ark might compare in size to the ships of today.

In my wanderings I happened into a planetarium and viewed a movie entitled *Genesis*. The information presented therein told me the earth was formed when a giant super nova exploded 20 billion years ago. Debris and gravity shaped the solar system, and the hot spot in the center became our sun, and so forth. Two years prior to all this, I saw another movie about the universe at the Denver Planetarium, also located in the Museum of Natural History, and although I don't recall the title of that movie, I do remember it told us the universe was created only 16 billion years ago.

In geochronology, "the currently accepted figure for the age of the earth, as deduced from radio activity of uranium and other elements, is about five to six billion years, with the solidification of the crust dated about 4-1/2 billion years ago."[7]

From an article entitled "The Age of the Universe" in the *Scientific Monthly*, "By examining the helium content of several meteorites, Paneth arrives at ranging their ages from 60 million to 7 billion years. Re-examining the evidence, Bauer arrives at a common age of about 60 million years for the meteorites examined by Paneth. This would give us, thus, a lower limit for the age of the meteorite, and also for the age of the universe."[8]

Whitcomb and Morris give their view:

> It has been difficult for astronomers and geologists to accept such a "small" age for the meteorites, in terms of any of the classical theories of the origin of the solar system. More recent and much more subtle calculations have been invoked to "reconcile" the discrepancy.
>
> When this is done, the age of the stony meteorites since solidification is found. The result is about 4.6 thousand million years. . . . Thus, merely by changing the method of calculation, one can increase the age of a meteorite from 60, to 4,600 million years! The latter calculation was made by the potassium-argon method, the first by the helium isotope method.[9]

Astronomer Dr. T.S. Jackson of the University of Washington, after discussing astromic methods of age measurements says: "The result is that we know nothing certain about the age of the universe."[10]

From what we've read of these few examples of dated conclusions, with large periods of disagreement in time, it seems we can assume that the statement by Dr. Jackson just about sums up the majority, if not the total of our dating knowledge, in whatever dating method used, beyond approximately 5,000 years. Perhaps newer technology will prove, or is proving to be more accurate.

"Microscopic study of growth rings reveals that a bristlecone pine tree found last summer, at nearly 10,000 feet, began growing more than 4,600 years ago, and thus surpasses the oldest known giant sequoia by many centuries. Many of its neighbors are nearly as old; we have now dated 17 bristlecone pines 4,000 years old, or more."[11]

The Genesis Flood says, "Since these, as well as the sequoias and other ancient trees, are still living, it is pertinent to ask why these oldest living things apparently have had time to develop only one generation since they acquired their present stands at some time after the Deluge. There is no record of a tree, or any other living thing, being older than any reasonable date for the Deluge."[12]

According to Whitcomb and Morris, authors of *The Genesis Flood,* "A careful study of the biblical evidence leads us to the conclusion that the Flood may have occurred as much as three to five thousand years before Abraham. This is taking into consideration the possibility of gaps in genealogy of Genesis chapter 11. Any longer period of time approaches impossibility when we consider the oral traditions of the Flood which have been incorporated into such documents as the *Gilgamesh Epic* of Babylonia."[13]

The *Gilgamesh Epic* is the documented record of Babylonia which pertains to the Great Flood and which I will briefly outline here. Bear in mind there are flood traditions existing in nearly every culture all over the world. Over 200 of them have been compiled and published.[14] The following are a few of them.

A close parallel to the biblical story of the Flood occurs in the Mesopotamian Epic of Gilgamesh. The epic centers around King Gilgamesh. Probably the deluge story, which is inserted on the 11th tablet of the Gilgamesh epic, existed in oral tradition before being committed to writing sometime in the remote Sumerian period. The tablet on which the deluge story is written comes from the library of a certain Babylonian patron of literature by the name of Assur-bani-pal, of the city of Nineveh. The tablet is now in the British museum and is dated to 2100 B.C. However, the story is of much greater antiquity.[15]

Gilgamesh, king of Erech (Gen. 10:10), sets out in search of the means of immortality. After sundry adventures, he is at last advised to betake himself to Utnapishtim, the

Babylonian Noah, who lives on a distant island and is reputedly immortal. Utnapishtim tells him that he possesses no such secret, but has been given immortality as a special and peculiar reward from the gods. By way of explanation, he relates the story of the deluge.[16]

Presumably, the warning of the deluge came to Utnapishtim in a vision. The voice of God said: Thou man of Shirippak, Son of Cubara-Tutu, pull down thy house, build a ship, forsake thy possessions, take heed for thy life! Abandon thy goods, save thy life, and bring up living seed of every kind into the ship.[17]

I did as I was bidden, drew up plans, built the ship and provisioned it. When all was ready, I caulked the outer side with bitumen and inner side with asphalt. Then I brought my family and possessions aboard. The same evening, the clouds — those princes of darkness — sent a prodigious rain, and a storm blew up. For six days and nights, wind and flood raged. On the seventh day, however, the battling wind seemed to exhaust itself and, suddenly, it died down, and the flood abated. I surveyed the scene. Not a sound was to be heard. Everything, including mankind, had turned to mud and clay.[18]

I bowed myself down, I sat down, I wept; over my cheek flowed my tears. I looked upon the world, and behold all was sea. — At length the ship came to rest on the summit of Mount Nitsir.[19]

An Egyptian story of a deluge is preserved in the so-called Book of the Dead. The god Atum announces his intention of flooding wicked mankind with the waters of the primeval ocean (Nun). The flood starts at Henensu, or Herakleopolis, in Upper Egypt, and submerges the entire country. The only survivors are certain persons who have been rescued in "the boat of millions of years."[20]

An Icelandic version of the tradition occurs in the Younger Edda, the great collection of ancient Norse myths and legends which was put together by Snorri Sturluson about A.D. 1222. We there read how the god Bor had three divine sons, Odin, Wili, and We, and how these sons slew the giant Ymir. From the wounds of the dying giant there gushed such a stream of blood that it drowned all the other giants except one, named Bergelmir, who escaped with his wife in a boat, and from whom the later race of giants is descended.[21]

A Welsh legend of the deluge runs thus. Once upon a time the lake of Llion burst and flooded all lands, so that the whole human race was drowned, all except Dwyfan and Dwyfach, who escaped in a mastless ship and re-peopled the land of Prydain (Britain). The ship also contained a male and female of every sort of living creature, so that after the deluge the animals were able to propagate their various kinds and restock the world.[22]

"The Mexicans," says the Italian historian Clavigero, "with all other civilized nations, had a clear tradition, though somewhat corrupted by fable, of the creation of the world, of the universal deluge, of the confusion of tongues, and of the dispersion of the people; and had actually all these events represented in their pictures. They said that when mankind [was] overwhelmed with the deluge, none were preserved but a man named Coxcox (to whom others give the name of Teocipactli), and a woman called Xochiquetzal, who saved themselves on a raft, and having afterwards got to land upon a mountain called by them Colhuacan."[23]

A Chinese legend also tells a folktale of a great flood whereby two people were to be saved by a boat as the land disappeared and was covered by a big lake. Sparrows, ants, and snakes were among the animals to be saved, but wolves along with men were not to be helped. When the boat landed, there was no sign of men anywhere, only mountains and hills.[24]

There is even an Australian Aboriginal myth of a great flood: "The animals struggled hither and thither in the blinding storm, seeking shelter, traveling up and up, and dodging behind trees and rocks and boulders on the mountainside, until they reached the summit, where they sought safety. Thus, the conference ended in desolation and death. It rained and rained. The valleys and the low-lying country were deluged. Nearly all life was destroyed in the great flood."[25]

The Hopi Indians tell us of a first world where life was simple and happy, but evil crept in and people strayed away from the Creator. The world ended with volcanic eruptions of fire. Not everyone died. There were still some left who believed in a Creator. Again the story repeated itself until the end of the Second World. "The world teetered off balance, spun around crazily, then rolled over twice. Mountains plunged into the sea with a great splash, seas and lakes sloshed over the land; and as the world spun through cold and lifeless space it froze into solid ice."[26]

The Flood and the Ice Age? In the previous chapter we discussed the possibility of the earth being moved exceedingly and reeling to and fro like a drunkard (teetering off balance). Also, the question of the Ice Age as a result of the Flood is dealt with. The Hopi legend continues, however, and tells of a water cataclysm since the time of the ice.

Some people again survived, and Hopi legend tells us there was a Third World. Again the people multiplied and populated the earth, and again there was corruption until destruction came by water. "Waves higher than the mountains rolled in upon the land. Continents broke asunder and sank beneath the seas. And still the rains fell, the waves rolled in." — Again some survived in the new land that surfaced, or pushed up, to live as they are now in the Fourth World.[27]

There is controversy in Egypt, and in scientific circles worldwide, over a new discovery. According to author John Anthony West and geologist-geophysicist Dr. Robert Schock of Boston University, the Great Sphinx is much older than the pyramids.

It is believed that the pyramids were built during the dynasty of the pharaohs when the climate was desert, such as it is today. Egyptologists claim the Sphinx was built during the period of the pharaoh Khafre (*Chephren* in Greek) around 2500 B.C. This would be in the same general time period of the building of the second pyramid. Both were built of the same limestone material. In fact, all the pyramids as well as the Sphinx were built of that material. It should be logical then, that weathering and erosion taking place over the years would be in the same way; that is, by wind and sand. However, much of the erosion on the Sphinx is by water. That is not the case with the pyramids.

A fascinating article from *Conde' Nast Traveler (Truth in Travel)*, a magazine incorporating European travel and life, which is entitled "The Sphinx, Clue to a Lost Civilization?" includes the following excerpts:

There is now a body of solid scientific evidence that holds that, unlike the pyramids around it, the Great Sphinx is, in fact, thousands of years older. This revelation is no mere statistical trifle. It means that the Sphinx was carved at a time when, according to accepted historical theories, humanity was in the rudimentary stage of hunters and gatherers, and civilization did not yet exist.

The implications are stunning. Suddenly, ancient history and the entire scenario we have drawn of the evolution of human civilization seem to require drastic revision.

A single line, buried within a paragraph in an obscure 1961 book by an obscure French scholar with an unpronounceable name, ignited the long fuse that, 30 years later, touched off the scholarly explosion:

> We have to acknowledge that a great civilization must have preceded the vast movements of water that passed over Egypt; it is this which is implied by the existence of the Sphinx sculpted in the rock on the western cliffs at Giza, this Sphinx whose whole leonine body, with the exception of the head, shows an indisputable water erosion.[28]

Subsequent to this article, a movie entitled *The Mystery of the Sphinx* (1993), seen on NBC and hosted by Charlton Heston, outlined the work of the author, John Anthony West, and geologist Dr. Robert M. Schock. Information given in the movie tells us that the head of the Sphinx is small in comparison to the body. The reason it shows no water erosion is because it was reshaped at a time long after the original carving. One can assume the head, too, in its original design, must have been badly eroded.

Charlton Heston narrates that the pyramids are 4,500 years old, but the Sphinx is from a time 9,000 to 10,000 years ago. If this is the case, then the history of ancient man will have to be rewritten. Darwinian evolution is challenged and put in question — the academic's worst nightmare. Heston narrates that the Sphinx may have been eroded by water from the Great Flood. A scientist on the program said, in essence, that the Sphinx could be from an antediluvian time, a time of a great civilization before the Flood.

By the end of the following chapter, old and new scientific evidence may give us not only the approximate date of the Flood, but that of creation itself!

EVOLUTION? CREATION?

John Morris, of the Institute for Creation Research, once wrote:

> The problem, very simply, is this: Evolution rests to varying degrees, on the assumption of uniformity. Uniformitarianism claims that, by studying and measuring present processes, and extrapolating these processes back into an assumed ancient past, the secrets of the past can be unfolded.
>
> Creationists maintain that the world had not always been the same, and likewise the processes have not been constant. They believe that, at a particular time in the past, a Supreme Being created both the world and its processes, both of which were greatly altered at the time of the Great Deluge, or Noah's Flood.

You may wonder why I'm spending so much time on uniformitarianism and evolution in a book about Noah's ark. The reason it is so much a part of this book, is really quite fundamental. First of all, this book isn't just about Noah's ark. It is also about salvation.

In order for me to believe that the reader will accept, or at least consider, what the Bible has to say about Christianity, I must first discuss as fairly, and yet as convincingly as I am able, the very foundation of the belief I am asking you, the skeptical reader, to study. I believe that the Book of Genesis, as it is written, is the very foundation to the rest of the Bible; to Christianity. Like the foundation of a house that gives support to the structure, a strong foundation, a belief in creation, gives a strong support to the overriding structure in Christianity. A foundation in evolution as we have defined it in this chapter, is a weak foundation, and Christian beliefs may be shaky at best. In other words, if you can't accept Genesis, can you accept the rest of it?

In this chapter I will give my opinion on issues which I think are of "grave" importance, so you can possibly be more informed in your understanding of the biblical account.

EVOLUTION?

Evolution is defined by Webster's Dictionary as "The scientific theory according to which higher forms of life have gradually developed from simple and rudimentary forms."[1] Now is a good time to introduce this definition in order to better understand the information to follow. When we think of theories of evolution, we naturally think of Charles Darwin, whose *Origin of the Species* had such an impact on the scientific community after 1859, and still commands a leadership role in scientific thought today.

However, "The idea of evolution did not begin with Darwin. Many scientists and philosophers believed evolution before Darwin's day. The idea of evolution arose first among the ancient Greeks; Anaximander taught that men had evolved from fish, and Empedocles asserted that animals had been derived from plants."[2]

In the year of Darwin's birth, 1809, Frenchman Jean-Baptiste de Lamarck published his *Theory of Transformation.* Lamarck believed that species evolved by transforming themselves into "higher" forms of life. For instance, "every animal that was 'low' on the scale of nature as it was called, had an innate tendency to transform itself, gradually into a 'higher' and 'more perfect' creature. Over long periods of time, a fish would naturally tend to become a reptile. The reptile had the same innate tendency to become a mammal, which was destined by nature to become a human being. Any gaps or imperfections on this evolutionary scale were attributed to the effects of adoption by a species to their environment instead of to the ideal."[3]

Darwin's theory is not much different. He says, in referring to the classification system set up by naturalists of his day, that all species which closely resemble each other belong to the same order, class, or phylum, and have descended from common ancestry. Darwin goes further to say, for example, "All members of the phylum of Chordates, have descended from some vertebrate animal that lived an immensely long time ago. Some of these primitive spined creatures evolved into reptiles, others into mammals."[4]

According to Darwin, man emerged from a unicellular organism, through shell, eel, fish, reptile and amphibian, to primitive mammal, monkey, and ape man.[5]

Darwin's theory of evolution is by a process he calls "natural selection." To continue with Darwin's theory, we must then define natural selection: The doctrine of survival of the fittest; in evolution, the process whereby certain types adapted to their environment reproduce their kind in emphasized degree, so that an improvement is being carried on gradually from one stage of development to another.[6]

Natural selection, according to Darwin, is a reality that can produce vast changes in living things over a period of time. Darwin says that small heredity variations crop up at random in the offspring of all living things, and through these changes by natural selection, the surviving species adapts to its environment. If a species is then unable to adapt to a changing environment, it might slowly lose out in the struggle for existence. Favorable variations over hundreds of thousands of generations constitute a new species. By the variations of one species into another, Darwin explains the origin of the species with evolution by natural selection.[7]

Problems in Darwin's theory are obvious. First of all, according to Darwin, evolution by natural selection results in living things beautifully adapted to their environment, all by random changes. By definition, random means "fortuitous, aimless, accident, chance, etc." Randomness, then, is without a purposeful plan or design. How can a great many random, purposeless changes eventually bring about a creature that looks exactly as it has been designed on purpose? It would be like believing that rocks rolling down a hill would not just end up in a pile, but rather would pile themselves into a castle![8]

For instance: What about the approximately three-pound wonder of organized matter we call the brain? Are the senses of vision, hearing, taste, and smell, along with our motorized functions of movement, simply a result of random chance? Are the sensations of touch, pain, and pleasure, which carry through our body's nervous system also a result of random chance? What about our ability to comprehend and remember? To put this in a nutshell, how is it that an educated person equipped with such an orderly and complex device as the human brain (which we all use so very little) can believe that his or her brain, and all the rest of the person, including the design of the human body seen by most of us through the eyes of intricate detail, and the emotions, such as love and hate, happened by random chance? Is it logical that such order can evolve completely from disorder, randomly and accidentally?

Another problem is the "sudden" appearance of fresh species of fossils in rock strata of different periods. Darwin admitted "the fossil record was the most obvious and serious objection which can be urged against the theory."[9] Transitional fossil forms between modern and extinct species cannot be found. Darwin said, "If this fossil record were a true account of the history of life, my theory must be smashed."[10] Darwin realized if the fossil record is true, then evolution is false. If evolution is true, then the fossil record is imperfect.

It does take a certain number of circumstances to fossilize a dead creature; for instance, a quick burial, so the animal is not allowed to decay or be consumed by scavengers. The mud and sediment from a flood could do that. Another point should be made in regard to fossilization. "Just because something is fossilized does not mean that it is millions, or even thousands of years old. Fossilization depends on the kind of materials that buried the animal. When the conditions and materials are right, fossilization can take place quite quickly. It mainly takes the right materials, quick burial, and the right amount of water. Scientists have found that chicken bones and wood can be fossilized in just five to ten years. A big dinosaur bone might take hundreds of years to completely fossilize; it all depends on the burial conditions over the years."[11]

Fossilized evidence for a Flood is extensive. For example:

Many fossil animals and tree trunks are found extending through several strata often 20 feet or more in thickness. The top parts of these "polystrate" fossils (those that cut through many layers of rock) are as well preserved as the lower part, showing that the whole tree was submerged in a short time by rapidly deposited layers of sediment. In some parts of the United States huge reptiles are found buried in this fashion. If the sedimentation had been at present rates, it would have taken 5,000 years for these animals to be covered.

Coal deposits provide evidence of a flood. Many facts suggest that the coal seams were formed when vegetation was uprooted and redeposited by flood waters, rather than slowly accumulating in a peat bog, as evolutionists believe. For example, upright tree trunks more than 10 feet in height have been found in coal beds. Some trees are positioned with their tops downward in the coal, and so could not have grown in place. Marine fossils have been found embedded in coal. Also, a 10-inch long, 8-carat gold chain, an iron pot, and a human skull were found buried in coal. These constitute evidence that a human civilization perished while the coal was being formed.

When a fish dies it usually floats to the surface, washes ashore, is eaten, or decays. It would take a rapid burial to preserve and fossilize a fish. There is a region in the hills of Italy where 100,000 fossil fish have been found 2,000 feet above what is now sea level.[12]

I am of the opinion that the evidence for a worldwide cataclysmic event as a Flood, has not been treated fairly by the evolutionists and uniformitarians of today. If this is indeed the case, to them I have one important question: What does it take for a scientist, or anyone who inquires, to actually look at the evidence and recognize it for what it is? What does it take to change the thinking of someone who has learned the wrong doctrine?

Here is an example. A geologist from Yale, Dr. Carl O. Dunbar said, "Fossils provide the only historical documentary evidence that life has evolved from simple to complex forms."[13] The reasoning here says we know evolution is true because of the fossil record. How did the fossil record prove evolution? Because when you find old rocks, you find simple fossils. This assumes that life evolved from the simple to the complex, and because of the time needed for this evolution to take place, only newer rocks would have complex fossils.

That's okay if you know how to date the rocks, so you know which is old and which is young, but how do you date the rocks? You date the rocks from the fossils found in the rocks. How do fossils date the rocks? Through stages of evolution, that's how. Simple fossils mean old rocks. That's okay if you know evolution is true. How do we know evolution is true? Because in old rocks, you find simple fossils. Then, how do you know the rocks are old? Because of the fossil record, and simple fossils are found in old rocks; and round and round we go! "In a vast circle of reasoning, the proof of evolution is the assumption of evolution."[14]

To sum up what we've just read, we see that the information which is taught to us today, as fact, tells us we know how old a rock is by the fossils found in it, and we know how old a fossil is by the rock it is found in. We assume vast ages and uniformities; we assume evolution, all based on theories a hundred or more years old, on evidence that can't even be dated.

The evolutionist needs fossils which indicate stages of transition between the species. They haven't been found. Even in the uniformitarian geologist's stratigraphic succession of geologic ages in the geologic column, this is still true. There may, in some circumstance, be a case for old fossils, but not for evolution.

Fish appear suddenly with no transitional fossils between them and the amphibians — mammals appear suddenly with no transitional fossils found. Even the trilobite, which is supposed to date to the Cambrian period of 300 million years ago, doesn't have any ancestry that can be found in the Precambrian layer just beneath it. And the trilobite has a complex eye structure that, according to evolutionists, should take somewhere in the area of 200 million years of evolutionary time in order to evolve to the complex structure that fossil evidence indicates it was.[15]

Dr. Morris says, "There are too many contradictions in this evolutionary uniformitarian model. From the premise and the buildup, to a conclusion, we find we must continually modify the model. When this happens, you should question the premise and see if there isn't a better model."[16]

Does the Bible give us a better model? We mentioned in our discussion of fossilization that a big dinosaur bone might completely fossilize in a matter of hundreds of years. Evolutionists tell us fossilized dinosaur bones are millions of years old. Is it possible that dinosaur bones may in fact be only thousands, or even hundreds of years old? Does the Bible make reference to dinosaurs, possibly even to the mythological fire-breathing dragon, which may in fact be a dinosaur?

The *New Universal Family Encyclopedia* by Random House, tells us the brontosaurus was an herbivorous (plant-eating) dinosaur capable of weighing up to 30 tons. It had massive pillar-like legs, a long neck and tail. This giant reptile of great size and strength spent much of its time in swamps, or near water.

In the Book of Job, God speaks to Job of "behemoth," a beast he made "with" man. A few of the verses in this chapter of Job give us this description of behemoth:

> Behold now behemoth which I made with thee; he eateth grass as an ox. Lo now, his strength is in his loins, and his force is in the navel of his belly. He moveth his tail like a cedar: the sinews of his stones are wrapped together. His bones are as strong pieces of brass; his bones are like bars of iron. . . . Behold, he drinketh up a river, and hasteth not: he trusteth that he can draw up Jordan into his mouth (Job 40:15–23).

Some commentators believe "behemoth," which in Greek means "river horse," refers to a hippopotamus. But Job 40:17 refers to an animal who *moveth his tail like a cedar*. I have seen the hippopotamus in the local zoo and in the African wild, and he does not have such a tail. A 30-ton beast such as a Brontosaurus, no doubt did have a pretty good-size tail; maybe the size of a cedar.

Finding a reference in the Bible of a beast which could describe the brontosaurus, brings the pre-history into the past history. Could it be possible that the brontosaurus has even a more recent past than of the time the Book of Job was written? According to a television documentary entitled "Dinosaur," by Philips-Marks Production, the brontosaurus may have been seen alive quite recently somewhere in deepest Africa. Also, the Loch Ness "monster" is probably yet another member of the "extinct" dinosaur family known as the *Plesiosaurus*, and may still be very much alive.

There is a book written by Paul S. Taylor entitled *The Great Dinosaur Mystery and the Bible* that tells of several possible visual accounts of dinosaur-like beasts. It seems, according to this book, that neither meteoritic dust in the atmosphere nor the Flood killed all the dinosaurs. At least one of the reports given us in this book can definitely be substantiated.

On April 10, 1977, the nets of a Japanese fishing ship, the *Zuiyo Mara*, fishing near Christchurch, New Zealand, snagged the decaying body of a large reptile. The remains, which were pulled up from a depth of 900 feet, measured 32 feet in length, and weighed approximately 4,000 pounds. The reptile had four fins, each of which was approximately three feet long. Photographs, measurements, and tissue samples all show that the decayed body was probably one of the great marine reptiles, such as the *Plesiosaurus*, of the "prehistoric" past.

> The evidence was examined and tested by a committee of high-ranking Japanese marine scientists. The Director of Animal Research at the National Science Museum of Japan said, "It seems that these animals are not extinct after all. It is impossible for one to have survived. There must be a group."

> So important was this find that the Japanese honored it with a commemorative postage stamp. As the scientific discovery of the year, the *Pleiosaur* was used as the official emblem for the 1977 National Exhibition, which celebrated 100 years of scientific discovery.

There is a photograph of the dinosaur's remains on page 47 of *The Great Dinosaur Mystery and the Bible*. Taylor goes on to explain that "like fish, the great reptiles of the sea could have lived through the Flood without being taken on the ark. Noah was told to protect the land-dwelling animals and birds, not fish and other creatures that could survive in the flood waters. Genesis 7:22, previously quoted, tells us that all that was in *dry land* died, not those creatures that lived in the water."

Taylor also says, "An ancient Hebrew legend says that the only animals to survive the Flood besides those on the ark were 'the giant Og, the monster reem, and the fishes.' The word 'Og' means gigantic and long-necked, a good description of the big *Plesiosaurs*."[17] Could this description also fit the "sea serpents" or "sea monsters" spoken of in ancient marine mythology? Possibly. If so, they have probably been seen from time to time by men, ever since the time of creation.

The entire crew of the English warship *Daedalus*, sailing between St. Helena and the Cape of Good Hope, reported sighting a sea serpent 65 feet long and extending 4 feet above the sea, on August 6, 1848.[18]

The earlier referenced encyclopedia tells us that *Tyrannosaurus Rex* was a huge bipedal dinosaur 50 feet long, 20 feet tall, and weighing around ten tons. He had a massive body and neck supporting a large head with dagger-like teeth. He was a carnivore with tiny forelegs and large muscular hind limbs equipped with big claws. Another meat-eating dinosaur is the *Allosaurus*, who was much like the *Tyrannosaurus*, except that it had larger forelegs.

From selected scriptural verses of Job:

> Canst thou draw out leviathan with a hook? Or his tongue with a cord which thou lettest down? Canst thou put an hook into his nose? Or bore his jaw through with a thorn? ... Canst thou fill his skin with barked irons? Or his head with fish spears? Lay thine hand upon him, remember the battle, do no more (Job 41:1–8).

"Leviathan" in this Scripture could, up to now, refer to a crocodile, but it is not clear. Verses 14 to 21 continue to add to the mystery:

> Who can open the doors of his face? His teeth are terrible round about. His scales are his pride, shut up together as with a close seal. One is so near to another, that no air can come between them. ... Out of his mouth go burning lamps, and sparks of fire leap out. Out of his nostrils goeth smoke, as out of a seething pot or caldron. His breath kindleth coals, and a flame goeth out of his mouth (Job 41:14–21).

Is a carnivorous dinosaur the animal referred to in ancient mythology, as the fire-breathing dragon?

> In his neck remaineth strength, and sorrow is turned into joy before him. ... When he raiseth up himself the mighty are

afraid: By reason of breakings they purify themselves. The sword of him that layeth at him cannot hold. . . . slingstones are turned with him into stubble. Darts are counted as stubble: he laugheth at the shaking of a spear. . . . Upon earth there is not his like, who is made without fear. He beholdeth all high things: he is a king over all the children of pride (Job 41:22–34).

Chapter 41, verse 25, says, "When he raiseth up himself, the mighty are afraid." If a crocodile "raiseth up himself," would "the mighty" be afraid? A crocodile is certainly a reptile to be given a lot of room. I've seen them in their natural environment in the animal preserves of Africa, and I did keep a certain amount of distance between us, you can be sure of that. Had I been closer, and one of the choices on their crocodile menu, then no doubt I would have expressed great fear, and hopefully great speed. If the same scenario would have occurred to one of "the mighty," whoever they are, would it necessarily cause an atmosphere where they would be afraid? Probably, depending on how much "the mighty" knows about the crocodile, and how close he or she was to it. One thing for sure, I can only imagine the increase in pulse rate and reaction of an individual (myself especially) if some giant reptile, such as a 20-foot tall, 10-ton carnivorous dinosaur, "raised up himself." If that would happen, then I think it quite possible that the verse, "the mighty are afraid," would be appropriate. If such a beast who is "made without fear" "raised up himself" with "flame [coming] out of his mouth," then I have an idea "the mighty are afraid" could almost be an understatement.

Scientists tell us that the dinosaur is extinct. Could the dinosaur have once existed during the same time as man?

When I last visited ark researchers and authors Mr. and Mrs. Eryl Cummings of Farmington, New Mexico, I noticed a cast of what clearly appears to be a very large human footprint in Mr. Cummings' office. He informed me that the cast was made from one of many footprints found in the Paluxy riverbed near Glen Rose, Texas. The footprint measures 15 inches long and 6½ inches wide, and along with others of the same type, was found next to, and in the same rock formation with several dinosaur tracks, which measured 30 inches across.

Mr. Cummings at one time had become involved in the research of the area, and was able to present casts of some of the footprints to a university located near the East Coast. The idea was for them to display the find. At a later date, he followed up on his generous donation, and went to see the exhibit. He found, through some searching, the casts and related information, tucked away in a box somewhere in the basement of the credited institution of higher learning; not exactly on display.

From the pages of *The Natural Sciences Know Nothing of Evolution,* by Wildersmith, we read this information:

> The dinosaur tracks in the Paluxy River, Glen Rose region of Texas, are well-known to geologists, and others. R.T. Bird of the Smithsonian Institute investigated them many years ago, and described what appeared to be man tracks in the same area. He surmised that the latter could not be genuine, since they occurred in the same formations as the dinosaur tracks, which would make man as old as the dinosaurs. Plainly, the New Darwinian evolution theory could not accept the genuineness of such human artifacts. A number of large saurian tracks were dug out and removed by Bird, the holes of which can still be seen at Glen Rose.[19]

That certain institute of higher learning near the East Coast no doubt suffered under the same delusion.

Carbonized remains of what apparently had been a burning tree branch was found in the same foundation, and study has led to the conclusion that it was laid down near the same time as the tracks. Carbon (C) dating was performed on the carbonized tree branch, and a date of 12,800 years ago was determined. Wildersmith says, "Any man tracks in those formations will bear the same age and that, if genuine, man and the sauriers lived contemporaneously. These finds, if confirmed, are of course totally fatal to evolutionary theory."[20] The problem we have here is whether or not a C-14 date can be accepted as accurate. This is the key to the discovery. Second to this is whether or not the C-14 date can be accepted as accurate. If these fossils are of tracks laid down before the Flood, then, as discussed earlier, the date may be in error due to different concentrations of C-14 in the atmosphere. Possibly there has even been a change in the atomic clock — an important point yet ahead in this chapter.

A SCIENTIFIC DISCOVERY

In this evolutionary-minded world, there obviously are newspaper articles printed from time to time that reflect evolutionary thinking. On September 24, 1987, I found an article in the *Denver*

Post about a fish known as the coelacanth, which was "believed to have died out long before the demise of the dinosaurs." The article was entitled "Deep Sea Film Records Movement of Rarely Caught Prehistoric Fish." There was a photograph of the fish included with the article. Several of the fish have been observed and photographed in their natural deep-sea habitat.

The article goes on at some length to explain the important evolutionary link the coelacanth is between aquatic and terrestrial vertebrates. I find it interesting that this "evolutionary link" is still a fish, is still living, and producing more of the same fish. Obviously, I have a difficult time in believing evolutionary theories.

On June 21, 1987, an article which was first printed in the *New York Times* appeared in the *Cedar Rapids (Iowa) Gazette*, entitled "Ocean Crater Tied to Death of Dinosaurs?" The article reads in part:

> A crater at least 28 miles wide and 1.7 miles deep, formed by the impact of a comet or asteroid 50 million years ago has been discovered on the sea floor 125 miles southeast of Nova Scotia, say Canadian geologists. The discovery may help solve a dispute over what killed the dinosaurs. . . . The crater lies on the outer Continental Shelf in 370 feet of water, rather than in an ocean basin with typical depths of 2 to 3 miles.

According to the article, the date attributed to this event has apparently been set by geologists at 50 million years. Earlier in this book we discussed the possibility that the interpretation of the data which is used to determine great ages may not necessarily be correct. If that point of view is considered to be accurate, we can then assume the date attributed to the collision of the earth and the comet, or an asteroid referred to in the *Gazette* article, could have just as easily been a few thousand years ago, rather than 50 million years. One thing I find curious about the point of this article is the attempt to explain the death of the dinosaurs as the eventual result of the impact, which is apparently believed by some Canadian geologists to have taken place.

In the article, a paragraph reads, "The discovery [of the crater] may bear on the controversy regarding the disappearance of the dinosaurs. One theory postulates that the impact of an extraterrestrial object at the end of the Cretaceous period 65 million years ago may have scattered debris into the atmosphere, changing the climate and causing the extinction of dinosaurs and other species."

The theory may be partially true. The impact of an extraterrestrial body may, indeed, have had a part in causing the disappearance of most of the dinosaurs. But I believe it was not by the scattering of debris into the atmosphere 50 or 65 million years ago, as some scientists try to explain, but rather by the timely breaking of the heavenly canopy encircling the earth at the time of the universal Flood of which the Book of Genesis speaks. The explanation of what happened to life during this event is given to us: "All in whose nostrils was the breath of life, of all that was in the dry land, died" (Gen. 7:22).

According to the newspaper article, "debris in the atmosphere changed the climate and caused the death of the dinosaurs and other species," while most other life apparently survived. Considering the material brought out in this book, it is easier for me to believe that a water cataclysm was the universal killing agent, rather than debris in the atmosphere.

There has more recently been found the possibility of a crater 100 miles wide not far off the coast near Cancun, Mexico.

CREATION

One of the basic laws of science is the first law of thermodynamics. This is the law of conservation of matter. It simply states that matter can be converted but cannot be created nor destroyed. More specifically, "energy/matter is neither created nor destroyed today."[21]

Another basic law of science is the second law of thermodynamics, which teaches us that "although the grand total of energy/matter within the cosmos remains constant, the amount of energy available to us for useful work is always, and constantly, decreasing."[22] "Even though nothing is being destroyed, things are running down toward disorder."[23]

Paul G. Hewett, professor, and author of *Conceptual Physics,* explains in his text the reason for this transformation in the law of conservation of energy. Again it reads, "Energy cannot be created or destroyed; it may be transformed from one form into another, but the total amount of energy never changes."[24]

Now, if these are two of the basic laws of science, then scientists must obviously agree that they are true. Experimentation by many brilliant minds must have proven them, and they have been accepted as fact in order to be laws of science.

If this is the case, then it is safe to assume from a scientific point of view, that matter and energy are no longer being created. It would seem to me that since we are here, and since we are matter and energy, which is no longer being created, that we must have been created sometime in the past, and the process of creation has since stopped.

In considering the big bang theory, a tremendous amount of heat must have been generated at the time of the explosion. George Gamow, an astronomer who escaped from Russia in the 1930s, "realized that as well as being extremely dense, the early big bang universe could have been very hot, thousands of times hotter than the center of the sun (currently estimated at 27 million degrees Fahrenheit)."[25]

What happened to all that energy? Since science tells us that our own earth has cooled, we can assume that the universe has cooled down since that explosion, if in fact that happened; according to our law of conservation of energy, the energy wasn't lost. Then, is the energy at rest? Are galaxies still being created, as witnessed by the activity in the heavens, or is energy and matter simply changing places as this law of conservation says it must?! Hoyle says, "We are not dealing with a universe which obeys the laws of Newton;[26] our universe is faithful to the laws of Einstein, in which matter and energy are interchangeable."[27]

So let's suppose we have a universe created with a tremendous explosion of heat and matter, and the laws of science stand throughout the universe. Dr. Henry Morris says the second law of thermodynamics tells us the universe has been running down.[28] This means the energy of motion is changing to another form, such as energy at rest, or matter. Now if this is so, then the energy of motion must have been greater at some time in the past. How do you guess all this motion/matter interchange got started? Is it logical to assume that something or someone, or a force outside the system, was needed to start all this in motion? Perhaps someone was there who did the creating, someone who made it all happen.

It would seem to me that a scientist should agree with this. The two basic laws we've talked about tell us that matter and energy are no longer being created, and that what was created is running down, therefore it must have been created at one time. Dr. Morris also says that if the universe was infinitely old, it would have run down by now. However, there obviously is sufficient energy left, therefore it must not be infinitely old. That is to say it hasn't always been here, and must have been created.

Let's look again at the law of conservation, this first law of thermodynamics: Energy/matter cannot be created nor destroyed; it may be transformed from one form into another, but the total amount of energy/matter, never changes.

Science knows this to be true, but do they know why? The Bible gives us an answer:

Thus the heavens and the earth were finished, and all the host of them. And on the seventh day God ended his work which he had made; and he rested on the seventh day from all his work which he had made. And God blessed the seventh day, and sanctified it: because that in it he had rested from all his work which God created and made (Gen. 2:1–3).

For by Him *were* all things created, that in heaven, and that are in earth, visible and invisible, whether they be thrones, or dominions, or principalities, or powers: all things were created by him, and for him (Col. 1:16, emphasis added).

Matter and energy are no longer created because the creation is finished, and God, when He ended His work . . . rested.

Of the creation, the Bible also tells us in Genesis 1:1: "In the beginning, God created heaven and the earth." Commentaries generally agree that God created the universe out of nothing, *Ex Nihilo* (Latin meaning). It occurs to me that a skeptical reader may have a difficult time accepting this possibility.

Physicist Stephen Hawking, in a *Newsweek* article entitled "Reading God's Mind," in his quest to "understand the universe, why it is as it is and why it exists at all," says that "the universe, according to some models, began with a singularity, which erupted into the big bang." Hawking, in postulating a property of black holes, as singularities, describes "singularities" as "point at which matter is not merely tremendously dense but infinitely dense — the remnants of a star collapsed to a point of zero size."[29]

An article in the same issue, entitled "Where the Wild Things Are," tells us of the big bang, "A single point of infinitely dense and hot matter, called a singularity, explodes spontaneously. This was not a burst of matter into space, but rather an explosion of space itself." The article tells us, "Before there were planets circling the sun, before there were stars in the night sky, before there were galaxies beyond end, there was nothing, nothing at all. In the greatest leap of imagination, most cosmologists now believe that the universe arose from nothing."[30]

I believe the scientific articles in *Newsweek* magazine are in general agreement with the biblical commentaries of Genesis 1:1.

Dr. Henry Morris, in a tape entitled "Modern Science and the Genesis Record," says:

Present processes don't tell us anything about the creative process, that process is finished. Present processes don't create anything. The only way we can learn about what went on is for someone to tell us about it, someone who was there.

God tries to do this in chapter 1 of Genesis. People just don't want to believe what He says![31]

With this comment, one may wonder again about the credibility of the written word as perceived by the skeptic. Would it make a difference if the information was written in stone by the finger of God himself for all to see? This could be exactly what happened!

The fourth of the Ten Commandments in the record given in Exodus 20:8 tells us, "Remember the sabbath day and keep it holy." God gave the reason for this to Moses on Mount Sinai, in verse 11 of the same chapter: "For in six days the Lord made heaven and earth, the sea, and all that in them is, and rested the seventh day: Whereby the Lord blessed the sabbath day, and hallowed it."

What about our study into the laws of thermodynamics? We have discussed the first part of the first law, why matter and energy are no longer being created, and decided that matter and energy are no longer being created because the creation is finished. What about the second part of the first law? Why is matter or energy not destroyed? Dr. Morris points out that in Hebrews 1:3 that "Jesus is 'upholding all things by the word of his power,' and He is now conserving that which He created until such time as He sees fit for the consumption of all things."[32]

So far, we've determined, for the purpose of this chapter, that the scientifically proven laws of thermodynamics have an answer in the Bible as to why they are so. We have a creation. For some reason, some highly educated individuals apparently do not believe this.

> But if our gospel be hid; it is to them that are lost: In whom the god of this world [Satan] hath blinded the minds of them which believe not, lest the light of the glorious gospel of Christ, who is the image of God, should shine unto them (2 Cor. 4:3–4).

Author A.E. Wildersmith, in his book *The Natural Sciences Know Nothing of Evolution*, says:

> Prior to Darwin, most educated people believed that our present universe consisted of three basic elements: matter, energy, (which revealed itself in the vibrations of chance movements), and information (planning, ideas, intelligence, teleonomy, or logos). But as the last element was always

associated with "spirit" (or God), one believed in those days in a "spirit" which acted as creator of matter, energy, and concepts. In order to form life from matter and energy, this "spirit" used intelligence, information, planning, or teleonomy (know-how). Today this older belief would be formulated in modern language in the following manner: Life consists of energy, matter, and know-how (concept, teleonomy, or information).[33]

Conversely, evolutionists profess matter, energy, and chance, without the purposeful plan of a creator — an "accident" — put life into motion. Wildersmith puts it this way:

Evolution is thus basically an attempt to explain the origin of life from matter and energy without the aid of know-how, concept teleonomy or exogenous (extra material) information. It represents an attempt to explain the formation of the genetic code from the chemical components of DNA, without the aid of a genetic concept (information) originating outside the molecules of the chromosomes.

New Darwinian theory attempts to explain the teleonomy and the systems of life in terms of the endogenous (internal) properties of matter and chance, and not in terms of any external concept.[34]

According to Darwin, "the laws of matter, chance, and natural selection alone have created us . . . chance is our creator."[35]

We read in the beginning of this chapter that Darwin, himself, said small heredity variations occur at random in the offspring of all living things. He also theorizes that through a process of natural selection, man randomly evolved from unicellular organism, through shell, eel, fish, reptile, amphibian, primitive mammal, monkey, and ape man. Life began randomly in the ocean. According to Wildersmith's interpretation of Darwin's theory, biogenesis occurred spontaneously and by chance, from amino acids and polypeptides in a primeval ocean. Wildersmith says this is taught in biology textbooks, but questions why, when even a superficial examination of this equation proves this to be definitely negative — that is, it couldn't happen. He goes on in great detail, to explain why it couldn't happen. I will not take the time here to go into this matter any further, other than to quote this statement: "The ocean is thus practically the last place, on this or any other planet, where the proteins of life could be formed spontaneously from amino acids."[36]

Sir Fredrick Hoyle has this to say about Darwinian evolution:

How has the Darwinian theory of evolution by natural selection managed for upwards of a century to fasten itself like a superstition on so-called enlightened opinion? Why is the theory still defended so vigorously? Personally, I have little doubt that scientific historians of the future will find it mysterious that a theory which could be seen to be unworkable came to be so widely believed.

Hoyle goes on to say later in the same chapter: "The Darwinian theory is wrong because random variations, (which the Darwinian theory requires) tend to worsen performance (as a mutation), as indeed common sense suggests they must do."[37]

Sir Fredrick Hoyle promotes a belief in evolution, just not the Darwinian evolution. He seems to believe the earth is an assembly station for life that did not originate on earth. He says:

Because properly working genes cannot be self-generated from within, they must come from the outside. The genes, the components of life, are assembled on earth from elsewhere, from space.

Instead of being the biological center of the universe, I believe our planet is just an assembly station, but one with a major advantage over most other places. The constant presence of liquid water almost everywhere on the earth is a huge advantage for life, especially for assembling life into complex forms by the process we call "evolution."[38]

Personally, I believe Sir Fredrick Hoyle's theory is but another diversion from the truth, and I cannot agree with it. However, the world-famous author does disagree with Darwin. For those of you who would care to know more about Hoyle's theory, I suggest you read his book. It is now a good time to check back in with Wildersmith, as he lists in his book the seven main postulates of the theory of evolution:[39]

1. Non-living matter spontaneously produced living matter at biogenesis. (Think about that for a moment.)

2. Spontaneous biogenesis, assuming to have only occurred once, so that present-day life descended from one single primeval cell. This assumption is supposedly supported by the fact that the genetic code is identical in all known forms of life (plant and animals). Only the information riding the code varies from species to species. The

identical highly complex code of life is unlikely to have developed by chance at different times under different conditions to produce separate microspheres with identical codes. For this reason it is assumed that this chance biogenesis which supposedly ended in the formation of the genetic code, took place once only.

    3. The different viruses, bacteria, plants, and animals are all descended from one another. They are all interrelated phylogenetically.

    4. Metazoa (multi-celled organisms) developed spontaneously, without plan out of protozoa (single-celled organisms), according to the principles of chance mutation and natural selection.

    5. The invertebrates are all phylogenetically interrelated.

    6. The vertebrates are all phylogenetically interrelated.

    7. All vertebrates are phylogenetically interrelated to the invertebrates.

These seven assumptions form the basis and foundation of the general theory of organic evolution. Not one single assumption out of the above can be proven experimentally.

Perhaps some of them might be repeated experimentally. But, this would under no circumstances prove that the biogenetic experiment actually took place historically.[40]

One could possibly say here that even though organic evolution can't be proven, neither can creation by God. Let's take a brief look into the very basis of life itself.

Two basic parts of every living system are DNA and protein. DNA is the famous molecule of heredity. This is the molecule that gets passed down from one generation to the next. Our characteristics, (hair color, eye color, etc.) are contained in the DNA molecule. Designed like a "string of pearls," this chain of repeating units[41] holds enough information to fill a thousand books of 500 pages each, in small print.[42] Each molecule, dividing every four minutes, forms another molecule with the very same information impressed on its units.

Proteins are the molecules of structure and function. Hair, skin cells, enzymes, and muscle parts are mostly protein. Proteins are also chains of repeated units with amino acids linking the chains.

The DNA code functions to tell the cell to make a protein such as hemoglobin for example, and that protein carries oxygen to the red blood cells. Basically that's the relationship between the two basic "parts" of every system. (In some cases an RNA molecule is present in place of DNA.) None of these molecules in the cell are alive. What gives life to the cell is the organization of several billion non-living molecules within that cell, into a precise order, structure, time, and amount. Life is a property of organization.[43] A. E. Wildersmith tells us there are 10^{87} ways to put together a cell using all the "parts," (that's a 1 followed by 87 zeros) and only one way it will work.[44]

Evolutionists believe that random chance in the DNA causes mutations that suit the organism better to its environment, by a process called natural selection. In actuality, mutations do occur, and are responsible for such things as genetic defects, certain kinds of cancer, and brain malfunctions.[45] Can mutations by random chance produce evolutionary changes?

Mutations occur on the average of possibly one per every ten million duplications of a DNA molecule; (that's 10^7). Our bodies contain approximately 100 trillion cells (10^{14}); there could be a couple of mutations in almost any gene. To get a series of related mutations, mathematics say the probabilities are one in 10^7 x 10^7 or 10^{14}. Two mutations may produce a fly with a bent wing. The probability of three related mutations is in the area of 10^{21}, and four mutations figure 10^{28}, and so on. Four mutations would not begin to turn a fish into a frog, or an ape into a man; and then they would have to be "good" mutations which by chance would benefit the organism.[46]

To give you an idea of just how large the number 10^{21} (the probability of just three related mutations in a series) is, it adds up to one chance in a billion trillion. Remember, we mentioned that there are 10^{87} ways to put a complex cell together, a much bigger number for chance to deal with (if, in fact, chance could deal at all). If you added up all the seconds of time in the 4.5 billion years that evolutionists say the earth has been here, you would only have 10^{25}, a one followed by 25 zeros.[47] With this information, some evolutionists have given up the classic idea of evolution, because it just plainly doesn't work.[48]

With the knowledge of the DNA molecule and the protein molecule in the living cell, and considering the biochemistry which takes place, and the mathematical probabilities of chance, it is suggested that "life" is the result of design by someone who knows how to put the properties of matter in a specific order, i.e., a creator. It is not logical that time and chance act on the inherent properties of matter and organize them into the complicated order, in a specific structure, in the right amounts and at just the right time, to give life.[49]

What do these numbers of probability indicate to you? Could

this alone be proof of creation by an intelligence, i.e., God, that knows how things work?

Dr. Wildersmith gives us two other scientific difficulties in the evolutionary theory, mainly in that the theory lacks experimental or theoretical scientific basis.

1. Paleontology gives no "experimental evidence for a phylogenetic evolution of one species to another higher one, that is, of transformation. Where are the missing links? Where are the intermediate stages? Geologists should have discovered them long ago in the geological formations. But they just do not exist. Even *Archaeopteryx*, the so-called intermediate stage between reptiles and birds, has been questioned regarding its phylogenetic evolutionary significance, and turns out to be far younger geologically than birds."[50]

Dr. Morris said on his tape, "Flood and the Genesis Record," that *Archaeopteryx* was simply a bird with teeth. It had feathers.[51] In his book, Hoyle has a photograph of a fossil of *Archaeopteryx* and both the feathers and teeth are clearly seen. Hoyle says this: "Even *Archaeopteryx*, the much acclaimed 'link' between reptiles and birds, is isolated in the fossil record. There are no steps in the record from reptiles to *Archaeopteryx* or from *Archaeopteryx* to birds, as the Darwinian theory requires. Indeed the situation is the opposite of what the theory predicts."[52]

2. "The laws of physics — the laws of thermodynamics, which we have just read about, also contradict evolutionary theory. For according to the experimental results on which these laws are based, matter alone tends toward chaos, or increased entropy (which is increased disorder). It does not tend toward auto-organization, even if one irradiates it with photon energy. Only with the aid of teleonomic energy-consuming machines (or intelligence), the construction of which require energy and planning, can entropy (disorder) be reduced in matter, and order and organization increased. But order and organization are the basis of life. Thus, according to the laws of physics, it is impossible for matter to have organized itself without the aid of energy and of teleonomic machines!"[53] Dr. Wildersmith is telling us that evolution is impossible, not scientific, and some intelligence had to put the system together.

If what we've read in this chapter so far is true, then why do so many highly educated men and women generally of a professional background, involve themselves and so many others in theories and doctrines, that by the basic laws of science prove to be false? Perhaps in some cases, it is because of what they were taught to believe.

Scientists are supposed to be objective, but is that always the case? Scientists and other people of the intellectual community are human. Being claim to that, they are subject to beliefs and bias just like anyone else.

For instance, if a person is an evolutionist, could he also be an athiest? If he is an athiest, then in his study would he be looking to the possibility of God for the answers? I doubt it. Is it then possible that the bias the scientist has influences what that person does with the evidence he or she has? If this could be the case, is the scientist being objective in his or her approach, or is that scientist being subjected to a prior influence, or dogmatism?[54]

Perhaps then, that portion of the intellectual community that is so involved in perpetuating beliefs in such theories and doctrines, do so because the alternative would be to address the question of God, or if a God, why does He allow certain things to happen? Not being able or willing to address this question, possibly because of prior bias (consequently not giving the question fair consideration), the evolutionary theories become quite attractive.

The apostle Paul said in his letter to Timothy, "O Timothy, keep that which is committed to thy trust, avoiding profane and vain babblings, and oppositions of science falsely so called which some professing have erred concerning the faith" (1 Tim. 6:20–21).

* * * * *

"Science" as a term, seems to be tossed around quite a bit, and is used to explain this or that, without really doing so. Such as, "scientifically" everything is explained in natural laws, thereby there is no evidence of God in nature. Science gets the lead, and God is out of the picture. Physics, biology, chemistry, and all the sciences have the answers, the laws of "Mother Nature" and "Father Time" have the explanations for everything and God is not included; except, of course, when someone files an insurance claim for damage caused not by Mother Nature, but by "acts of God." Then, God is included.

Isn't it incredible how man takes the credit and God gets the blame?

Personally, I have no trouble seeing evidences of a Creator. In fact, almost everywhere I look, I see a testimony to His creation. The Bible has this to say in Romans 1:20: "For the invisible things of Him from the creation of the world are clearly seen, being understood by the things that are made, even his eternal power and Godhead; so that they are without excuse."

What does that mean? "For the *invisible things* of Him from the creation of the world are clearly seen." Dr. Morris says, "These are the things in the structure of nature, the things that scientists study, [author: such as the DNA and protein molecules previously discussed] being understood by the things that are made, that is, a convincing testimony to the nature and power of God, "even his eternal power and Godhead."[55]

We have previously read that although the universe is still expanding, the system is running down. Therefore, the universe cannot be infinitely old, as it would be run down by now; it was created, it had a beginning. Therefore, the source of the power must be an *eternal power,* outside of the system it created. This will be further explained as we read on, and I make my point. But, first we'll continue and attempt to understand the Scripture in Romans 1:20.

Godhead — what is the Godhead?

> In the beginning was the Word, and the Word was with God, and the Word was God. . . . And the Word was made flesh, and dwelt among us, (and we beheld his glory, the glory as of the only begotten of the Father), full of grace and truth (John 1:1–14).

> Jesus said, I and my Father are one (John 10:30).

> The Lord our God is one Lord (Deut. 6:4).

> Go therefore and teach all nations, baptizing them in the name of the Father, and of the Son, and of the Holy Ghost (Matt. 28:19).

> For there are three that bear record in heaven, the Father, the Word, and the Holy Ghost: And these three are one (1 John 5:7).

The Godhead is three in one. How can we understand that? How can we believe that even the Godhead is clearly seen? Is this beyond our ability to understand? Do we just accept this in faith ? "We walk by faith, not by sight" (2 Cor. 5:7).

Dr. Morris explains it somewhat this way (paraphrased). The Godhead is a trinity, and each part is distinct in itself, but there is still one God. A model is seen in the universe, as it is a tri-universe. It is made up of the matter, energy, or phenomena that takes place; and space and time. Phenomena taking place in space and time. Phenomena, space and time, all distinct and individual in itself, and each as a whole, but not as parts of one universe. The whole universe is matter and energy, the whole universe is space, and the whole universe is time. A trinity is not the sum of three parts. In the trinity, each is the whole. This is the universe, this is a model of the Godhead.[56] If we can accept this explanation, then we can possibly see that Lord God has shown us a model of himself in the creation of the universe.

Individual interpretations to Scripture seem to vary to some degree, and each interpreter may show some support for one particular avenue of human thought which is not quite the same as that of another, yet both profess Christianity. We may see some of this in the different church denominations. It is not my intention to take part in an argument of any degree, over different interpretations of Scripture, or make any denominational stand.

In regard to this issue, the Bible says, "No prophecy of the scripture is of any private interpretation. For the prophecy came not in old time by the will of man: but holy men of God spake as they were moved by the Holy Ghost" (2 Pet. 1:20–21). It also says, "All scripture is given by inspiration of God, and is profitable for doctrine, for reproof, for correction, for instruction in righteousness" (2 Tim. 3:16).

In the Bible, the Book of Deuteronomy, chapter 6, verse 4 tells us, "The Lord our God is one Lord." If Jesus and the Father are one, as we have read, then Jesus is also our one Lord. The Bible tells us, "God is a Spirit" (John 4:24). Understanding that, for me, is possible only if I believe that there must be a oneness of Spirit in the persons of God. If Christ then, is our One Lord, and in a oneness with God, and if by his sacrifice we have the opportunity to eternal life (discussed in chapter 14) and if God is omnipresent through His spirit, then personally, I don't detect an argument. He moves freely in His creation, in space and in phenomena. He moves in time. He is everywhere. He is omnipresent.

My opinion on the issue is this. It seems to me by the information we've read so far, that there is a Creator, i.e., God. If so, then the Bible is definitely a book written with knowledge pertaining to information of the subject, God. To be able to determine for oneself answers to any questions a person may have, then, as he or she would do in the study of anything else, that person should wish to study the best information on the subject available. In this case, I think the Bible, as it is written, would get the most votes.

One of the questions raised by a skeptical reader, may be to express a certain wonder as to why so many of the brilliant minds of this world would disagree with the biblical Scripture, if the Scripture is the best information available on the subject of creation, and a Creator.

Let us go back to creation, and Romans 1:20. "So that they are *without excuse*." Dr. Morris puts it this way: "Men who don't see God in nature have no apologetics or defense. To be an atheist, one has to be utterly unscientific to reject the testimony of every phenomena science deals with because they all point to the necessary truth of creation."[57]

> Because that, when they knew God, they glorified him not as God, neither were thankful: but became vain in their imaginations, and their foolish heart was darkened. Professing themselves to be wise, they became fools, And changed the glory of the incorruptible God into an image made like the corruptible man, and to birds, and four footed beasts, and creeping things. . . . Who changed the truth of God into a lie, and worshipped and served the creature more than the Creator (Rom. 1:21–25).

Hence, theories of evolution.

> For the preaching of the cross is to them that perish foolishness; but unto us which are saved it is the power of God. For it is written, I will destroy the wisdom of the wise, and will bring to nothing the understanding of the prudent. . . . For after that in the wisdom of God the world by wisdom knew not God, it pleased God by the foolishness of preaching to save them that believe (1 Cor. 1:18–21).

Think about it.

*   *   *   *   *

So, what about the six days of creation, and when was the beginning, and how long was the day?

From Genesis 1:1: "In the beginning God created the heaven and the earth." I think at least some of the scientific community would agree that first of all, there was a beginning. Perhaps the one theory we've mentioned, the big bang, was the beginning. The Bible says, "That by the word of God, heavens existed long ago, and an earth formed out of water" (2 Pet. 3:5). Maybe the big bang was the Word of God. "And the earth was without form and void and darkness was upon the face of the deep" (Gen 1:2). Scientists might say this description fits one of a dark nebula. (A cloudlike celestial phenomenon consisting mainly of vastly diffused gas — vagueness; indistinct; formless.)[58] In fact, "this verse has been quoted by Dr. Alter, director of Griffith Planetarium, as being the best description of a dark nebula that has ever been written."[59]

There are theories that attempt to bring compromise between the science view of long ages and the Scripture. The "gap theory" says that between Genesis 1:1 and 1:2 there was the original chaos with formless matter, and there is the judgement interpretation that says it was a period of satanic rebellion after the creation and the world was recreated.[60] I won't go into that here, I will only mention that that interpretation exists. There is the "day age theory" which tells us the day could be another period of time other than a 24-hour day.[61]

> And the Spirit of God moved upon the face of the waters. And God said, Let there be light: and there was light. And God saw the light, that it was good: and God divided the light from the darkness. And [according to our English Language Bible] God called the light Day, and the darkness he called Night. And the evening and the morning were the first day (Gen 1:2–5).

Science may look at this as a stellar sequence, and the forming of the solar system. First the dark diffused nebula, which does preceed a stellar sequence, then the gas contracts, it becomes dense, measuring in mass producing heat, and eventually the light of the sun greets the first day. With the aid of gravity, and physical law and order, the sun and the planets are formed.[62] The earth revolves around the sun and rotates about its axis, and there is day and night.

> And God said, Let there be a firmament in the midst of the waters, and let it divide the waters from the waters. And God made the firmament, and divided the waters which were under the firmament from the waters which were above the firmament; and it was so. And God called the firmament Heaven. And the evening and the morning were the second day (Gen. 1:6–8).

According to Stoner and Newman: "First the water covered the hot earth in dense clouds above it. As the earth cooled, much of the water condensed to the surface with a space of air (firmament) between; a necessary stage a planet must go through as it cools."[63]

Second Peter 3:5 helps us to understand some of this. It says in part, that "By the Word of God the heavens were of old, and the earth standing out of water and in the water." A translation easier to understand says, "Long ago by God's Word the heavens existed and the earth was formed out of water and by water" (NIV). The Bible is apparently telling us the world was in universal flood stage from the beginning.

The firmament was the space between the waters, where the birds flew as in Genesis 1:20, "And God said, let the waters bring forth abundantly the moving creatures that hath life, and fowl that fly above the earth in the open firmament of heaven." To understand the "firmament of heaven" which is referred to, we know first of all that Scripture refers to three major realms of heaven.[64] One is the atmospheric heaven. An example is in Deuteronomy 11:11, which refers to rain from heaven. "But the land, whither ye go to possess it, is a land of hills and valleys, and drinketh water of the rain of *heaven*" (author's emphasis).

There are the celestial heavens, mentioned in Genesis 15:5, concerning the stars. The Lord is talking to Abram: "And he brought him forth abroad, and said, Look now toward *heaven*, and tell the stars, if thou be able to number them: And he said unto him, so shall thy seed be" (author's emphasis).

And there is the believer's heaven, the abode of God. Examples are mentioned in the following:

> Look down from *heaven*, and behold from the habitation of thy holiness and of thy glory (Isa. 63:15, author's emphasis).
>
> John answered and said, a man can receive nothing, except it be given him from *heaven* (John 3:27, author's emphasis). (The "firmament of heaven" is the atmospheric heaven.)
>
> And God said, Let the waters under the heaven be gathered together unto one place, and let the dry land appear. And it was so (Gen. 1:9).

As the earth cooled (assuming it was in need of cooling), and with a "shrinkage" taking place, the resulting tectonic forces raised the continents above water. Note, that it is generally agreed that "in its earliest stages, the surface (of the earth) was quite smooth and of nearly uniform height."[65] This seems to say that there were no tall mountains at that time.

Curiously, there was light on the first day, yet "God made two great lights; the greater to rule the day, and the lesser light to rule the night: he made the stars also," on the fourth day (Gen 1:16).

In *Science Speaks*, Peter Stoner and Robert Newman provide us with a possible answer to this puzzle by incorporating a Scofield translation to Genesis 1:16. "God made 'to function' two great lights — the stars also." Here is the logic: If the earth was covered in dense clouds as we previously discussed of the firmament created on the second day (Gen 1:6–8), then although the sun was in place and provided energy (greenhouse effect) for the vegetation of the third day (Gen 1:11–13), the sunlight itself did not shine on the earth until there was a break in the clouds on the fourth day. The sun was "made to function" in that the sunlight, also moonlight and starlight, reached the earth when the dense cloud cover of the creation allowed an opening.[66]

The sequence of events of the creation which we have read on the previous pages all add up to, no doubt, some pretty long days from a scientific point of view. Obviously, the longer the period of time science can "assign" each day of creation, or what is considered prehistoric time, the more it strengthens acceptance of the evolutionary theories by students in their quest for knowledge. The current scientific theories seem to put dates of millions and billions of years ago to anything pertaining to prehistoric time and events.

When considering prehistoric time, it's an interesting thought that if the Bible is correct, and God recorded the history of creation, then there is no such thing as prehistoric time.

Stoner and Newman tell us, "This period of time, day, in Genesis may have been a 24-hour period, or it may have been any other period of time, even a fraction of a second, or a geological age. Psalm 33:6-9 reads (in part), "By the word of the Lord were the heavens made; and all the host of them by the breath of his mouth. . . . For he spake, and it was done; he commanded, and it stood fast." This passage seems to indicate that the acts of God occupied very short periods of time. Furthermore, the periods of time in Genesis may have been separated by other and long periods of time. God is counting periods of time in which He was doing work on this earth. If, after the the first act of God, the first period of creation, a million years elapsed before He acted again, this second act would still occupy the second period of time in God's creation. "He spake, and it was done; He commanded, and it stood fast," lends strong support to the interpretation that the days of Genesis are, in part at least, short, intensive acts of creation, separated by long geological periods of time. This makes perfect harmony between science and the scriptures."[67]

Could this also give a certain harmony to creation and the time needed for a God-directed plan to design within certain boundaries of variance, the family, species, or kind of living organism, by guiding changes necessary for survival in a horizontal kind of evolution? Probably not. Stoner and Newman did not have, or may not have considered, all the data.

I will go on to remind the reader, as Morris and Whitcomb pointed out in an earlier chapter, that it isn't the data of recognized earth's history that is in question, so much as it is the interpretation of that data. To make this point, let us first notice with interest that our modern-day scientists seem to have confirmed the order of things as was written by Moses some 4,000 years ago.

For instance, when God said, "Let the waters bring forth abundantly the moving creatures that hath life, and fowl that may fly above the earth," he put them in order and on the fifth day. On the sixth day, God said, "Let the earth bring forth the living creature *after his kind* cattle, and creeping things, and beast of the earth after his kind, and it was so" (emphasis added). Science has the fish in the Devonian period on the geologic column, and birds in the Jurassic period. This is in the same order that Moses put them in. These periods are both in the Mesozoic era (the fifth day?), creatures and mammals are mentioned in the Cenozoic era, which is later than the fish and birds.[68] (The sixth day?) According to science, these periods date back a considerable number of millions of years. At this place in your thinking you may be believing that to be the case. I ask you to thoughtfully consider the day and the week of creation as you read and study to the completion of this chapter. Again we deal with the interpretation of data and dating systems we've already discussed.

All of the above assumes a constant speed of light. So, how long is a day?

SPEED OF LIGHT

Recall in this chapter how we have discussed the second law of thermodynamics; that the universe is running down. Recall also that time — like space and phenomena, is the universe. If the universe is running down, then time must be as well. How is this possible? What does this have to do with the speed of light?

Dr. Walter T. Brown, director of the Center for Scientific Creation in Phoenix, Arizona, has a Ph.D. in engineering from M.I.T. Dr. Brown says:

> Has the speed of light always been 186,000 miles per second, or, more precisely, 299,792.458 kilometers per second? The most obvious way to answer that question is to

search out and compare the historic measurements of the speed of light.

During the last 300 years, at least 164 separate measurements of the speed of light have been published. Sixteen different measurement techniques were used. A detailed study of these measurements, especially their precision and experimental errors, has been made by astronomer Barry Setterfield of Australia. His results show that the speed of light has decreased so rapidly that experimental error cannot explain it.[69]

So of what significance is this? It is in time!

Enter the time scales and astronomer, geologist, physicist, lecturer Mr. Barry Setterfield of Blackwood, South Australia, as presented to this author:

THE THREE DIFFERENT TIME SCALES

In everyday experience we have become accustomed to three major time-scales that are frequently used. The first of these is our usual calendar in years A.D. or B.C. These calendar years are, in fact, orbital years based on the earth's movement around the sun. The second clock that we are familiar with keeps atomic time in millions of years, Before Present (B.P.). It is the clock used by the scientist to measure the age of the rocks, fossils, planets, and stars. Finally, there is the time scale used by the Bible, which counts time in years After Creation (A.C.). Incredibly, these three different time scales can be harmonized, as a result of a new scientific discovery.

At first sight, a harmonization of these three seems absolutely preposterous. On what basis can three such diverse time scales be synchronized? How can millions of atomic years B.P. possibly correspond to a few thousand historical years B.C.? To answer this puzzle, let us examine those three time scales beginning with our usual orbital or calendar clock.

It is normal for us to measure time in this way. One year on an orbital clock is the time it takes for the earth to go once around the sun. This clock runs at a constant rate. This system of measuring time is the basis for our years A.D. or B.C. on the calendar or in history. The Bible also uses this unchanging time scale. Genesis 1:14 explicitly states that the sun, moon, and stars were given to measure time. In fact, the Scriptures count actual orbital years of elapsed time After Creation, or years A.C. These years can be deciphered from the father to son listing of descendents from Adam in Genesis 5 and 11.

But there is a third way, often used by scientists, to measure time. It is called the atomic clock. This clock frequently dates the age of objects in millions of years B.P. (Before Present). It is called atomic time, as the movements of particles within the atom determine how fast it ticks. You will have heard of the atomic clock under different names, such as carbon 14 dating. Another form is the caesium clock, used today as a standard atomic timekeeper for the world. It is by these atomic clocks that scientists measure the age of the rocks, fossils, planets, and stars.

Without consideration of the biblical time scale, science has implicitly assumed that these two clocks (orbital and atomic) run at the same rate. Certainly, it has been assumed that radioactive decay processes have remained invariant over the history of the cosmos. It is here that light speed enters the discussion.

ENTER THE SPEED OF LIGHT

Again, Setterfield to the author:

Now here is the crucial point: it used to be thought that the atomic and orbital clocks were running at the same constant rate. For example, if a rock was atomically dated as, say, one million years B.P., it was thought this equalled one million orbital years. Recently, however, Dr. Thomas Van Flandern of the U.S. Naval Observatory in Washington, showed that one clock was running faster than the other.

In a research report from Stanford Research Institute published in August 1987, Trevor Norman and I demonstrated the reason why. The atomic clock is affected by the behavior of the speed of light, and the speed of light has not been constant! Scientists usually abbreviate light speed with the letter "c." Light speed c must therefore be reckoned with to discover how many ordinary years have elapsed. For example, when c was ten times its current speed, the atomic clock ran ten times faster, and ticked off ten years in one of our ordinary orbital years. Obviously, if we knew how c had behaved we could correct the atomic clock to read actual calendar years.

Light speed can also be found by comparing known orbital dates for various artifacts, corals, and tree rings with their date on the atomic clock. It is customary for some to ignore atomic dates for these items, as they seem so different to actual historical dates. The change in light-speed is the reason why they differ.

In other words, the atomic clock would register that ten years had passed in one of our ordinary years. This happens because the orbital clock remains completely unaffected by these changes that the atom and c undergo.[70]

Dr. Brown, again:

Although the decreases in the speed of light during the past three centuries has been only about a percent or so, the measurement techniques are so precise that extremely minute and yet significant changes can be detected. Of course, the measurement errors are greater the further back one looks in time. However, the trend of the data is startling. The speed of light apparently was much, much faster the further back one looks in time. The pattern of this apparent decrease is almost exponential — that is, as one moves back in time, the speed of light increases at an accelerating rate. One can select several mathematical curves that seem to fit these three centuries of data. Projecting these curves back in time, the speed of light becomes so fast that it is conceivable that the light from distant stars could reach the earth in several thousand years.[71]

Again, from Setterfield, as given to this author:

A DRAMATIC NEW DEVELOPMENT

When the speed of light was higher, all atomic processes were correspondingly faster. As stars burn by atomic processes, this has an important effect. When c was ten times its current speed, a star would emit ten photons of light where only one photon would be emitted today. However, the energy of each of these ten photons would be lower, so the energy emitted per unit area per unit time (the energy flux) does not change. In other words, the energy flux from the sun and radioactive sources would be the same for high c values as it is now.

THE IMPORTANCE OF THE RED SHIFT

This approach has one very important result. When light speed is higher, the energy of each emitted photon of light is lower. But when the energy is lower, the wave length of the photon is longer, or shifted down toward the red end of the rainbow spectrum. This red shift, as it is called, is very noticeable in light from distant galaxies: it is a well-known astronomical effect. The more distant a galaxy is from us, the further down into the red end of the spectrum is its light shifted. Although there have been other explanations for this, it seems that this red shift effect is entirely due to c variation alone.

When this scenario is followed through in mathematical detail, an amazing fact emerges. The light from distant objects is not only red-shifted; this red shift goes in jumps, or is "quantized," to use the exact terminology. For the last 15 years, William Tifft, an astronomer at Arizona Observatory, has been pointing this out. His most recent paper on the matter gives red shift quantum values from observation that are almost precisely that obtained from c-variation theory. As a consequence, we now know from the red shift how far away a galaxy was, and the value of c at the time its light was emitted. We can, therefore, find the value of c right out to the limits of the universe.

Shortly after the origin of the universe, the red shift of light from distant astronomical objects indicates that c was about 11 million times faster than now. At the time of the creation of the universe, then, this high value for c meant the atomic clock ticked off 11 million years in one ordinary orbital year. This is why everything seems so old when measured by the atomic clock.

In referring to several graphs and linear displays, a method in which Setterfield exhibits his work, this astronomer is able to correlate atomic and dynamic time in a pattern which is quite easy to understand. Mr. Setterfield makes this statement:

When the atomic clock has been corrected, an amazing fact emerges. By an integration procedure, it can be shown that the 15 billion-odd years for the age of the cosmos on the atomic scale terminates around 8,000 years ago. In other words, this is the origin date for the cosmos. This astounding result precludes any possibility of the gene pool expansion, or the evolutionary scenario being viable, as this date can be corrected to years B.C.[72]

From Setterfield to this author:

CORRECTING THE ATOMIC CLOCK

Knowing how light speed has behaved, we can correct atomic time to actual orbital years as shown on our calendars. Bible chronology then fits into astronomy and geology, and all three time scales harmonize into one beautiful whole. Since the main c decay pattern is linear, the correction is easy to apply.

When this procedure is followed through, it becomes apparent that the dates obtained for the catastrophic divisions of the geological column form an important sequence. In fact, the dates obtained also correspond to catastrophic events in the Bible. Indeed, precise red-shift data from astronomy, plus the atomic time scale from geology independently combine to give a perfect harmonization of geological, astronomical, and biblical events. All fit into a time scale given by the Bible for the creation of the cosmos and Adam. The derived chronology is in exact accord with the scriptural text and chronology quoted by Josephus, Christ, the Apostles, and the early church.

When the light-speed correction is applied to the atomic dates obtained for the geological eras, a conversion to actual dates B.C. can be obtained. The converse is also true. If we take as our baseline the correspondence of dates noted above,* our baseline becomes 14.8 billion atomic years ago, or 5792 B.C. for the origin of the cosmos. This accords with both astonomy and Scripture.[73]

Barry Setterfield is able to use this data to correlate any historically documented event. I will mention only a couple in this text. The early life geological period known as the "Archeozoic Era ended at the 600 million year mark with the first catastrophe. That date becomes 3536 B.C. when the c correlation is applied."[74] That is the date of Noah's flood![75]

At the time of the Flood, the speed of light, according to Setterfield, was 2 million times its current rate, having dropped from 10.6 million times c now at creation. Does this sound to be a bit unrealistic? "More startling yet is the work of V.S. Troitski, a Soviet cosmologist at the Radiophysical Research Institute in Gorky. He has concluded, independently of Setterfield, that the speed of light was 10 billion times faster at time zero."[76]

Statistician Alan Montgomery says, "In regard to Setterfield's early, preliminary (1983) data on c-decay, it is beyond coincidence, in my opinion, that all these numbers should show definite trends, in the appropriate direction and in the appropriate amounts. There is no data for the rational mind to reject Mr. Setterfield's conclusion of c decay and every statistic leads the reasonable mind to accept it."[77]

Geophysicist Lambert Dolphin says, "One of the most important atomic constants found to vary in proportion to c is the decay rate of radioactive nuclei! Radioactive decay data is the principal reason scientists have had for believing in a very old earth. It now appears that all the radio clocks have been giving times that are far older than time as measured by gravity clocks! The notion that radioactive decay rates have always been absolutely constant is one of the most sacred cows in physics! Yet the c-decay evidence is that the so-called geological ages of millions or hundreds of millions of years, as measured by radioactive decay processes, may be compressed into actual calendar (dynamical) times that do not exceed 7,000 or 8,000 years of earth history![78]

Again, from Setterfield:

> The base of the magnificent mountain Ararat covers an area of at least 2,500 square kilometers. As such, it is probably the largest single mountain mass anywhere in the world. Other big mountains are usually part of a whole range. The name "Ararat" literally means "Holy Ground." the Latin word for a sacred altar, *Ara*, comes from the same root. Both point to Noah's altar of sacrifice on Ararat, and God's rainbow covenant with him and the whole human race. In a cave high on the northern face of the mountain, some pre-cuneiform pictograms have been discovered. The translation reads: "God's sacrifical covenant of the bright bow (rainbow) is to go forth, be fruitful, multiply, and have children."[79]

Now, consider again the mountain — more than that, consider the rock, consider the granite: conventional wisdom says granite was formed naturally out of a molten state as the earth cooled over millions of years.

Dr. Robert Gentry has shown through his many years of research that this cannot be the case. Consider polonium. Polonium is one of the last steps in the normal decay process from uranium to lead. A polonium radio isotype has a fleeting existance. Polonium 218 exists for only a few minutes before decaying into something else. Conventional wisdom also says polonium cannot exist without its parent, uranium, but it does.

Polonium haloes are found in the mica of granite all over the world. They shouldn't be there according to conventional wisdom. They would have decayed in minutes, a long, long time ago (billions of years). The fact that they are there indicates that the granite did not form naturally through cooling over millions of years, but was created almost instantly.[80]

If he is correct, and his work has been subject to peer review for over 25 years without anyone contradicting or being able to disprove it, this invalidates the uniformitarian principle, which is the glue that holds the evolutionary theory together. Gentry has given us proof that the granite, the foundational rock of the earth, was formed in minutes. There was a creation, and it was quick. Polonium haloes are the signature of God — written in stone.

Assume for this discussion on the argument of time, that the six days of creation, are as six, literal, 24-hour solar days.

When God gave the Ten Commandments to Moses, he explained the reason for keeping the Sabbath Day holy.

> For in six days the Lord made heaven and earth, the sea, and all that in them is, and rested the seventh day; wherefore the Lord blessed the Sabbath Day, and hallowed it (Exod. 20:11).

Did God give man an example of a six-day work week and a day of rest, in six literal 24-hour days of creation?

Dr. Henry Morris says, "The Bible record itself makes it plain that the days of creation are six literal days, not long indefinite ages."[81]

> And God saw the light, that it was good: and God divided the light from the darkness. And God called the light Day, and the darkness he called Night. And the evening and the morning were the first day (Gen. 1:4–5).

Having separated the day and night, God had completed His first day's work. *The evening and morning were the first day.* This same formula is used at the conclusion of each of the six days; so it is obvious that the duration of each of the days, including the first, was the same. Furthermore, the "day" was the "light" time, when God did his work; the darkness was the "night" time when God did no work — nothing new took place between the "evening" and "morning" of each day. The formula may be rendered literally: And there was evening, then morning — day one: and so on. It is clear that, beginning with the first day and continuing thereafter, there was established a cyclical succession of days and nights — periods of light and periods of darkness.

Such a cyclical light-dark arrangement clearly means that the earth was now rotating on its axis and that there was a source of light on one side of the earth corresponding to the sun, even though the sun was not yet made. "And God made two great lights, the greater to rule the day, and the lesser light to rule the night; he made the stars also" (Gen. 1:16).

It is equally clear that the length of such days could only have been that of a normal solar day.[82]

Are the six days of creation meant to be taken literally? Could an all-powerful God do this, in order to give us a basis for our work week and day of rest?

On the third day of creation the lands were uplifted and on that same day, land plants appeared. And God said, "Let the earth put forth grass, herbs yielding seed, and fruit trees bearing fruit after their kind, wherein is the seed thereof, upon the earth: And it was so" (Gen. 1:11).

Morris and Whitcomb say, "As now formed, a soil requires a long period of preparation before becoming able to support plant growth. But here it must have been created essentially instantaneously, with all the necessary chemical constituents, rather than gradually developed over centuries of rock-weathering, alluvial deposition, etc. Thus, it had an appearance of being 'old' when it was still new. It was created with a appearance of age!" This means that fish and birds created on the fifth day, and animals, insects, and man, on the sixth day were created full-grown and placed in an environment already perfectly adapted to it.[83] A week of six literal days, being created with the appearance of age! The geologic column would then be incorrect, and what is taught to be millions of years of evolutionary time would be seen in the sediments of the year-long Noachian flood.

Evolution, Ancient Man, and the Ark

When I was in college, I can remember sitting in an anthropology class and wondering, in a sort of pseudo amazement, how an anthropologist or paleontologist could take a single bone fragment, a skull cap, a bone to a foot, part of a jawbone, or even a tooth, and reconstruct the likeness of a beast-like creature and then state that this was the look of our early ancestors. Some paleontologists claim they can do this and determine the height, weight, and even sex of their object of study. If sufficient evidence is found, no doubt this is possible, but is a bone fragment sufficient evidence? I wondered at that time how much of their findings were simply the result of a subjective conjecture on the part of an individual scientist, and how much was factual.

On this matter, Professor E.A. Hooton of Harvard University, writes: "Some anatomists model reconstructions of fossil skulls by building up the soft parts of the head and face upon a skull case, and thus produce a bust purporting to represent the appearance of the fossil man in life. When, however, we recall the fragmentary condition of most of the skulls, the faces usually being misleading, we can readily see that even the reconstruction of the facial skeleton leaves room for a good deal of doubt as to details. To attempt to restore the soft parts is an even more hazardous undertaking. The lips, the eyes, the ears, and the nasal tip leave no clue on the underlying bony parts. You can, with equal facility, model on a Neanderthal skull the features of a chimpanzee, or the lineaments of a philosopher. These alleged restorations of ancient types of man have very little, if any, scientific value, and are likely only to mislead the public. So put not your trust in reconstruction."[1]

Let's take a step back in "evolutionary time" to *Robustus Australopithecus Africanus* (meaning "southern ape of Africa") and the lineage to *Homo habilis, Homo erectus* to *Homo sapiens* as we are now called by science. What about all the forms of stone age types as the Neanderthals and the "hunters and gatherers" and cavemen the anthropologists also tell us about? This, of course, is the evolutionary theory again, the incredible string of "accidents," in fact, Darwinism, and any other evolutionary theory that comes to surface.

C.E. Oxnard, scientist and author of *Human Fossils: The New Revolution, and The Place of the Australopithecine in Human Evolution: Grounds for Doubt?* has proven by mathematical analysis that the bone shapes of *Australopithecus* resemble apes far more than man. Oxnard has pointed out how the reconstructed bones of the foot, which were made to look like man's, can be reconstructed to look like a chimpanzee's also. The bones of the hands resemble the hands of various apes in seven features, while man in only three ways. The shoulder blade has been confirmed in recent years to be more like an orangutan than anything else.[2]

In the proposed lineage to modern man, *Australopithecus Africanus* is supposed to have lived long before *Homo habilis*. The theories of uniformitarianism and evolution would lead us to believe that the older fossils of *Africanus* would be found in older strata than that of *Homo habilis*. Richard Leaky has found more "modern-looking" creatures in supposedly "older strata." For instance, Leaky found that *Homo erectus*, which supposedly follows *Homo habilis* on the evolutionary chain, was actually walking the African plains at the same time of *Australopithecus*, which is supposed to be the ancestor to *Homo habilis*. This was interpreted to show that *Australopithecas Africanus* could not be man's ancestor, and the evolutionist went back to the drawing board for another theory.[3]

It would seem to me that by the very definition of evolution by natural selection, the earlier species would have not survived. It also occurs to me that apes and monkeys still very much exist today, so by the natural selection method, how could they be our ancestors?

Apparently some evolutionists believe that a line of the Dryopithecus Ape split in various branches and man is one result.

The Flood could, no doubt, be responsible for a great number of the animal-like fossils being found deep in the various sedimentary deposits and strata. Perhaps some are animal, some human, and some of them are of a species now extinct. No doubt, the influence of the evolutionary theories have been responsible for all this opinionated conjecture. One, for instance, is that of the aforementioned Neanderthal man, so named because the skeleton was found near Neander, Germany, in the soil of a cave.

The find was reported in 1857, two years before Darwin's *Origin of the Species*, and soon became controversial. Within a few years the evolutionists would seize upon Neanderthal as their missing link between the apes and man. Neanderthal Man was reconstructed to show how he walked with a stooped gait, with his head set far forward. This appearance gave this man the characteristic ape-ish look. Since evolution was just then being proposed, the ape-ish reconstruction was destined to eventually lend support for Darwin's theory.

All was not rosy, however. Several voices were raised in dissent. Rudolf Vichow, a pathologist, studied the fossil material and concluded that the man had had rickets. [Rickets is an infantile disease marked by defective development of bones. It is caused by a lack of Vitamin D.]

Currently, Neanderthal is considered a homo sapien. His elevation to the status of a man, rather than an ape, occurred reluctantly in spite of evidence, because earlier workers (evolutionists) needed Neanderthal as an ancestor.[4]

I've met Dr. Clifford Wilson, an archaeologist, theologian, linguist, psychologist, educator, writer, lecturer, and world traveler. He comes to the United States from Australia, and the Australian Institute of Archaeology. I have read one of Dr. Wilson's many books, *The Bible Comes Alive*, Volume I, and I hope to have the opportunity to read more of his work. The following several pages contain quotes from the result of his study on Genesis in Volume I.

Remember first our discussion of evolution, and consider, for instance, Neanderthal Man. Dr. Wilson writes that "Neanderthal Man was fully human, so named because some of them were found in the Neander Valley in Germany. It appeared they endured food and vitamin deficiencies and had problems such as rickets."

About the Olduvai Gorge in Tanzania, Dr. Wilson writes, "Dr. Louis Leakey and his wife, Mary, found the skull of *Zinjanthropus Bosei* (East Africa Man) at the Olduvai Gorge, and it attracted worldwide attention — Leaky claimed that it was the earliest pre-human skull ever recovered, being nearly two million years old. Leakey eventually admitted two things: (1) the skull was apparently no more than 10,000 years old, and (2) it was not human but was a variety of *Australopithecus* ("southern apes"). It is an unfortunate fact that a documentary indicating that this was a sensational find was still being presented over American television years after Dr. Leakey had died of a heart attack."

Mentioned in Dr. Wilson's book are *Gracile Australopithecus* and *Astralopithecus Robustus*. The skull named "Lucy" (skull #71) and a more robust looking skull (skull #48) which came from Swartkrans in South Africa, were examples of the larger and stronger, or more robust, of the two *Australopithecines*. They were thought to be of the same species, male and female. They are now considered to be "not man and wife after all, but separate ape species. For many years anthropologists claimed that the various forms of *Australopithecines* were transitional forms between apes and humans. . . . Subsequent findings have caused many scholars to turn from these creatures as ancestors to man: their brains are much smaller than those of humans, and their skulls, jaws, and ears are distinctly ape-like. Even their supposed bipedal upright walking is explained on the same basis that modern apes also walk uprightly. . . . They *(Australopithecines)* were as far removed from apes and humans as apes and humans were from each other. . . . Humans don't become apes, and apes don't become humans."

Other examples: Piltdown Man, found by Charles Dawson in 1912. "It was hailed . . . as a missing link between apes and men. . . . The scientific establishment finally exposed Piltdown Man as a fraud." It took 40 years, but it was proven that "a faked skull was carefully constructed by making use of altered and stained bones from an orangutan and a modern man. The teeth were filed down." Bone fragments were used in the construction. "During 1990 the perpetrator of the hoax was named as Sir Arthur Keith."

Java Man, or *Pithecanthropus erectus* ("upright ape-man"), was discovered by Eugene Dubois, a Dutch physician, in 1891 and 1892. "A few teeth, a skull cap, and a leg bone were found" in one site. "The leg bone was found about 45 feet or 14 meters from the skull cap, but they were linked together by Dubois to make a 'missing link.' . . . The leg bone he displayed was probably human, the skull was more ape-like. Two human skulls were found first at the same site . . . but Dubois did not give this information to the scientific world until nearly 30 years later in 1920. Dubois himself eventually admitted that the skull was probably that of a giant gibbon."

Bangalore Man is another example of misinformation given to the public. A man photographed alive in 1952 by Dr. Wilson himself was heralded by a newspaper as "the twin brother of Neanderthal Man." The truth is that the Bangalore Man (as Dr. Wilson pointed out) was "simply a poor fellow with a congenital deformity that had left him with virtually no brain capacity. . . . He was fully human, but with a deficiency. There are many known cases of children being born with virtually no brain. Such was the case with Bangalore Man — not a missing link between apes and men, but a person who was fully human."

Keilor Man, found in the suburbs of Melbourne, Australia, was at one time declared to be a missing link 150,000 years old. Carbon dating has recently given Keilor Man an age of 9,000 years, "and that is not necessarily final."

Colorado Man was considered to be an "early man." It was eventually discovered that he was a "tooth" that came from the horse family. That is right — a tooth.

Nebraska Man also turned out to be just a tooth, but this one proved to be a peccary, or an extinct pig. Does one sense a decline in scientific integrity here? There was also *Ramapithecus*. He was an extinct ape.

Dr. Wilson writes that "Java Man, Piltdown Man, Heidelberg Man, Rhodesia Man, Peking Man, and others used to be offered as proof of 'missing links,' pointers to man's evolution. They are nowadays all but ignored in anthropological discussions. Neanderthal Man and Cro-Magnon Man are universally accepted as *Homo sapiens* today."[5]

Apparently there are certain people in circles of influence that didn't get the word. In the July 1997 edition of *National Geographic* there is an article titled "The First Europeans," where another discovery is mentioned.[6] A one-and-one-half-inch-long splinter and other small splinters were found, pieced together, and now we have another missing link. They call him the Ceprano Man, and tell us that he is 900,000 years old! In that article, the Neanderthals are said to have existed 230,000 years ago, having evolved from the Heidelbergenis. Humans are believed to have set foot in Europe about 500,000 years ago, and had evolved from *Homo erectus* which had evolved in Africa two million years ago! The article goes on and on until I can no longer finish it. I have a problem with this thing called "evolution of the species."

* * * * *

If there was a universal Flood, then since that time of the Flood, as the earth was again being repopulated, I expect there could have been communities of people living in an age of development, utilizing stones and whatever else the state of civilization at that time could provide. They hunted and they gathered, they grew and explored the earth and built villages and cities. I have little doubt that they did all this and more. I believe that in certain circumstances they were also cast out of those villages and cities, and were forced to live any way they could in order to survive.

I am of the opinion that civilization, after the flood of Noah, had to start all over again. Some knowledge was carried over by Noah, but a new earth and new people had to start from the beginning.

In discussing, from a personal viewpoint, the reasoning behind evolutionary thought, it occurs to me that the widely accepted theories of evolution, as in a vertical progression from simple to complex life forms, are presented to us by just a few learned people who have been able to influence the teachings of our educational system.

The student, with this educational background, then perhaps overwhelmed by all the various species of life forms, can accept no other explanation for their existence than what he interprets as logical reasoning. Since learning through the teachings of our present educational system (which only recently, and in only selective areas, has offered creationism in their curriculum) has all but eliminated the possibility of another answer, evolution is accepted as fact.

Besides, certainly the vast numbers of wildlife must boggle a person's mind. How then, can anyone expect that all these animals could have possibly crowded onto one wooden boat? A global flood would not be thought of as logical.

There are many, many species of wildlife on the earth today. It certainly is difficult for most of us to think that all species could have been represented on the ark, even if God had sent them all to Noah. Let's consider this possibility.

The Ark on Ararat, by LaHaye and Morris, gives us some information that I believe is very important to our discussion:

> The first thing we must determine is the modern equivalent of the Genesis "kind." The first mention of "kind" appears in the creation story in Genesis 1, where ten times it is stated that God created the animals "after its kind." We don't know exactly what this "kind" was, but no doubt it represented the boundaries of variation of each plant or animal. Certainly adaptation and variation have occurred and are occurring today, but there always seem to be limits beyond which no variation is possible.

Some have felt, and with good reason, that "kind" approximates our modern classification of "family," and if so, the maximum number of animals represented on the ark would be about 700. But since taxonomy is in many cases quite subjective, it is difficult to be certain, and that number should be considered a bare minimum. For our purposes, and to answer any argument raised by the skeptic, we feel it more realistic to use the number of "species" instead of "families." This figure would certainly be the maximum number on board the ark estimated by any knowledgeable taxonomist, and if the ark could accommodate the maximum, it could certainly handle a lesser number.

Ernst Mayr, probably the leading American systematic taxonomist, has provided the following table listing the number of animal species.

Mammals	3,700
Birds	8,600
Reptiles	6,300
Amphibians	2,500
Fishes	20,600
Tunicates, etc.	1,325
Echinoderms	6,000
Arthropods	838,000
Mollusks	107,250
Worms, etc.	39,450
Coelenterates, etc.	5,380
Sponges	4,800
Protozoans	28,400
Total Animal Species	1,072,305 [7]

Of all these 1,072,305 animals, not all of them needed to be on the ark in order to survive. Only the land animals needed to be there.

Fishes, tunicates, echinoderms, mollusks, coelenterates, sponges, protozoans, most arthropods, and most worms, could have survived outside the ark. Many of the insect species among the arthropoda could have survived, particularly in their larval states, but those which needed to be on board would not have taken up much volume at all. The amphibians, and many of the reptiles and marine mammals, could also have survived without the aid of the ark.[8]

If we take the number of animals which could have survived outside the ark, as represented on our chart, and subtract that number from the total number of animal species as determined by Ernst Mayr, then we come up with this computation: 1,072,305 minus 1,051,205, which equals 21,100 animal species on the ark. For the sake of simplicity, if we figure that two of every kind were represented on the ark, the total number of animals would then be 42,200. I think this could still be a conservative number, so to be possibly more accurate I'll add on a few to account for the species which are now extinct, and then more to cover for the "clean" pairs not included in our estimate. Let's assume 50,000 animals were on the ark. Now about the clean pairs.

The Bible tells us, "And of every living thing of all flesh, two of every sort shalt thou bring into the Ark, to keep them alive with thee; they shall be male and female" (Gen. 6:19). The Bible goes further to tell us, "Of clean beasts, and of beasts that are not clean, and of fowl, and of everything that creepeth upon the earth, there went in two and two unto Noah into the Ark, the male and the female as God had commanded Noah" (Gen 7:8–9).

The point here is to show that God had differentiated between clean and unclean beasts and fowl. God says, "Of every clean beast thou shalt take to thee by sevens, the male and his female: and of beasts that are not clean by two, the male and his female. Of the fowls also of the air by sevens, the male and the female; to keep seed alive upon the face of all the earth" (Gen. 7:2–3). What we have learned here is that there were not just two of every kind brought aboard the ark as is generally accepted. There were actually seven pairs of some beasts, and seven pairs of some fowl brought aboard the ark. These were the "clean" ones. This explains why Noah would sacrifice a burnt offering to the Lord immediately after having left the ark. He could not have done so if he had had only two of each clean beast and fowl. "Every beast, every creeping thing, and every fowl, and what so ever creepeth upon the earth, after their kinds, went forth out of the ark. And Noah builded an altar unto the LORD, and took of every clean beast, and of every clean fowl, and offered burnt offerings on the altar" (Gen 8:19–20).

Leviticus chapter 11 explains that the clean beasts and fowl are the ones that man was allowed to eat, and he was not allowed to eat those that were not clean. It would defile the body and be dishonoring to God to do so. Leviticus 11:3 explains in the New International Version of the Bible, which is in this case easier to understand:

"You may eat any animal that has a split hoof completely divided and that chews the cud." This would have included cattle, sheep, and deer. Leviticus chapter 11 doesn't tell us much about clean fowl, just those that are unclean. The unclean are any kind of bird that eats flesh. A fowl that does not eat flesh, such as a grouse, duck, chicken, or a dove would be clean. The food in Noah's day was much like ours today.

Exactly how many kinds of clean beasts and fowl, or animals and birds if you prefer, there were on the ark is not clear. However, it is possible our first estimate of 42,200 total animals would fall short. It depends a lot on the definition of "kind," whether it means family or species, or if there is another classification that approximates the meaning more closely. It is only a guess at this point to assume 50,000 total animals on the ark as a fairly accurate maximum figure. It's a nice number to work with, so we'll use it for our computations.

There are some very large animals which would require a considerable space, but there are far more that are very small and would only occupy a limited area. It is reasonable to assume that even the larger species of animal would have been represented by young healthy ones of that species, and not the older and possibly larger animals which could have been less likely to survive the ordeal in order to reproduce its kind. If God was able to order the animals to the ark, then He would have been able to be selective. Let's assume that the average size of all the animals was the size of a sheep.

If one was to convert the volumetric capacity of Noah's ark to the equivalent capacity within a number of standard American railroad stock cars, the concluding figures are significant in getting a better idea as to the probability of the ark being large enough to house 50,000 animals.

Let's remember that at the time of this writing we do not know the size of the cubit that was used in the ark's construction. The ark may be much larger than we now imagine. Do not discount this possibility. If such a structure is found on Ararat, even if it is broken in two or more pieces, by knowing the length to width ratio of the ark is 6 to 1, we will then be able to figure the size of the ship as well as the cubit. In this example I am using a conservative approach to answering the question of "How could all of these animals and birds possibly be crowded onto one wooden boat?" I will use an 18-inch cubit rather than one of a much larger size. The idea here is that if all the animals could fit on a boat built with a smaller cubit, then they certainly could fit on a boat built with a larger cubit.

The late Ronald L. Lane of Guilderland, New York, and Longwood, Florida, an engineer friend of mine, made the following calculations. The biblical measurements for the ark were 300 cubits x 50 cubits x 30 cubits, or 450 feet x 75 feet x 45 feet. Using an 18-inch cubit, he came up with a capacity of 1,518,750 cubic feet for the ark. This number, divided by the space within a standard American railroad stock car of 2,670 cubic feet, equals 568.82, or nearly 569 stock cars. Current shippers can cram 240 sheep into a standard stock car, with each animal having a space of 2' x 2' x 2'9.4". If that small space was used for the average-sized animal, then the ark could have handled 136,500 animals of that size, or 50,000 animals in the space of 208.33 cars, with the space of 361 cars left for food and other areas required by Noah and his family. The animals would live in 36.5 percent of the ark. Obviously, with creatures of different sizes, the space required for some of them would have been larger, and for some the requirement would have been less. The example used represents what is thought to be an average-size animal, with all sizes considered.

I would imagine the small individual space of 2'x 2'x 2'9.4" used in the calculation would have been a bit tight, and probably more space was needed. If that space was doubled for each animal, using this example there would still be the space of 152.16 stockcars, or 406,267.2 cubic feet left for storage of food and other uses. The animals would live in 73 percent of the space within the ark, with 27 percent of the space left. The right answer probably lies somewhere close to this second figure.

Being in a small space would no doubt be somewhat of an unfavorable living condition, especially over such a long period of time as a year. It is suggested by Morris and Whitcomb that the animal world has two means to cope with unfavorable environmental conditions. They migrate, or they hibernate. If this is so, and since migration was out of the question, then hibernation would have been the alternative. The animals and birds may, for the most part, have generally suspended their functions in a state of hibernation during the year-long captivity.

The *World Book Encyclopedia* says: "Hibernation is an inactive sleeplike state that some animals enter during the winter. Animals that hibernate protect themselves against the cold and reduce their need for food. A hibernating animal's body temperature is lower than normal, and its heartbeat and breathing slow down greatly. An animal in this state needs little energy to stay alive, and can live off fat stored in its body."[9]

With the protective canopy of water and carbon dioxide over the earth and its subsequent greenhouse effect (discussed in chapter 11) before the Flood, climates may not have been so harsh and varied as they are now. There may have been little need for hibernation in a more uniform climate. God may have imparted these powers in an intensified form to the animals at the time of stressful living conditions in the ark.

If it is indeed possible that the animals and birds, during the convulsive period of the Flood, were, due to the stress of the environment, in such a physiological state of inactivity to the point of hibernation, then caring for and feeding the animals would have been relatively easy, and not much room for the animals would have been required. The room remaining for storage of food would have been sufficient.[10] It seems, under these conditions, that there was enough room on the ark for its described load.

This should answer the question for those who believe in an evolutionary past, or at best a local flood, because of the reason that not all the animals would be able to fit on the ark. Even using a conservative approach with an 18-inch cubit, there was enough room. Perhaps today there are more species of birds and animals, but even if the variations which are occurring today in a species, for instance pigeons and doves because of interbreeding, indicate to us a type of evolution, it is a horizontal movement and not a vertical one. As Dr. Henry Morris put it, even though there have been different types of dogs, "a dog is still a dog."[11]

Again, as mentioned earlier in this chapter, I'm not refuting the evidence that man has lived in more primitive societies, and in some cases still does. We didn't start out flying jet planes and driving taxicabs right after the creation or the Flood. Those things had to be developed just like the bow and arrow were in their time, during man's progression over thousands of years. What I am saying is, I believe we are here as a matter of purposeful creation, rather than an evolutionary accident.

As long as we're on the subject, I believe there is another discovery of evidence that is worth our time to discuss. It is explosive evidence for catastrophe in the aftermath of the eruption of Mount St. Helens. A video, narrated by Dr. Steve Austin of the Institute for Creation Research, should, in my opinion, be required viewing by any scientist of our day.[12]

On May 18, 1980, at 8:32 a.m. Pacific time, the effects of an earthquake reached the surface of Mount St. Helens in Washington state, and a nine-hour eruption released the energy equivalent to 400,000 tons of TNT blast energy. The 9,677-foot tall volcano lost 1,300 feet of height, or approximately one-half of a cubic mile of itself down its north slope with approximately one-eighth of a cubic mile of trees and debris landing into the once picture perfect Spirit Lake, located at the mountain's northern base. The splash sent a wave 860 feet up the nearby hillsides, tearing trees out by their very roots. the energy of that 400,000-ton TNT blast and eruption was equivalent to more than 30,000 Hiroshima-type atomic bombs — one every second for nine hours! It was not a small event.

A mature forest was leveled in seconds. Branches burned off almost immediately in the 550°F surface heat with millions of logs littering the hillsides and inundating Spirit Lake with an estimated one million logs. A mud flow 30 feet deep scoured the landscape of a valley to bedrock, leaving deposits 15 feet deep, one-fourth of a mile wide — and that was a small one. Strata was eliminated in certain areas and redeposited with mud flows and ash in layers to a height of 600 feet. Solid rock was eroded to a depth of 140 feet to form new canyons. Steam explosion pits, gully topography, and a catastrophically designed landscape resulted — and there was more. But it's the aftermath of this catastrophe that gives us a tremendous amount of information, some of which I will mention here.

A geologist might have expected the deposits left by the event to be in one homogenized mass, but that is not the case. The deposits were in layers. The uniformitarian model of geology tells us that it takes long periods of time for deposits of sediment to form layers. The eruption was a catastrophic event. Pumice flows, pyroclastic flows, mud flows, and air flow deposits show minute layering, as if it settled in pulses. Deposits were 15, 25, and even hundreds of feet thick, and layered — not over long periods of time as the uniformitarian model suggests, but in minutes and hours.

Canyons were formed, complete with drainage basins and a river. The standard uniformitarian theory tells us that rivers create canyons, that is, the canyons are a result of the river. The Grand Canyon is the number one example given to us by mainstream uniformitarian geology. They tell us that it took millions of years for the river (the Colorado River) to cut its way through the rock and form the Grand Canyon. But here at Mount St. Helens we see that the canyon provided a place for the river. The river then, is a result of the canyon, which is just the reverse of the traditional point of view. The canyons formed by the flows of mud and debris have given us a 1/40th scale model of the Grand Canyon, and it was formed in a matter of hours!

Floating logs in Spirit Lake, perhaps over 20,000 of them, have settled upright at the bottom of the lake. With each of those upright logs, one end of the log became heavier because of the root structure and the ball of earth around it, and the heavy end began to sink first, causing the log to settle in a vertical position. They settled at different times in the past few years since the eruption. Some logs would sink and lay on the bottom of the lake horizontally. Others would sink vertically. It is the logs that sank vertically that are of interest. One log would sink, then sediment, tree bark, and other debris would settle to form a layer a few feet thick. Then another log would sink, then more sediment, and the process continues, giving the appearance of forests of upright trees at different levels on the lake bottom.

If the lake was drained, it would look much like Specimen Ridge in Yellowstone National Park that geologists claim is proof of a colossal amount of geological time. They see what appears to be the remains of 27 layers of forests in petrified tree stumps. This is the claim of uniformitarian geologists, despite the fact that when one digs down to the base of the stump, which has been done in several locations, there is no root structure to indicate that the tree grew there. The evidence indicates that the trees were simply redeposited in an aftermath of a big flood!

Like those in Spirit Lake, the upright logs on Specimen Ridge in Yellowstone National Park probably settled upright while under water. If this is so, then they are there as a result of a great cataclysmic event, deposited over a period of only several years, and not as a result of 27 forests over a period of millions of years.

Dr. Austin has introduced a "floating mat" model of the way peat is deposited and coal is formed. He says that coal beds in places such as Kentucky, for instance, came to be as the result of bark from a log mat floating above the surface. In Kentucky? Yes, as a result of the biblical flood. Sound preposterous? Not at all. In Spirit Lake more than a million logs floating together as a log mat have rubbed their bark off, and the bark has accumulated on the bottom of the lake. This is known because Dr. Austin went scuba diving in Spirit Lake. That's right — Dr. Austin and a diving partner went to witness the position of the upright logs on the bottom of the lake, and when doing so discovered layers of tree bark in the sediment on the lake bottom. He discovered something else, too. The result of the layers of tree bark is seen in peat beds that are being formed out of this tree bark. He witnessed this in a period of only five to six years after the eruption.

As sediment covers the layers of tree bark, now the beginnings of a peat bed, pressure results, and coal will eventually form out of the peat. This is why one can many times see layers of what appears to be bark in pieces of coal freshly dug out of the ground. Coal is formed out of peat which is formed out of tree bark. At least that is what is happening in the case of Spirit Lake. It follows Dr. Austin's "floating mat" model to a tee; or perhaps I should say, to a tree. This challenges the traditional swamp theory of the formation of coal over an eon of time by the traditional uniformitarian geologist. What the eruption of Mount St. Helens has given us is a model of a major catastrophic event.

What we have here is a living laboratory, a model that gives us a series of canyons over 100 feet deep, with rivers as a result of the canyon. This was done in a few hours. It was not over an eon of time through the wearing away of rock by one river as the geologists claim happened in the Grand Canyon. We have logs floating upright and settling at different times in the sediment of the lake bottom that would give us the appearance of different levels of forests, if the lake somehow lost its water. The redepositing of these logs in this upright manner has happened in a matter of a few years and not over an eon of time as the geologists claim about the history of the trees at Specimen Ridge in Yellowstone National Park.

We have a laboratory in Spirit Lake that shows us just how peat and coal are formed. They are formed not over an eon of time, but in a matter of only a few years. We have a small scale model of the biblical flood and the events that followed as the waters moved over a dramatically changing landscape.

Realize this also: Darwin based his theory of evolution on his perception of geological gradualism. He noticed how the Santa Cruz River in Argentina appeared to have cut its way into the landscape, and he assumed that the small amount of water would take a long time to cut the canyon out of the earth. He concluded that the change in the canyon by the action of the river was very gradual over a very long time.

Then Darwin went to the Galapagos Islands and observed that the reptiles and finches were surviving by a process he called "natural selection and survival of the fittest." He considered what he thought to be the truth in his theory of geological gradualism and then concluded that there must also be biological gradualism. He based his theory of biological gradualism on the long periods of time in his theory of geological gradualism. Had he not first concluded that there was a theory of geological gradualism, he may well have not concluded there was also a theory of biological gradualism. Upon the completion of his journey he then wrote his book *The Origin of the Species*, which has influenced the world since the 1860s. Geologists later realized that the Santa Cruz River in Argentina was caused by drainage from glaciers in a catastrophic fashion in a short period of time. Darwin was wrong!

* * * * *

It constantly amazes me, when I stand on the sidewalks of a city, any city, and observe the countless numbers of people — beautiful, intelligent to varying degrees, many of them no doubt in possession of brilliant minds, moving flawlessly about in the pursuits of their daily lives. If questioned, most of them would probably profess to believing their ancestral heritage is simply apelike, and totally accidental. I wonder how it is that these many people, I believe complete human beings, not mutants of an evolutionary time clock, can then accept that they have purpose in their lives, not only in their daily pursuits, but even in their long range plans, when they had, according to their own beliefs, such a purposeless and low-life beginning. Will beliefs, or could beliefs, ever get a truthful boost?

I did have a strong sense of encouragement recently as I walked to a small newsstand on a San Francisco sidewalk. There I picked up the local *SF Weekly*, dated June 20–26, 2001. The front page, which got my attention, displayed cartoon-like drawings of what I'm assuming is meant to be God and two of his angels dressed in lab coats, with pockets full of pencils, and handling test tubes and a chart. The featured article was titled, "Looking for God at Berkeley." The article was written by Mark Athitakis, who I assume is employed by the weekly paper. The well-written article tells us of a molecular biology researcher by the name of Jed Macosko, who has come to the conclusion that "intelligent design" is evident in bacteria. Although his current research was the *E. coli* bacterium, he states, "Indeed, any microscopic organism — is a sophisticated dance of proteins and amino acids interlocking and working together. Many molecular bioligists find it utterly dazzling that something so small yet so amazingly complex could have evolved in nature. . . . It's so incredibly complex that it couldn't conceivably have formed through evolution. The only reasonable explanation, he says, is that these systems and their processes were deliberately created by an 'intelligent designer.' "

The author of the article says of scientist Jed Macosko, "He is inspired by what he claims is growing evidence that Charles Darwin's theory of evolution — the very bedrock of biology — has collapsed on the molecular level."

Athitakis writes that "Macosko and his colleagues are studying how genetic material — RNA, DNA, enzymes, and protein — goes about its business. . . . DNA, the double-stranded molecule that carries genetic information and makes up chromosomes, reproduces when RNA makes a copy of a DNA strand. In this way, cells make proteins that help the cell do any number of things, including reproduce, or they make proteins that are essential to the life of the organism. . . . This process begins with an enzyme called RNA polymerase, the focus of Macosko's work."

The article is in depth, unbiased, and very informative. I do not intend to quote the entire article here, only to include a couple of points. "Macosko believes this system to be what he calls 'irreducibly complex.' . . . In the case of Macosko's research, the theory of irreducible complexity says that even the slightest change in the composition of RNA polymerase and its course of action in the cell would make the whole system nonfunctional; furthermore, the arrangement of amino acids in the system is so complex that they could not have evolved."

Through the author of this article, the scientist Macosko tells us "Darwinism isn't science so much as a closed-minded materialistic viewpoint that needs rethinking. The common thread is an incendiary claim: People are being misled — or outright lied to — about the theory of evolution's power to explain the whole of nature, and that room needs to be made for something that is, if not the hand of God, then outside of our accepted notions of scientific evidence."

All the while Macosko works, traditional scientists at the university are prone to laugh at the concept of intelligent design. "In the minds of most scientists, however, intelligent design is simply a more insidious way of packaging creation science; intelligent design theory, they argue, is little more than the latest twist in an ongoing attempt to wedge religion into public schools, and besides, it's not much of a theory at all. It's just bad science, they say, which makes specious, deceptive, and unprovable claims about the nature of the universe."

So, the battle goes on at Berkeley. Fortunately, Macosko isn't alone. He is joined by Jonathan Wells, a biologist who wrote *Icons of Evolution* and who went to UC Berkeley specifically to smash Darwin's theories.

There is Phillip Johnson, a retired professor of criminal law who taught at Berkeley, who speaks of " 'intellectual bankruptcy' of the mainstream scientific community" as that community debates the credentials of Jonathan Wells (who holds two Ph.D's). Johnson wrote *Darwin on Trial.* From the article: " 'Darwin could not point to impressive examples of natural selection,' Johnson wrote, and neither have thousands of scientists hence; oft-cited examples of natural selection like fruit flies and Galapagos finches, Johnson said, are just 'convincing circumstantial evidence.' Johnson was looking for direct evidence that natural selection had produced a new species or a new organ." All he found was to be considered "unsatisfactory."

Other universities are now seeing legislation directed toward the teaching of some form of creationism in schools. In Michigan, for example, "A bill proposes that intelligent design be taught alongside evolution, and that 'a public school official shall not censor or prohibit the teaching of the design hypothesis.' "

This is a wonderful thing. It is what I ask for; it is part of the "why" that I've talked about. Let the truth be taught.

THE QUESTION OF GOD

Teach me to do thy will (Ps. 143:10).

What about this question of God? Is there in fact a certain faction of the scientific community that is so biased by its own personal beliefs, that in its own search for answers the possibility of finding them in a creation by God isn't even considered? Do they even believe there is a God? The doctrine of uniformitarianism and theories of evolution become as fact, and are taught in the classrooms of our schools while God and prayer are tossed out. Why is this so? Is it because of a satanic cloud over our thoughts? Is it apathy? Is it disbelief?

The Scriptures tell us:

But if our gospel be hid, it is hid to them that are lost: In whom the god of this world [Satan] hath blinded the minds of them which believe not, lest the light of the glorious gospel of Christ, who is the image of God, should shine unto them (2 Cor. 4:3–4).

As far as I'm concerned, there is no question of the existence of God. That is fact. The evidence we've read about should bring us to that realization. For the skeptical person, the finding of the ark may help. For some, the books on the Shroud of Turin helped. But we shouldn't require a "sign" in order for us to believe. The Bible says "we walk by faith and not by sight" (2 Cor. 5:7). And Jesus said, "Blessed are they that have not seen and yet have believed" (John 20:29). It is the change in the believer's life that stands as the testimony to his beliefs, not the "sign" he or she waits for. The Book of John tells us in part, "We know that he abideth in us, by the Spirit which he hath given us" (John 3:24). I know this is true in my own life, even with the many troubles of the day. In other words, as "rough" as I still am, I know to the very depths of my "inner man," there is a change going on. When you take a step in faith and accept Jesus Christ as your Savior, then by the Word of God the Spirit of God abides in you. I challenge each and every reader to try and prove me wrong; but, to do so you must first take this step of faith and find out for yourself.

What is faith? The apostle Paul writes: Faith is the substance of things hoped for, the evidence of things not seen"(Heb. 11:1), and "Without faith it is impossible to please him: For he that cometh to God must believe that he is, and that he is a rewarder of them that diligently seek him" (Heb. 11:6).

If this is so, then what about those who diligently seek him, and things still seem to go wrong? In fact, why should I believe and trust in a good God despite the evidence to the contrary, such as a personal family tragedy, and a look at the world around me?

It would seem that to have faith, or to believe in God, can be somewhat difficult to do when a terrible tragedy strikes and something bad happens for which there seems to be no good explanation. In some cases, no explanation is possible. We suffer and try to grow through these seemingly scheduled tapestries of troubles, and then we ask the always ever-present questions: If there is such an all-loving God, why is there so much hurt, hatred, violence, and misery in this world? Why do the children die? Why is there suffering, sickness, and handicaps? Why is life not fair? Where is God when we need Him? Does He care, or are we just here to fend for ourselves? Does He exist? What good is faith? Faith in what? Does this "faith" deny one of our highest faculties, the ability to weigh evidence and then to make logical decisions based on that evidence?[1] In other words, does "faith" deny our ability to think for ourselves? Without the answers, the questions always come up, and expectedly so.

A big question to me is why do the little children suffer and die; why is it they so many times do not even seem to have a chance in life before tragedy strikes; and what about the people who die before we think their time should be up?

Jesus said:

Verily I say unto you, Except ye be converted, and become as little children, ye shall not enter into the kingdom of heaven. Whosoever therefore shall humble himself as this little child, the same is greatest in the kingdom of heaven. And who shall receive one such little child in my name receiveth me. But who so shall offend one of these little ones which believeth in me, it were better for him that a millstone were hanged about his neck, and that he were drowned in the depth of the sea (Matt. 18:3–6).

It is obvious to me that by this Scripture, the little child enters into the kingdom of heaven.

I have not experienced the unexpected tragedies that so many people have. Therefore, I cannot personally relate to the sorrow that must be felt. That day may come, I certainly hope not, and I dread the thought of even that possibility. Perhaps there is comfort in what Jesus has told us as it relates to the children, to the converted, and even in the knowledge of the demise of those who have offended — I believe it means physically, mentally, or spiritually harmed in any way — the little children.

> For we must all appear before the judgment seat of Christ; that every one may receive the things done in his body, according to that he hath done, whether it be good or bad (2 Cor. 5:10).

> Whatsoever a man soweth, that shall he also reap (Gal. 6:7).

In Genesis 6:6 it says, "And it repented the Lord that he had made man on the earth, and it *grieved* him at his heart" (emphasis added). In Hebrews 13:8, the Holy Spirit, through Paul, writes, "Jesus Christ the *same* yesterday, and today, and forever" (emphasis added). These verses tell me that, as in the time before the Flood when the Lord grieved in His heart, and since He is the same today as He was then, that He grieves now, right along with us — that He can feel in his heart just as we do now.

Then why doesn't He stop it? For the little child, and I will go so far as to say I believe even for the aborted, and for those of us who are old enough to decide for ourselves and are converted, the Scriptures tell us the kingdom of heaven is on the other side of death's door. Therefore, death must be better for the victim than the tragedy is. Before I go any further, be assured that I don't advocate ending this life just to find out. Our life is a gift, we don't throw it away. I don't think the "giver of life" would be at all pleased if we did that. We each have a certain amount of time given to us, and after that, as the apostle John writes in the Book of Revelation, "God shall wipe away all tears from their eyes" (Rev. 7:17). I believe this is good for all who inherit the kingdom of heaven, be their earthly tribulations great or small. But now, what about the tragedy

— where is God's love and power, and why doesn't He put a stop to it?

Previously we talked about time, as a creation of God, and He is probably able to go back and forth in His creation. If this is the case, then He knows what is to take place. Why does He allow the tragedies to happen? And what about this love of His? A.E. Wildersmith, in his book *Why Does God Allow It?*, has this to say: "At this point, the question may arise that if God saw in advance the chaos and awful possibilities of misery, hate, and suffering conferred on man with the gift of free will, why did He proceed to create us? Was He not rather sadistic to have persisted in those plans, if He knew in advance the shocking results? Would it not have been better to have dropped the plan of creation before starting to create, if it was going to work out as terribly as it has?"[2]

This type of questioning can arise everyday in our own personal lives. For instance, in our decision to get married . . . when we make that decision, we normally choose a person we love. We get married, and if we would think ahead we would know that separation through death is inevitable. This, of course, comes if we don't fall down on our own, and do manage to stay married to each other until that time of death comes. Apparently, it is God's plan that we do. Our marriage vow says, "Until death do us part." Scripture backs this up; when that time of death comes, it is expected that there will be a time of sadness. If, by our own choice we don't make it that far as a couple, then there is another misery, but I don't think it is God's intent. When we stay together, we accept the inevitability of separation through death because of the experiences in the love we intend to share along the way. Even if this experience of love is for just a short time, it must be worth more to us than the ultimate misery and loneliness we will experience at the end of the marriage. If this were not the case then, except for the time necessary for propagation of the human race, why would we do it?

A.E. Wildersmith says God apparently feels the same way. In order for God to have the love and fellowship with us, He has accepted the hatred and violence which is also very present in the world He created. This hatred and violence is present because we, as humans, have been given the right to choose and make decisions for ourselves. Some choose to love God and seek His will, others do not. Wildersmith says it's a question of balance and God must have been convinced that even a little true love is worth more than the bitterness of suffering.[3] The reasons for this matter of true love and the right to choose, or free will, deserve further explanation, and will be discussed on the pages ahead.

In opposition to love, there is indifference, hatred, and consequently, rejection. Evidently even the Almighty God of love has a limit when He is constantly rejected. The results of His subsequent anger is given to us in the history of the Noachian flood, as written in the Book of Genesis. Only one man and his family, who were capable of making the decision to love God, did so. Only that family, the family of Noah, along with a cargo of animals incapable of free will decision, survived. The rest of the world's population, according to the Bible, perished. Is there a contradiction here in the wrath of a God of love?

Sin entered the perfect world created by God. I'm sure He knew it would happen, especially if He is indeed able to look ahead in His own creation. Yet, I do not believe it was God's will that sin entered the world, but rather that of the devil. We all know the story of Adam and Eve in the Garden of Eden in Genesis chapter 3.

Think of this possibility — that throughout the time before the Flood, men and women had their free will, and were even then able to make their own decisions to accept God or not to accept him. The time came when only Noah and his family were righteous before God, and the rest of the world chose not to accept Him. Instead, there was only violence, hatred, and all types of sin. If Noah would have given way to the ways of a sinful life, then the world of people, created by a God of love, would have in its entirety chosen the way of sin, the way of the devil, and mankind would have been lost. What was God to do?

Henry Morris says that nothing less than a total cleansing had to take place in the baptismal waters of a Great Flood. This had to take place before the demonic wickedness could gain control of every man, woman, and child throughout the entire world, thus destroying God's redemptive promises.[4] Noah and his family were the last. It sounds to me as though a loving God waited until the last moment, continuously being rejected by everyone else, before his judgment commenced. And He did this to keep His promises of redemption, that not all mankind be forever separate from the love of God. I don't see any contradiction at all.

I think the trials, misery, and suffering of this world are facts of life because of the sins in a world in which we are able to make our own decisions. These trials, miseries, and sufferings of the present life probably will be ended at death. What happens then? For those who enter the kingdom of heaven, where God is love (1 John 4:8), it stands to reason that love continues to love on forever. In this time of God's grace, the Bible tells us love will continue on for us if we have chosen to accept His gift of eternal life through our acceptance of Jesus Christ. If a God of creation allows us the possibility of love by our own free-willed choice, then the freedom to love must certainly be worthwhile, even though a lot of suffering accompanies us along the way. "For love is the greatest of all virtues, and far surpasses the misery which the freedom to love may entail."[5]

Why do you suppose a God who created us would even allow free will, knowing all the problems that would accompany that free will? Would it not have been better for God to eliminate our ability to make our own decisions, and prevent the troubles associated with the hatred and violence resulting from our wrong decisions?

What would, in fact, be the result if God had not allowed our free will, and we were only capable of doing His will? Would real love exist in God's creation if we were automatically virtuous, loving, kind, and incapable of sinning? For example, "Just as a lock opens when one turns the correct key, or as a vending machine delivers the bar of chocolate when the correct coin is inserted. If man had been so constructed that he delivered love and goodness whenever God pushed the right button, would he be capable of love or any other virtue?"[6] If God, in order to be guaranteed of our love, eliminated the possibility of hate by simply taking away our ability to make decisions through free will, if we were designed to simply deliver love, even worship, whenever it is requested of us, like the candy machine delivers a chocolate bar when the button is pushed, then could there ever be any real and true love experienced in such a creation? If we couldn't hate, could we really make our own personal choice, and really truly love? "The necessity for absolute free will in making decisions — to love or to hate — is inherent in any creation in which love and virtue are to exist."[7] "Love is only satisfied when returned free-willed. God is not constructed in any way to love us, He just loves us because He is love. Such divine love does not force us to return His love. The very attempt to do so would destroy the basis of all real love and all real virtue."[8] Does this answer, at least in part, our question, "Why does He allow the tragedies to happen?"

If God is omnipresent in space and time, He knows our future. Could He change it? Could He stop a tragedy, or is He a God who just doesn't interfere? If God is all powerful, and he knows our future, then He is in control. If He is in control, then could He change the events? If this is even remotely an option, what then could we do to possibly influence Him in our behalf? How can we be in His favor, or can we? I believe we can make known our desires, but we should first make the effort to be in His will, to prove ourselves, if you will.

For instance, a preacher may tell us of certain conditions that should be met, such as ridding ourselves of sin, fear, guilt, bitterness, negative attitude, and the like, which would thus allow God to work in our lives, and consequently turn things around for us. I believe it basically all boils down to a lack of communication on our part. Consider a marriage that is running rough, and divorce seems to be the logical and maybe even the welcome answer. Many, if not most of us, are at certain times guilty of these thoughts or actions, and may be able to relate. We distance ourselves from the ones who love us, and until there is a reconciliation, there's a problem in communication, and consequently in the relationship. In the marriage, when we fail to patch things up, if, because of our own shortcomings we are unable or unwilling to communicate to our spouse, how then can we apologize and forgive where need be, and get back on the track? We just plod on, sometimes "fed up" with the situation, choosing to do and see things our own way.

A difference in the two relationships is that the marriage may not work out. Any number of variable reasons can enter in, and the "family" foundation of that particular marriage crumbles, and one or both spouses may wish to terminate the relationship. This is not God's wish in our relationship with Him, nor in our marriage. Neither is it His provision for us to live together in bitterness. It takes two willing people to make a marriage work. Attitude, behavior, respect, and love are variables of influence. It takes one willing person to establish a relationship with God. The Bible tells us God is waiting and willing. He stands at the door of our lives and knocks, waiting for us to open that door and ask Him in (Rev. 3:20). The variable here is just in our willingness to do what God asks.

Basically, I think the crumbling of a relationship comes about because of a lack of effective communication between the spouses, in the case of marriage, or between each of us and God, in our prayer life. When this happens, troubles come. Sometimes it seems that trouble comes anyway, and it appears to us as a great inconsistency in our lives. In the Lord's Prayer we ask God to forgive us as we forgive others. Fortunately with God, if we communicate, that is, "If we confess our sins, He is faithful and just to forgive us our sins, and to cleanse us from all unrighteousness" (1 John 1:9). As in the marriage, our relationship with God is up to us. As in our relationship with God, in a marriage there must be forgiveness. I believe we should strive to be happy, but we must keep in mind the Bible tells us we are going to have trouble. Maybe it is because we have this right to choose. We can believe, accept, and love God, or choose another way, if we so desire.

The animal kingdom doesn't have that right. They get along on instinct, and by their design into the ecosystems, they seem to fit into the tapestry of life as they are intended to do. We are the ones who have the trouble.

Certainly, I don't know all the answers to the questions. If I did, I wouldn't have so much trouble. In fact, I don't know any one human individual who does know all the answers. Sometimes I even wonder what answers there could possibly be to all the controversial questions that may arise concerning matters of such a personal nature. But when things that happen seem to cause me to get a bit mad, or somewhat disgusted, when I get to the point I don't want to do what I know I should, then at that time I know I must pray. I must open up to God. I know, too, I should reflect on what I've learned from the past events of my life, and what I've observed in the lives of others. It's a time to consider advice given to me by someone who is in a position to advise me. If I take that time, and if I choose to do that, I weigh that advice and then I act, sometimes correctly, sometimes not. There should be little doubt that with all the variables in human behavior, we will have trouble.

The apostle Paul says, "All things work together for good to them that love God, to them who are the called according to His purpose" (Rom. 8:28). We may question, "Am I one of the 'who'?" In some cases, like with a child tragedy, what purpose is in that? Maybe, in some cases, this Scripture comes true on the other side of death's door, as the Scriptures go on to affirm, "For I am persuaded, that neither death, nor life, nor angels, nor principalities, nor powers, nor things present, nor things to come, nor height, nor depth, nor any other creature, shall be able to separate us from the love of God, which is in Christ Jesus our Lord" (Rom. 8:38–39).

There are questions for which I cannot find the answers. But really, how important can the questions be, if what we've just read is true?

I believe a secret of this life is "hope," and to quote a familiar axiom, hope that "the best is yet to come." With this hope, I am betting my life on one answer I have found, and thank God, so have many others. I am betting that God made His choice known when Christ hung on a cross for us — He chose to love. "For God so loved the world that he gave his only begotten son, that whosoever believeth in him, should not perish, but have everlasting life" (John 3:16). And that is the bottom line. Jesus commanded us to "Love each other as I have loved you" (John 15:12), but it is our choice, and there's where the trouble comes in. We all are faced with a variety of trials and troubles. This book is dedicated to those of us who accept that fact, and still believe in the saving grace of the Lord Jesus Christ.

Jesus tells us in John 5:39 to "search the scriptures — they testify of me"; and He says in John 14:6, "I am the way, the truth and the life, no man cometh unto the Father but by me." Jesus is telling us there is a way out of this troublesome mess, if we choose Him.

Jesus also tells us that before He returns, there are some things that must happen. For instance, "And ye shall hear of wars and rumors of wars." We certainly know there are wars. As a Vietnam veteran, I can assure you there are. "For nation shall rise against nation and kingdom against kingdom: and there shall be famines, [ever hear of Africa?] and pestilence, [Webster: infectious or contagious deadly disease (AIDS?), destructive, wicked, harmful to morals] and earthquakes, [remember Mexico City?] in diverse places" (Matt. 24:6–7). There have been more earthquakes in recent years than in all recorded history. People wonder how there could be a loving God when these things happen. They fail to search the Scriptures.

The president of the United States read this verse to our nation during one of his televised messages to us, sometime in 1983. "If my people, which are called by my name, shall humble themselves, and pray, and seek my face, and turn from their wicked ways: then I will hear from heaven, and forgive their sin, and will heal their land" (2 Chron. 7:14).

The nations begin with the individuals, and each of us has that God-given right to choose. In making that choice, we are putting our love where our priorities are. True love is a personal choice. God gave us His Son, He would expect nothing less than our best.

If there is one main question to be answered, it is not a question of God. His testimony is obvious, and we have talked a lot about it in the chapters we have just read. There are many Christian testimonies to His existence. The churches are full of them. The question we are dealing with here is about us. What are you and I going to do about it — accept the testimony or reject it?

It is tough when you've been taught one way and then become faced with a decision to believe yet another. It is also tough when your faith is shaken, as your life seems to fall apart because of personal problems and heartaches of all sorts. Your world may be shattered, and we cry out, "Oh God, why!?"

The Bible doesn't say these things won't happen; on the contrary, it assures us they will. But it also says, "Blessed are they that mourn; for they shall be comforted" (Matt. 5:4). We can expect that the tragedy may happen, and pray that it won't. If it does, we can go to our knees before God and receive that comfort, even amongst all the anger and tears, if we believe. With time and prayer we can grow through what may be a devastation in our lives. We can also choose another avenue of behavior. We can choose to hide behind a "shield" of anger and blame. We always have trouble, some worse than others. Comfort may be the personally chosen blessing to be desired. If this is your choice, then let your prayer be, "Teach me to do thy will; for thou art my God. . . . For thy righteousness' sake bring my soul out of trouble" (Ps. 143:10–11).

I've learned that I must spend time in prayer every single day, not just on Saturday or Sunday when time for church rolls around. Occasionally I've sat somewhere in the back rows of the church, and let my mind wander across the problems of the day or the week, whatever they may be, and even missed the message the pastor was preaching, remembering almost none of it as I left the building. That certainly is not being in a very prayerful attitude. One Sunday I decided to move to the very front row seats, and the pastor, in a very loud and convincing style, let the congregation know that he, too, gets mad or angry when he sees certain things happening. He had my attention.

The verse of Scripture that follows "Blessed are they that mourn; for they shall be comforted," says, "Blessed are the meek: for they shall inherit the earth" (Matt. 5:4–5). Now I had never understood the meaning of "meek" before, and in no way did I want to be identified with being "meek," as I perceived it to mean.

Pastor Del Roberts, in a solid, clear voice, boomed that "Meekness does not mean 'mush'! It does not mean you lose your spirit, your drive, your energies and desires; it means you allow the Lord Jesus Christ to help and guide you, and together you overcome the problems."[9] I understood him. It takes faith; it takes communication through prayer, through reading His encouragements in the Bible, and belief. It takes communicating in a right mind and spirit, to be in the will of God (Phil. 2:1, 2, 5). Without this action, the problems can be overwhelming. With this action, the Bible says, "If ye abide in me, and my words abide in you, ye shall ask what ye will, and it shall be done unto you" (John 15:7).

It's communication, it's prayer every day, but as in a marriage, sometimes our communication falls short. Then, so does our relationship.

Keep in mind, neither you nor I know how much longer we are going to live on this earth. Any decisions that could well be eternal, probably should be your highest priority. In referring to this life span of ours, the Bible says, "It is even a vapor, that appeareth for a little time, and then vanisheth away" (James 4:14) where eternal life with God is "from everlasting to everlasting" (Ps. 90:2). . . . I'd decide now.

The apostle Paul, in his letter to Titus, spoke of the "hope of eternal life, which God, that cannot lie, promised before the world began" (Titus 1:2). It is a promise, but you must believe it and do what is necessary to gain it.

The Scriptures tell us "the natural man receiveth not the things of the Spirit of God: For they are foolishness unto him" (1 Cor. 2:14). This verse tells us that the skeptic will have a rather tough time believing the Word of God as it is written or spoken. It makes much more sense for him to believe the highly educated scientist who has determined "what really happened," in the history of the earth, and where man came from, regardless of whether it is in contradiction to the Bible or not.

Our main topics in the recent chapters have had to do, in part, with discussions of the theories of uniformitarianism and evolution. Darwin's evolutionary theory, for instance, has been taught and generally accepted by many, for more than a century. Darwin tells us life began completely by accident in a primeval ocean. One thing led to another, accidentally, and eventually man arrived on the scene. We have discussed this before. I don't know about you, but I prefer to believe it took a God to create me, that there is purpose for my life, and not that my ancient ancestors crawled out of an ocean in a rather low form of life, which was simply an accident from the start, and has continued to be so till this very day. For if the latter is the case, impossible as it is, then there is no purpose, no reason but chance, no cause for order, no sense in morality. There is no hope, no spiritual tie with the Creator, there are only evolutionary mutants, chaos, and death.

The Scriptures tell us, "Your faith should not stand in the

wisdom of men, but in the power of God" (1 Cor. 2:5). "For it is written, I will destroy the wisdom of the wise" (Cor. 1:19). What follows in this next paragraph should be worthy of your attention.

The Scriptures tell us in speaking of Jesus Christ, that "there is none other name under heaven given among men, whereby we must be saved" (Acts 4:12). The Book of Romans says, "That if thou shalt confess with thy mouth the Lord Jesus, and shalt believe in thine heart that God hath raised him from the dead, thou shalt be saved" (Rom. 10:9).

"For by grace are ye saved, through faith, and that not of yourselves: It is the gift of God: not of works, lest any man should boast" (Eph. 2:8–9). The Scriptures tell us that when we accept the gift, we become as children of God: "For as many as are led by the Spirit of God, they are the sons of God. For ye have not received the spirit of bondage again to fear; but ye have received the Spirit of adoption, whereby we cry, Abba, Father. [A term of great affection, Interpretation of ancient Hebrew gives Abba, the meaning of 'Dad' or 'Daddy'.] The Spirit itself beareth witness with our spirit, that we are the children of God" (Rom. 8:14–16). What does an affectionate father give to his child?

"As it is written, eye hath not seen, nor ear heard, neither have entered into the heart of man, the things which God hath prepared for them that love Him" (1 Cor. 2:9).

To me, it is quite clear, the most important decision a person can ever make, is a simple act of the will, a personal choice. We cannot work our way into heaven, we can only choose to accept the gift. I care not to imagine the consequence of making some other choice.

The Scriptures tell us, "It is appointed unto men once to die, but after this, the judgment" (Heb. 9:27). For those who are not prepared to meet the Lord, "There shall be weeping and gnashing of teeth" (Matt. 24:51).

For some of us, it hasn't been easy to surrender to the faith and hope that we will get out of this world spiritually alive; that is, to live forever in the glorious presence of God. For me, it is no longer a choice to make. The alternative does not excite me much. I have made my choice, even amongst all the troubles. Have you? It is your responsibility, and you have everything to gain.

Jesus never said it would be easy, in fact, quite to the contrary. I have an idea that being nailed to, and hung from a cross, wasn't easy either. He did that for you and me. Remember to thank Him — and then humble yourself and praise Him.

* * * * *

In these previous chapters we have pondered the purpose of a person's existence, and if we were but an evolutionary accident. We questioned why a God would create us in the first place, if He knew of the misery the human life was to experience. The question is, in short, "why are we here" — by accident or on purpose — and if for a purpose, what? Evolutionary thought, through the channels of science, tells us we are an accident, a chance beginning.

The Scripture verse Revelation 4:11 reads like this: "Thou art worthy, O Lord, to receive glory and honor and power: For thou hast created all things, and *for thy pleasure* they are and were created" (emphasis added). The way I understand it, the purpose for our creation then, and for the creation of all things, is entirely for giving pleasure to the Creator. I doubt it is simply for His amusement as it may sound to some, but rather it is a pleasure in the ultimate triumph of God's own will. Maybe we are players on the center stage of earth, in a great drama between good and evil, between the will of God and that of Satan; a drama for all the universe to witness. I suspect then, this verse means we are to have fellowship with Him, that is, to pray, to love Him, and to praise Him. The Scriptures tell us "For it is God which worketh in you both to will and to do of His good pleasure" (Phil. 2:13). We know He loves us, because He forgives us and Jesus paid the price. And, if we accept that fact, then in turn, He has promised us we will live with Him forever.

It occurs to me, since God, according to the Scripture, is love, and since God can *grieve*, since God can know *pleasure,* and by the Scriptures we know God can be *angry,* and feel pain in His heart as He did when He saw the violence on earth before the Flood, and since God made man in His own image, and desires personal relationship with us through His Spirit — He sounds almost as though He is one of us, like part of the human family; the Father of the family. I don't believe a father would want to see his children suffer; by the Scripture, He grieves, and feels pain right along with us. He did so before the Noachian flood. Genesis 6:6, referenced earlier in this chapter, says so. The baptismal cleansing Henry Morris spoke of became necessary, and God grieved. God sounds as though He has a very strong sense of emotion. By the Scriptures, we know Jesus certainly did. And Jesus told us, "I and my father are one" (John 10:30).

The Bible doesn't tell us what God did before the creation, therefore any further reason for creation I would include would be simple conjecture on my part. Perhaps there is a greater purpose in a great master plan, to be unveiled to us at a later time. I don't know. It satisfies me to read in the Scriptures that we were created for the purpose of His pleasure. Does this answer the question: Are we here by accident, or is there a purpose? . . . You decide.

THE BIBLE PUTS IT THIS WAY

And the flood was forty days upon the earth; and the waters increased, and bare up the ark, and it was lift up above the earth. And the waters prevailed, and were increased greatly upon the earth; and the ark went upon the face of the waters. And the waters prevailed exceedingly upon the earth; and all the high hills, that were under the whole heaven, were covered. Fifteen cubits upward did the waters prevail; and the mountains were covered. And all flesh died that moved upon the earth, both of fowl, and of cattle, and of beast, and of every creeping thing that creepeth upon the earth, and every man. All in whose nostrils was the breath of life, of all that was in the dry land, died. And every living substance was destroyed which was upon the face of the ground, both man and cattle, and the creeping things and the fowl of the heaven; and they were destroyed from the earth: and Noah only remained alive, and they that were with him in the ark. And the waters prevailed upon the earth a hundred and fifty days (Gen. 7:17–24).

The Bible tells us the ark floated for five months before it landed. But there was a considerable length of time to pass before Noah, his family, and the cargo of animals were to leave the ship.

And the ark rested in the seventh month on the seventeenth day of the month, upon the mountains of Ararat. And the waters decreased continually until the tenth month: in the tenth month, on the first day of the month were the tops of the mountains seen (Gen. 8:4–5).

And in the second month on the seven and twentieth day of the month, was the earth dried, and God spake unto Noah, saying, Go forth out of the Ark, thou, and thy wife, and thy sons, and thy sons' wives with thee. Bring forth with thee every living thing that is with thee, of all flesh, both of fowl, and of cattle, and of every creeping thing that creepeth upon the earth; that they may breed abundantly in the earth, and be fruitful, and multiply upon the earth (Gen. 8:14–17).

The Bible tells us that somewhere in the area of 220 days or 7 months and 10 days after the ark landed, only then were they able to leave the ark, and all this time the waters were decreasing continually.

It does stand to reason that they certainly must have landed on the top of what was, even then, a very tall mountain.

> Bless the Lord. . . . Who laid the foundations of the earth, that it should not be removed forever. Thou coverest it with the deep as with a garment: the waters stood above the mountains. At thy rebuke they fled; at the voice of thy thunder they hasted away. They go up by the mountains; they go down by the valleys unto the place which thou hast founded for them. Thou hast set a bound that they may not pass over; that they turn not again to cover the earth (Ps. 104:1–9).

The mountains rose and valleys were created. The surface of the earth changed. The waters receded, the climates changed, and the theory presented tells us the glaciers formed. Thousands of years passed while civilization and wildlife were again multiplying upon the earth, and the glaciers receded. History is now being recorded. Theories are being conceptualized as to the origin of it all. Uniformitarianism becomes popular and the thoughts of creation are snubbed by the intellectuals. All the while, in a state of preservation, frozen and petrified, Noah's ark rests and waits high on a mountain in eastern Turkey.

Did it really happen this way? Is the ark there? If so, where?

EXPEDITIONS

1984 — MY FIRST SEARCH

Wednesday, August 15, 1984: At 7:00 a.m. I left Denver on a Frontier flight bound for Chicago to connect with Lufthanza to Ankara via Frankfort and Munich. I arrived in Ankara and the Mola Hotel by 5:00 p.m. on August 16. I was to wait in Ankara until Jim Irwin and John Christensen arrive. The three of us, plus a guide, would make up our climbing team.

Friday, August 17: I had breakfast with Watcha McCullum, a heliocopter pilot and member of a team led by Marv Steffins of International Expeditions out of Louisiana, and Jim and Martha Davies, two ark explorers from Bend, Oregon, who had just returned from Ararat. Our conversation related to Watcha flying a heliocopter, Jim and Martha's climbing experience, and a discussion about other climbers involved in the search. The Davies informed me that no one was being allowed to climb the north side of the mountain. Also, the snow line on Ararat was more conducive to a search than it had been in the past 25 years. It had melted back to at least 13,000 feet. I asked what is probably the number one question: *If the ark is there, why don't the Turks find it?* The answer I received from Jim Davies was: *City folks don't care or believe, small town folks can't afford to look for it, to scratch out a living takes all their time, and there's apathy.*

On Saturday, I learned that Marv Steffen, whom I had only spoken with on the phone, and Watcha McCullum had left Ankara and were enroute to Erzurum. They expected to have problems using the heliocopter. A two million dollar insurance policy and Turkish pilots were a probability, and were not necessarily part of the current plan.

Air Force Chaplain Jack Richards, a friend of Jim Irwin's, is stationed at Bulgat Air Station in Ankara. I contacted Chaplain Richards upon my arrival and he is keeping me informed of Jim's progress. Apparantly Jim has missed his flight, and now his itinerary has changed somewhat. Instead of arriving in Ankara this evening as previously planned, Jim will arrive in Athens, Greece, at 10:30 tonight. When he finally does get here, Jim is expected to speak at the military bases located at Sinop and Erzurum. The air force will try to provide transportation for him in order to speed up his travel time. Still, with this delay, I am beginning to sense a tightening of the schedule, and time on the mountain will be shortened. This may get to be a bit frustrating. From what I understand, the red tape and permits yet to deal with have caused others some grief. Five-day sports climb permits have been issued in lieu of research permits previously promised. A sports permit does not allow one to research the mountain, only a hike up, then down. The time it could take to resolve these problems would no doubt be costly to us by further limiting our time on the mountain. Schedules to be kept in other areas of our lives will force us to leave Turkey on certain predetermined dates, regardless of whether we climb or not.

A Turkish *hammon*, or bath, took part of my afternoon, an experience I'll not repeat soon. A muscle-bound moose rubbed me to the limits of my endurance, and there were no dancing girls. What an embarassing turn of events it would be if I had to report back home that I had been unable to climb the mountain because I had broken a few bones while taking a bath.

Jim and Martha Davies and I had dinner at the Officer's Club at Bulgat Air Station. Jack Richards permitted us to use his name to sign in. At the time, I did not know that Jack was a colonel, and when the doorman asked his rank, I signed him in as a captain. I'm glad the chaplain has a sense of humor.

Church in the base theater and brunch at the Officers Club took care of Sunday morning, the 19th day of August. Jack Richards called at 4:00 p.m. and informed me that Jim had missed another flight. Time is being wasted. The Davies tell me that all climbers are using the south route. The reason may be for the protection of the climbers, as bandits are reported to be on the east and north sides of the mountain. I am curious as to what impact this protection will have on us as we attempt to research the remote areas of the mountain. Time will tell, but for now I must be patient.

Late Sunday night Jack Richards received a message that Jim Irwin was on his way. Jack picked me up at the hotel, and we went to the airport to meet him. Jim and John Christensen arrive together, but separately. They were both on the same crowded plane but each did not know the other was there. Jack Richards knew that Jim was on the plane but the whereabouts of John was uncertain. Consequently, not knowing John was on the plane, we left him at the airport. John later made his way to town, but without his climbing gear, which for some reason failed to make the trip.

Jim was accompanied by an explorer by the name of Ron Wyatt, from Nashville, Tennessee. Ron is independent of our team. His reason for being in Turkey is to search out a boat-shaped object found in the Tendurek Hills some distance from Ararat. He has seen this object before and is convenced that it is the ark.

Early the next morning, Monday the 20th, Jim and I jogged and talked about the expedition ahead of us. Then I had breakfast with Jim and Martha Davies and checked out of the hotel. John and Ron picked me up in a taxi and we three were on our way to the airport with the intention of flying to Erzurum. John made the flight; Ron and I missed it. The plane was full of passengers. Initially disappointed, Ron and I made our way back to the city and gladly accepted an invitation to stay at the home of Kasim Gulek for the night. Later, members of the press arrived at the Gulek home. There must have been a dozen or more, all doing their job. Jim was interviewed, there were photos taken, and much discussion of the expedition to follow.

On Tuesday, August 21, Ron and I picked up Orhan Baser, a Turkish military officer. Orhan was Jim's guide on a previous climb, and he may be our guide this year. At the very least, since Orhan speaks English, he will help us to communicate with the Turkish authorities. Orhan's wife and son will accompany us as we leave for the airport and, hopefully, this time for Erzurum. Jim goes with the military to speak at Sinop. He will meet us in Erzurum.

On Wednesday, August 22, we were up at 7:30 a.m. and on our way to the boat-shaped object — Ron Wyatt's Tendurek Hills site. Mount Ararat, rugged in appearance, towering majestically as a place of refuge high above the Anatolian landscape, stands in full view in the splender of the morning. Except for photographs, this is the first time I have ever seen the mountain. I'm without words to accurately describe the beauty of this ice-capped giant. For my first impression, it is simply awesome.

The day is warm and beautiful, the sky's clear, the promise of great weather lies ahead, and the army is kind enough to do the driving. Iran is apparently between three and six miles away, according to Ron, and the boat-shaped formation is in sight. The bow of the object looks like a boat shape, and not the barge-shaped structure of which the reports of mountain sightings speak.

Is this just a clay push-up in a mud flow and the results of the 1959 earthquake in this region? Is it a lava push-up, covered with mud and soil in an old decayed lava flow also pushed up by the earthquake? Or, is something under there? It looks like a boat. There is a rock outcropping that must be explained in the center of the object. Ron thinks the boat was transported downhill in a lava flow, broke and rested against the rock, settled around the rock, and was buried by the lava.

According to Ron's research, it is possible that the Armenians built a copy of the ark in A.D. 300. If so, could this be the copy or could this be the ark? At present, I'm not convinced that it is anything other than a geological formation. Excavation, carefully and professionally executed, is necessary. Ron's metal detector indicates something is in the object, and he says he has found evidence of wood in the object during a previous trip. He's been here at least twice before. Villagers in the area say it is a boat, but as far as I can tell, they can only see what I can. Ron, possibly with Orhan's help, may do some digging. It depends on legality and permits through the Turkish government.

We're back from the boat-shaped object at 10:25 a.m., and the day calls for Jim dealing with permits, guides, police, and the politics of the situation. If anyone will be successful in this endeavor, it will be Jim Irwin. Orhan will be with Jim to help with language translations. John waits for his climbing gear which still has not arrived. It's time to repack, have breakfast, pray, and ponder.

It's been over a week since I left Denver. I'm frustrated because of all the delays. Our time on the mountain will be shorter than planned. I'm ready to go, and now I find that our first day of climbing will be only to 3,200 meters — 10,500 feet — where we will sit around and acclimate. The plan now is to climb Thursday and Friday, search Saturday, Sunday, and Monday, and come back down on Tuesday. That's Jim's schedule. Maybe I'll be ready to return then and maybe not. With the snow line back more than it has been in perhaps 25 to 30 years, now is the opportunity. I believe that we will be successful in our search. If this will not be the case, then we will have to wait on the results of excavation, and the dating of the boat-shaped object at Tendurek. To call the object the ark, I am not at this time persuaded to do, and unless there is extremely convincing evidence I will probably not be persuaded. In my opinion, to call the object near Tendurek the ark would be like a dry water glass, anticlimactic, a silent victory.

John still waits for his climbing gear, but in the meantime he has been lining up any equipment he can borrow. It seems his gear has been misplaced by the airlines, and its whereabouts is uncertain. Jim fills in part of the afternoon jogging, and I am stuffing in pills to kick a cold I've picked up. I must be rid of it by tomorrow.

Wednesday evening comes and Ron offered to take us to look for sea anchors which he has supposedly found not far from Ararat. Jim and John chose not to go, but Marv Steffen and I did. Marv has also seen the boat-shaped object. The possibility of its being the ark is the topic of conversation for the evening. Marv believes it shows more promise than anything he's ever seen on the mountain. I'm sure he is sincere in his belief. At this point, I prefer to believe that the ark is somewhere on Mount Ararat. It was getting dark and we did not locate the sea anchors. At 11:25 p.m. we packed, prayed, ate a watermelon supper, and were ready to go early the following morning.

Thursday, August 23: We left the hotel at 6:37 a.m., and now we are on our way to Eli village near the base of the mountain. By 8:20 a.m. the horses are being saddled with our packs. The friendly Kurdish folk at the village are filling us full of juice, and the members of the press and photographers who have accompanied us are in fine form.

Jim mentioned yesterday how a shepherd boy had come to his rescue when he was faced with a probable attack by dogs. A rock was Jim's sole weapon. Perhaps the Lord sent the good shepherd. Somehow, that sounds familiar.

At the village, during the photo session, the lady of the main household of Eli village was asked to pose with Jim. She originally declined but decided that since Jim was a good believer, she would allow her picture to be taken with him. John and I handed out gum and candy to the children. There were many of them who came back several times holding out both hands for our offerings. That was fun. I noticed that John was particularly good with the kids, and they seemed to love him. I believe it is his gentle, kind nature that attracts the kids to him. In my case, I suspect it's the gum.

Leaving the village at 9:15 a.m., our four-man operation, plus reporters, photographers, and followers, totaled 16 people and three horses. By 9:30 a.m. we were at low camp, about 10,500 feet (3,200 meters) or so. I'm told that it is time for a light lunch and rest. The plan now is to sit around all day and get acclimated. I'm very impatient, but Jim is wiser than I and agrees with the guide that we're to sit tight. I must keep in mind that it's God's timing that will take us to the ark, not mine; but I hope it's soon.

On our way to this place we endured three rest stops so the Kurds could have a cigarette break. These breaks were announced as five-minute stops, however, my watch indicated close to 15 minutes.

Orhan decided not to climb, so we have acquired Redvan Karpoos as our newly assigned guide. He says a thousand people have climbed the mountain this year. This is more than ever before; however, sport permits were issued to nearly all of them. They simply went for a hike, and stayed on one path only. We are actually the only group which has supposedly been given complete freedom of the mountain. This thought occurs to me: Due to a problem getting the required insurance, the heliocopter won't be flying, the snow is melted back, the weather is great, and we still (although just barely) have enough time. We must be in God's favor. If the ark is to be found, I, perhaps selfishly, believe that we will be the ones to find it.

It is now 7:25 p.m. on Thursday. We went to a river and filled our water bottles. The water was cold and dirty. We had to purify the drinking water with iodine tablets — a must from now on. It's interesting how, all of a sudden, water is of such importance. It is one of those things you seem to take for granted back in the States, or in any area of plenty. We had supper, and Jim answered more questions for JoLee, a female reporter who had accompanied us thus far. Allie, the traveling photographer (who rode a horse most of the way up to low camp) took the pictures.

When you are in the company of Jim Irwin you find yourself treated quite well, and cameras come from everywhere to get him on film. This is our first camp. Tomorrow we go to the high camp and beyond; then three and a half days for the Lord to show us the ark, if that's His plan. I know, for sure, it's ours.

Friday, August 24 at 6:30 in the morning: We're up and breakfast is underway — a quick one to be sure. We're leaving a duffle bag full of stuff behind, and still we seem to be taking too much with us. The Turks and Kurds kept us awake well into the night; there must have been a party of sorts.

It's 9:00 a.m. and we're finally underway. It's a slow start. (So, what's new?) The reporters are left behind, still one photographer sticks with us. By noon we are at 4,200 meters, which is as far as the horses can go. That's somewhere around 13,800 feet. We made good time this morning, now we will carry our own packs. Our high camp will be at 4,900 meters, which is approximately 16,000 feet. There are a lot of loose rocks and it's a difficult climb. Water is at a premium. It amazes me how these Kurds can smoke so much and still climb like they do. We have a break now, then the toughest climb to come.

Another journal entry, Friday the 24th, at 6:15 p.m.: We've climbed for two days, had the horses for a day and a half, and we're still three hours from where we will make our high camp of operation, next to the ice. It's very slow going, and I'm somewhat disappointed that it is. We left the horses at 1:00 p.m. and climbed until 3:10 p.m., then stopped and made camp among the rocks. A total of four hours and 45 minutes of actual climbing today — two hours and 35 minutes climbing with the horses and two hours and 10 minutes on our own. It doesn't sound like much, but you have to have been there. The packs were heavy. At one point, I fell and John helped me to my feet, then took part of my load. I was loaded far too heavily, I imagine close to 90 pounds . . . a dumb mistake.

In our Bible study a couple of weeks ago, John was seen as being the mule. If that means taking on a heavy load, he is beginning to fulfill that part. Today was a rough day for me; tomorrow will be another day. We must be above 14,000 feet now. Perhaps God will show us the ark on Sunday or Monday. I feel good about that possibility; I'm still confident.

The sun is sinking behind the mountain and it's time to crawl into the sleeping bag, as it will be getting cold soon. It's time for prayers high on the side of a mountain.

Saturday, the 25th of August, 6:45 a.m.: The sun is peaking over the mountain and the skies are clear. I've been in this bivy sack for 12 hours and 15 minutes. That's the time of no sunshine — a long night. Jim went to bed early and has been in the sack nearly 14 hours. Redvan and John are in a tent, and I hear them awake now. My thermometer says 25° F. A little ice is on the packs and bivy sacks. As soon as we thaw out and eat, we'll be on our way. This is the third day of our climb, and by the size of my pack, it looks like it will take all day. Still, my attitude is great, and I expect great things. My thoughts are to praise God, for I believe He is with us.

By 9:40 a.m., Redvan and I are on top of the first of two hills between last night's camp and our future base of operations, the high camp. John and Jim are right behind. I'm pleased with myself and our progress as a whole. I feel stronger today than yesterday. We have a short rest stop here. The wind is cold, but the skies are clear.

It's 11:00 a.m., and we've reached high camp after only two hours and 20 minutes of climbing this morning. Our plan is to use this camp for the next three nights. God will grant us good weather . . . I believe this. We see the ice cap, but it seems like such a long way away. Also, it is my observation that Inonu Peak, which is reported to be approximately 16,000 feet tall, is still quite a ways above us. This being the case, the high camp we're at, which is known as the 4,900 meter (16,000 feet) camp must actually be closer to 4,700 meters. This would put us approximately 15,400 feet up. I believe this estimate is the more accurate of the two.

It is now Saturday night, August 25. This is an overview of the day and plans for tomorrow. Today was a busy day. We left our camp of last night and climbed to somewhere between 4,700 and 4,900 meters, and set up our high camp by noon. We rested until about 1:10 p.m., then we hiked to the west glacier and looked it over from above. We then climbed a finger glacier to search for the wood sighting of which Jim was made aware last year. We found it — a pair of skis and poles at 16,000 feet on Inonu Peak. We reached that summit with crampons and ice axes. We don't know why the skis are here. I can't imagine anyone actually trying to use them on this mountain. A photograph of the skis at a distance would cause them to appear like pieces of wood sticking out of the ice. Were they planted to bring Jim back? I wonder why they are there.

Redvan, an expert mountaineer, conducted a lesson in ice belay and self-arrest, after which we returned to camp, most of the way on ice. We're actually camped not very far from the edge of the ice, and tomorrow we'll climb up the ice to the 17,000-foot peak named Ataturk. Jim wants to see the site where Dr. Charles Willis, who believes the ark is very high and near the summit, has discussed cutting into the ice in his search for the ark. Then we'll be above the Ahora Gorge and the northeast area of the mountain. This is what I've waited for. I pray we give it a good search and the Lord will reveal the ark to us. The weather on top today was a bit rough and windy. I hope tomorrow is nice, and I expect it will be. It's 6:50 p.m., Saturday night, August 25, 1984. The sun is behind the mountain, and I'm in the sack. The temperature is 28° F. and dropping.

Into my notes, the next entry: It's just past midnight, early Sunday morning, August 26. I find it hard to sleep at night; 12 hours is too much. Anticipation of tomorrow is great, and I'm slept out. The temperature is 22° F., a mild evening, and the sky is incredible. Stars are everywhere like I have never seen before. Like the lines in a Robert Service poem: *Night's holy tent, huge and glittering with wonderment.*

I thank God for good weather. Without it, it would be a challenge to survive. The night wears on until now, and it's 6:00 a.m. German climbers and guides, 18 of them, wake us on their way to the top. They have a sports permit. They stopped briefly and one or two of them posed for a picture with Jim as he stuck his head out of an iced-up bivy sack. They had started their day's climb at 2:00 a.m. They've got to be tough.

The skies are clear and we were underway at 8:00 a.m. sharp. It's now 11:35 a.m. We've been around the west side on the ice, the north side above the Cehennem Dere, above the Ahora Gorge, and across the Abich I and II glaciers to the saddle between Ataturk peak and 2nd peak (Cakmak), and now at the place where Willis was to dig in the ice. This year didn't work out for him, but I understand that he may have dug here in the past. We're somewhere close to 16,500 feet now, and we're above the east side of the Ahora Gorge. The exploration of the northeast area is next, and what I've waited for.

It is now Monday, the 27th, at 8:55 a.m. I'm not sure where or how to begin. A lot has happened since my last entry. I'll try to begin where I left off. We were on the saddle between Attaturk and Cakmak peaks.

For the first or only time on the expedition, I felt that we were not all in one accord. Perhaps it was due to the powers and principalities the Bible tells us about. Perhaps it was God's will the following events took place, but if that was so, why do I feel so empty? Maybe it was no one's will and we just blew it. Maybe we made the wisest decisions possible within the boundary of our limitations . . . maybe not.

Discussion took place on how to reach the northeast side. We had to descend at least 2,000 feet to be near the edge of the ice where I'm sure the ark must rest.

Redvan and I unroped and took a walk to look down the ice and snow fields that were to be negotiated. His wish was not to take us down there. I understood him to say it was too hazardous, perhaps there was another reason I missed. It is true that the area looked fairly steep, but in my impression as I look back on it, we could have made it. To me, it appeared as though the trip down would have been easy enough, hopefully not too fast. Climbing back up again, however, may well have been another matter. At the time, I was beginning to become confused. The northeast area was an area to which I felt we had to go. It was a must, but now, all of a sudden, we couldn't get there.

John and I agree that the area needs to be searched. Jim wants us to be able to search the area, therefore we all agree to that. But Jim knows we cannot get down and back up before dark. Now what? Jim has a plan, or maybe it was was Jim and John who had the plan; anyhow, it makes sense to me, even in my emotional, impatient state of mind. Because of the terrain to be negotiated, the best way to get to where we want to go is from the bottom. The plan is to descend the mountain, circle it, and climb up from that side. It's an interesting idea, but certain problems were not being fairly dealt with, I think, by any of us. First of all, could we legally get to the northeast side of the mountain? Did I understand earlier that the northeast side had been closed to all climbers? Would that include us, since Jim had been given complete search privileges of the mountain? Second, if we could go there, would we require additional police approval from Dogubeyazit, the town and area whose jurisdiction we are apparently under, and subsequently pick up additional delay? Thirdly, Redvan mentioned something indicating it would take more time than we had, in order to negotiate a hike to that side, search, and return. When was it first realized that it would take four days to do the job, and Jim and John had only two days left?

Nevertheless, we all agreed to the plan . . . call it a lack of oxygen. One major problem that I should mention, is that we were just in the wrong place to begin with. We were camped on the south side of the mountain, and our original plan of being mobile didn't work. We were packed too heavily, and I was probably the worst one of all. Looking back on it now, hindsight seems to say that we should have made ourselves mobile for at least two days, and descended the snow and ice fields on one day . . . camped, and climbed back out on the following day.

Just before our return to the south side camp and subsequent descent of the mountain, we did a very human thing and climbed to the summit of Ararat, the 16,945 foot peak named Ataturk. We took some pictures, put our names in the book of the mountain (encased in a metal container in ice on top) and then started our journey down. What a trip that turned out to be.

We left the summit at 12:45 p.m., and reached high camp by 1:30 p.m. At 2:15 p.m. we were packed up and gone. It would have been earlier, but I was a few minutes slower than the rest. The trip down was an exhilarating experience. At 4:00 p.m. we reached 4,200 meters, where the horses had left us only two days before. There were no horses there to meet us, as we were two days early. The packs pushed and dragged us, until we staggered into the base camp at 3,200 meters at 6:10 p.m. . . . four hours and 40 minutes to descend what took us two days to climb. We dropped our packs and ourselves for a few minutes' rest. Then, in preparation for the rest of our day's journey, we changed boots and clothes while drinking several bottles of pop that a few enterprising young kids had packed in and offered us for a price. After Jim finished with the reporters who were waiting for us, we started down toward Eli village. We left the base camp at

6:50 p.m. and expected to be in Eli by 9:00 p.m. However, it was 10:10 when we arrived. Neither John nor I could negotiate the rocks very well in the dark, and twisted ankles, sore knees, and blisters took their toll. Jim did better. Redvan and the Turkish policeman that had accompanied us from base camp, I would imagine, were somewhat disappointed by our slow going. We were just experiencing too much of a good thing . . . the Turkish countryside.

When we finally reached Eli village, we were greeted with a lantern to show the way, homemade bread, yogurt, and great hospitality. The ride to Dogubeyazit started out in a pickup, then changed to a police van. Along the way, the Turks filled the van with smoke (they smoked like there was no tomorrow), and the man riding shotgun tried to shoot a coyote or wolf out of the window of the vehicle. Several back roads later we arrived at our hotel and dinner. The press was waiting.

It's Monday, August 27. News that a British climber was shot somewhere on the north side of the mountain while climbing alone has reached us. Reports of who shot him or why vary from the military, because of improper papers, to bandits or villagers, for any number of reasons.

I'm sitting on the balcony of the hotel, alone, drinking some sort of juice, watching the mountain and waiting for our packs to arrive. The packs were to be picked up at the 3,200 meter camp by horses and brought to us. No doubt they are on their way. I'm frustrated to a point. I'm somewhat confused as to how things are turning out, and I'm deep in thought, and in a conversational prayer. I have only questions to ask. Why have I not been able to complete my task, or have I? I should say "we," but right now I'm more concerned with "me." What lessons did I learn? Do I go back up the mountain now, or later, or what? My prayer was for God to take me to the ark. Is the ark the boat-shaped object in the valley, and has He done what I asked, or is it on the mountain? Did we almost get there and fall short on our own? Many more related questions travel the channels of my mind, and through prayer, sleep, and even a dream, through calculations amidst confusion, I came to this conclusion.

First of all, I'm very proud and thankful to have been a member of this expedition, and I hope the association with Jim and John will continue even to the point of another expedition, if that is God's will. At this point, I'm not sure how I will determine whether or not it is God's will. Maybe it is up to Jim and John.

Second of all, I believe that within the boundaries of our limitations, some of which we set ourselves, we did the best we could do. I have peace in that knowledge, but I still have a tremendous unrest in my soul that says the job is not done. The confusing bottom line is that I am dissatisfied.

Third, I am thankful that we all can learn, and should we try again we'll know better how to go about it. There is one area of the mountain, I believe by mutual agreement through previous research, that should have been searched. That is the northeast side. Mistakes were made, but then so was the attempt, and it is important that we were not afraid to try, and even to fail.

Fourth, I knew that I was going home. For me to stick it out alone, since Jim and John were adhering to their schedules and leaving Turkey, would not be a wise move, only an emotional one. I will choose the wise move and go home.

I will not labor this report any further with details of our trip back, only to say we were treated very well by the American military and Major Walsh in Erzurum. Also, the press lived up to the expectations we hold of them, in their quest for news. The end of this trip is to say we returned home, after due travel time, and I saw no reason to keep further notes.

This conclusion pretty well sums up my personal observation along the way. I can only add that although we didn't accomplish what we set out to do, we did not come back empty-handed. With Turkish approval and with the dirt sample confusion cleaned up, Ron Wyatt was able to leave the country with a few of the samples. Is it possible that the boat-shaped object in the valley is the treasure which we so desired to find? We will be awaiting the completed results of any testing to be done on possible artifacts of the boat-shaped object. How these findings will influence further thoughts on the subject of Noah's ark is yet to be determined. I believe it is possible that Noah's ark still rests in hiding, high on the slopes of Greater Ararat awaiting God's chosen time to be revealed. I think it is, therefore, also possible that God had something completely different in mind than we did when he brought us, or at least allowed us, to come this far. Maybe His will has been fulfilled in some obscure way. Reports of the ark search have been in the news now, and maybe for perhaps the first time, a few people of little or no faith in biblical scripture, have begun to wonder about the possibility of any truth to the Genesis account. At the very least, there has been some exposure in the press, maybe more this year than in the past. The thoughts and subconciousness of maybe a few have been touched. In this possibility, positive thoughts concerning the reports of our experience, and optimism toward the future, begin to surface.

Maybe this expedition has prepared the way just a little more than that which has been done in the past. Not to believe this would be, in my opinion, to accept a defeatist attitude. If I have a choice, then I would prefer to believe there is a silver lining somewhere in the clouds of dissatisfaction, and purpose in considering possibly another expedition next year.

THE 1993 ATTEMPT

I went to eastern Turkey again in 1989. John McIntosh was there as well. We spent time and effort, but weren't allowed to climb. I didn't record the events of the year. Basically, we tried to get permission when we arrived, and it was denied. We left Turkey having again not accomplished our goal of searching for and locating the ark. It was a fairly quick trip in 1989. It was the year I finished my book, *The Ark, a Reality?* I did not return to Turkey again until 1993. Why not? I'm not sure. Maybe I didn't feel led to do so, or maybe I was just tired.

There were other expeditions during the years in which I didn't participate. Chuck Aaron and Don Shockey each had teams. Jim Irwin was there again. Now Jim is with the lord. His heart stopped beating 20 years and one day after his return from the moon. It was August 1991. That hurt. I miss Jim Irwin and think about him from time to time. Also, I've thought again of Ararat.

Ararat and the search had been on my mind every year since 1989. Still, I probably wouldn't have gone in 1993 except that I had been encouraged by a few people to lead a team on another search. I must have been ready because a considerable amount of planning went into the expedition. Not that the previous expeditions went without considerable planning, but I really jumped in with both feet this time.

The team was organized, and although much could be said of each member, for the sake of brevity I will introduce them by name, or by name and state only. On the team as originally organized were John McIntosh, Ray Anderson, Ron Lane, Al Jenney, Bob and Margarat Roningen, and myself, who as veterans of previous expeditions made up a combined 30 trips to Turkey. The Roningens, not previously mentioned in this book, are from Minnesota and were members of an expedition led by Dr. Charles Willis in 1988. Also on the team are Joe Presti from California, Gary Duce from Wisconsin, Barnett Duce from Ohio, Rick Perkins from California, and Ross Wutrich from Virginia. They were on their first expedition.

Our plan was to fly in a helicopter and land on the ice cap of

Mount Ararat. We would then search for the location of Noah's ark visually and, if necessary, also with the aid of a subsurface radar unit. We would locate the structure, document its location, and record its exact coordinates using a Global Positioning System. We would measure, record, and photograph our find, then get off the mountain and notify the authorities and the scientific community of the discovery.

Despite our efforts and intentions, all things did not go as planned. There was trouble. Here is an idea of what happened.

We originally consisted of 12 people and called our expedition "The Search for Truth." Well, the truth is that it began to unravel the day before we left the States. Through some freak accident during transportation, a subsurface radar unit which was to be used on the ice of Ararat had been electrically shorted out against the bed of a truck. This rendered the radar unit inoperable. Upon discovering the problem, the Roningens, who were to operate the radar unit as well as photograph the expedition, frantically tried to have the unit repaired in time to join the group. They gave it a valiant effort, and eventually succeeded in the repair. However, because of the problems we had trying to obtain the proper permission, the Roningens remained in the States. The rest of us intended to meet on August 16 in Newark, New Jersey.

Eight of us were present at that meeting. They were Gary Duce, Barnett Duce, Ray Anderson, Al Jenney, Rick Perkins, Joe Presti, John McIntosh, and myself. Missing was Ross Wutrich, whose flight was late, and Ron Lane who was delayed because of a sore back, actually a fairly severe problem. Ross would join us in Antalya, Turkey, a day later, and Ron would join us in two days, still with a sore back.

Although a final decision had not yet been made as we started the trip toward Europe, Al Jenney was preparing to go to Moscow. He had a contact in New York who made a Moscow connection possible. Flight 50 departed at 8:00 p.m. for Frankfort, Germany. During the Atlantic crossing Al and I discussed the value of any information regarding the ark that he could turn up in Moscow. We thought that since Al had a contact in Moscow, and if he could connect with him by phone from Frankfort, that he should make the trip. Arrival in Frankfort was right on schedule. Al made the phone call, made the decision, and made the trip.

Seven of us arrived in Antalya, Turkey, on August 17 and met with Mehmet Noyan of Attalos Travel and Trade, Inc. We chose Antalya for a couple of reasons. First, the helicopter company (Attalos) was located there, and second, because it was somewhat out of the way.

When we arrived in Turkey, the Kurdish Workers Party with the name of Peoples Kurdistan Kurtulus (means "liberty" — considered by Turkish authorities to be an illegal workers party and also a terrorist group otherwise known as the PKK) had increased their offensive action dramatically. Thirteen foreign hostages (tourists) had been taken and quite possibly at least 11 of them were on Mount Ararat. Several people were killed in the area of eastern Turkey. This includes local residents (mostly Kurdish) and Turkish military along with members of the PKK. The situation had become explosive, and that turn of events was definitely not in our favor.

There was fear on the part of some Turkish and U.S. officials that should the PKK capture a handful of Americans, they would use the captives in attempting to apply a definite leverage on any future negotiations. Much of this type of reasoning was used as stumbling blocks in our attempt to get the necessary permissions to complete our expedition. This is understandable and will be brought out later in this report. However, I still believed we would get permission.

Before our departure from the United States, I had asked Mehmet Noyan to go to work in our behalf to ensure we would have the necessary permission to complete our expedition. During my discussions on the phone and via fax with Mehmet Noyan in those weeks before our departure, I learned that because of his efforts in Ankara, Mehmet was 95 percent sure of our obtaining permission for the expedition through the Turkish Ministry. Mehmet had hand-carried our applications to each and every office and had spoken with the appropriate authorities in those offices. There were possibly two problems. One would be with the University of Ataturk at Erzurum because they had been given the final say as to approval of any scientific expeditions, and the second would be with the army chief of staff because of the conflict with the PKK.

We were working on both of those problems. The University of Ataturk could possibly be swayed with a letter from a university in the United States. This seemed to be a requirement in order to be considered. John McIntosh had worked hard on this problem before our departure. It proved to be a formidable problem. Secular universities seemed to have a tough time with our request. Pastor Kenneth Long of Phoenix, Arizona, would provide us with a letter from Southwestern Bible College. We would receive it when in Turkey. However, we would have to remove the word "Bible" from the letterhead. The Bible is not the most read book in this Moslem country and this was to be a scientific expedition and not a religious one.

On the other matter, we had hoped our contacts with senators and congressmen in the United States would help persuade General Dugan Gures, the Army Chief of Staff of Turkey, to see things our way. We had letters of support from two senators and two congressmen to help in this effort. Believing, we went to work with this.

During the first few days in Antalya, Mehmet Noyan, his partner, Eran Ilhan (a former army officer and now an enterprising businessman), Gary Duce, John McIntosh, and I made several phone calls and sent fax messages to the ministry offices in Ankara. We contacted the offices of the congressmen and senators who supported us, and we again contacted various universities in the United States. We also contacted the universities in Ankara and Erzurum, Turkey.

We discussed the operation of the MI-8 helicopter with the pilots. The MI-8 helicopter is a Russian-made aircraft and was the equipment operated by Attalos Travel. The helicopters, however, were owned by a parent company by the name of Em-Air, which is located in Ankara. In my previous in-depth discussions with the management of the company in Ankara, as well as in Antalya, I was assured the MI-8 could do the job I contracted for: namely to land a team on the ice of Ararat and take us off again. Now I hear a different story. Apparently, according to the pilots, the aircraft couldn't do the job as I was originally led to believe. I am told there was a communication problem of some sort between Mehmet and his chief pilot during the time of our previous in-depth discussions. A larger helicopter would have to be found. Mehmet and Ersan knew of an MI-17, but it was in the Ukraine. Ersan would try to establish contact with them. In the meantime, Mehmet phoned the Civil Aviation Authority and did in fact receive verbal permission to operate an MI-17 over Mount Ararat. He was told that written permission would soon follow.

We received the letter from Southwestern Bible College of Phoenix that supported our research team. The letter asked that every consideration be given to us in our attempt to discover the location of the ark. It was addressed to Dr. Bayruktutan of the Department of Geology, Ataturk University, Erzurum, and signed by the academic dean of Southwestern, Dr. Phillip Schafran.

We faxed the letter to Ataturk University in Erzurum and subsequently found out that Dr. Bayruktutan was on vacation. The man in charge during Dr. Bayruktutan's absence was Professor Hamza Atan. We contacted Professor Atan by phone. Mehmet did the talking and the professor was persuaded to give us the written approval. He sent the approval to the Office of Foreign Affairs in

Ankara, and I believe it went either to Mr. Cevdet Ozgun or Mr. Akin, the "number two man" to the chief of staff and now specially assigned to this foreign affairs office. We had the university approval – that was a good start. Mehmet and I then decided it was time to go to Ankara.

I spent a week in Ankara bouncing between offices of the Turkish Ministry trying to obtain the necessary paperwork. This was actually my second trip to Turkey in 1993. The first trip, a month prior to this one, was in part to meet with members of the Gursan family of Em-Air who owned the helicopters. It was also to insure that the required permissions for our expedition would be granted. There was no guarantee then, but there never has been. I think you probably are getting a feel for that now. A difference this year, however, is that I had the assistance of Mehmet Noyan who was to walk our applications through the proper channels of government for me.

On that first trip of this year I had also met with the U.S. ambassador to Turkey, Richard Charles Barkley. It was my intention to inform him of the planned expedition and to ask for his support. This I did. Be assured that I was very graciously received at the American embassy. It was an honor for me to speak with the man representing the United States in Turkey. Concerning the support, he did not say no. It is also true that he did not promise his support, rather he told me that the embassy's function was to protect American citizens traveling in Turkey. The ambassador then asked that I inform the embassy when I return to Turkey with the expedition team.

Now on this second trip I'm told by the embassy that the problem with the PKK in eastern Turkey is getting worse. The problem, as I understand the embassy sees it, is that the PKK are taking foreign tourists as hostages in eastern Turkey. Why are they doing this? Apparently any foreign person who doesn't have a visa for "Kurdistan" is being detained. At least this is one line of reasoning I've heard as to why people are being taken hostage. The problem is, there is no such thing as a visa for Kurdistan! The tourists in this predicament are from Germany, Italy, Britain, and New Zealand. So far there are no United States citizens in the hands of the PKK and the embassy would like to keep it that way.

I am told by a Turkish source that there is also a more involved international plan to open a pipeline that has been closed since the Gulf War. Briefly, I understand that to open the now-closed pipeline, some restrictions would have to be lifted on Iraq because some of the pipeline is in their country. Opening the pipeline would stop the loss of money for Turkey (and Iraq) that its closing caused. You can see there is a problem here. There is also a plan to build a pipeline that would go either through Iran and Nakhichevan or through Georgia. This is all very deep and involved and "secret." Apparently the PKK doesn't want Turkey to prosper, at least until their demands are met. Therefore they don't want the United States and the United Nations to allow the pipeline to open. They probably don't want a new one to be built either for the same reasons. It may be felt that nine American hostages might give the PKK some leverage. If this is even close, then I can understand the embassy's concern for our safety.

I want it to be understood that I explained to the embassy officials that I do not intend to put the team in a situation where becoming a hostage would be likely. Those who had been taken as hostages were on the ground either walking or possibly in a vehicle. We have no intention of making ourselves so available. Our plan is to fly in a commercial helicopter, land on the ice cap of Ararat, do our work, then fly away. The PKK operates far below the icecap of Ararat and wouldn't have the time to reach us before we would be long gone. Also, we would be in constant communications with Turkish military authorities.

Mehmet and I then returned to Antalya. Along the way I thought about the incredible spaghetti-like tangle of red tape that shackled our progress with the Turkish Ministry. I wondered how we would ever be able to cut through it all. I decided if we were supposed to accomplish anything worthwhile then God would have to open the shackles, and the door. All we could do is our absolute best, stay positive, and go forward with no hesitation, believing our permission to fly would be granted.

Now it is Friday morning, August 27, and I am in the office of the chief pilot, Mehmet Sakir. He and a Russian captain and I are studying the manuals and talking about what his twin-engine MI-8 helicopter could actually do. They seem to be stuck on this 4,000 meters figure with only three people on board (plus the pilots) for a high-landing capability. I'm doing my best to convince them there is a safety factor built into the performance charts and the aircraft would perform better if they pushed it just a bit. We added in a wind factor and found that just 15 knots of wind would allow the MI-8 to make the landing at 4,400 meters with three people plus the pilots. They were reluctant still, thinking they wouldn't have 15 knots of wind, but I assured them that I believed we would. It's windy on mountaintops! There is a way and we were making progress; however, there was no way I would accept a landing at 4,000 meters.

That's PKK country, and below that, ice at 4,000 meters would put the team and the chopper in jeopardy. I wanted 4,800 meters (15,800 feet), but 4,400 meters (14,500 feet) would be a satisfactory compromise. I was giving serious consideration to the MI-17.

Here is some data that may give you a brief technical difference between the two aircraft. The MI-8 helicopter has two 1,500-hp engines. It has a service ceiling of 4,500 meters (14,850 feet) at a gross weight of 12,000-kg (26,400 lbs.). If the MI-8 was not loaded to gross weight, it could fly higher. (A service ceiling is basically calculated to be the maximum altitude an aircraft is capable of attaining under standard conditions pertaining to variables of air density, altitude, ambient temperature, gross weight, etc.) The MI-8 has a three-hour range at a speed of 225 km/h (125 mph).

In comparison, the MI-17 has two 2,200-hp engines. It has a service ceiling of 6,000 meters (19,800 feet) at a gross weight of 13,000-kg (28,600 lbs.). The MI-17 has a three-hour range at a speed of 240 km/h (133 mph). The MI-17 is a more powerful aircraft, being able to travel a little farther in the same time period, climb higher, and, according to the manual, land and take off at 4,400 meters with a nine-member team and two pilots easily. Naturally I would prefer the MI-17, but for reasons mentioned in this report, I am working with the pilots on trying to determine the capability of the MI-8.

If the MI-8 were used, we would land three of us, then the chopper would shuttle a second three-man team to follow the first three. The second team would be a four-man team if the wind was strong and the chopper performed well above their expectations. Two men would not get on the mountain, but they would be able to see Ararat as we all would on the initial fly-by. All nine of us would then be on board. I knew that the fly-by was possibly all we would get. With the concern over safety of our team regarding the PKK, the shuttle would have to originate in the security of the Kars Airport just over 40 miles away from Ararat.

The first three-man team would be Gary and Barnett Duce and myself. I believed the Duce brothers to be fast and strong with a good amount of ice-climbing experience, and I knew where we had to go. The second team would be John McIntosh, Joe Presti, Rick Perkins, and Ross Wutrich. Ron Lane and Ray Anderson, because of possible health reasons, would not climb the ice. Ron still had a sore back, painfully sore, and it was tough for him to walk, sit, or lie down. He could stand just fine and standing he was — standing strong and there with us no matter the pain he had to endure.

As the pilots and I discussed the necessity of landing on the ice cap, I attempted to be positive and convince them the job could be done. When I was told it was "impossible," I let them know with absolute certainty that is was indeed possible and would be done. (I hate the word "impossible." I don't like the word "no." I heard them a lot on this trip.)

Mehmet and Ersan were brought into the discussion as we went from office to office and the discussions occasionally reached a feverous pitch. The meetings ended favorably and Ersan later informed me the pilots agreed to try. He had offered them a $1,000.00 bonus.

Today is Saturday, August 28. The Turkish government offices, like those of the United States, close down for the weekend, and Monday is a holiday. Wednesday, the first of September, is the day we have targeted as our day of decision. That's the day we either fly or pay the bills and prepare to go home.

During this day I received a message that Al Jenney, our team member in Moscow, had been called home. It was business at the request of the U.S. government. During his stay in Moscow, Al did a good bit of research and had articles published in a science/religious magazine as well as being interviewed for an article published in a newspaper. He even managed to have part of my book published in the Russian language. It's all part of the search for the ark.

Ron Lane and I went to the Attalos office today. We met with Ersan and then with Mehmet. We discussed the time we had remaining and the possibility of the M-17 arriving from the Ukraine within that time frame. It had to be here by Tuesday in order for all the team members to be a part of the expedition. Beyond Tuesday, the MI-8 was the only option, and the only way the travel company would make a substantial profit would be to land on the ice cap. I'm not paying the full, originally agreed-upon price when the company cannot do the job originally agreed upon. In short, the touchdown on the ice is worth $10,000. Over and above his expenses, just a fly-by will not net the company the profit they had hoped for.

We were told the pilots flew to 5,000 meters (16,500 feet) with a group of eight tourists on board. They tested the machine and found that they could reach that altitude and could therefore make the flight with the MI-8. Well, I knew that! The fact remains, in order for Attalos to make the profit they want to make, we have to do the job as agreed upon.

Sunday, a day of rest; a day of reflection; a day of sightseeing and a museum. I am a tourist on this day. I sit alone in an outdoor café above the bay, the ancient harbor of Antalya. The café, named Kalebar Café, is built on a foundation wall that dates back to King Attalos in about 150 B.C. The walls were rebuilt during the ninth century. I understand this to be the period of the Seljuks. The purpose of the walls was to keep out invading forces of the enemies. A light breeze provides motion to a red and white Turkish flag.

It's a warm day. All the days have been warm and the heat seems to comfort me as I look to the sky — blue, cloudless, and complete in its perfection as is the abode of God which is where I direct my prayer. Tomorrow is Monday. It's a holiday. I'm told it's Victory Day. It commemorates a day about 70 years ago when Kemel Ataturk beat the Greeks. Ataturk is considered the father of modern Turkey. I think that is what the name implies. I am looking now to my Father — the one in heaven. I too want a Victory Day. We must fly on Tuesday. We must get the permission.

Monday, August 30. This morning I wore a jacket and tie to the Attalos Travel office. I told everyone at breakfast that it was an "attitude change day." I was doing my best to hide a deep concern; the positive outlook was probably going to do me more good than anyone. I asked Ron and John to join me and we went to the Attalos Travel office where we met with both Ersan and Mehmet, and there was some discussion about the flight. It is determined that the MI-17 will not be available. Paperwork, money, distance, and time. The MI-8 is now the obvious choice. Sakir, the Turkish chief pilot, was there, and again he falls back to the concern surrounding the landing. I'm tired of dealing with this as a problem. Ron and I simply laid it on the line. Basically it went like this: "We are landing at 4,400 meters. Period! You figure out how you're going to do that, but that's what we will do!"

I then told Mehmet that we expected a green light in the morning. We wanted the flight to take off at 11:00 a.m. We would fly to Erzurum and on to Ararat with two fuel stops along the way. (We had already considered our reroute of flight and were ready to file it with the Civil Aviation Authority.) I said, "Tomorrow is the last opportunity for the entire group. We have to fly tomorrow. Plan on it!"

Tonight I will pray with the team and plan our flight. I will share it with them that we will have the word by 11:00 a.m. and will leave then. It's a faith thing. We still don't have permission.

Tuesday, August 31. I'm in Mehmet Noyan's office by 9:00 a.m. and we're on the phone to Mr. Akin in Ankara. I asked him, "When can I expect the permission?" He replied that one of the ministries had said "no." He wouldn't tell me which ministry. The phone call ended.

Okay, now that we've gotten that answer, how do we get around it? I need a miracle! Then Mehmet got mad. He phoned the president of tourism in Turkey, Mr. Basaram Ulusoy. I don't understand that language. I do know that whenever a Turkish man operates a telephone in an agitated state of mind, he gets very loud! I so believed we were going to get this permission that I think I had convinced Mehmet as well. We actually had the pilots standing by to take the team to the airport, and we still didn't have permission.

Mehmet ended his phone call in utter frustration that nothing could be done.

THEN THE DOOR OPENED!

Mehmet Sakir, the chief pilot, informed us that the governor of Erzurum had gone on holiday and a very good friend of his was the army commander of that region. Mehmet said the commander was now in charge of everything that happened there with regard to permissions out of Erzurum. We knew that we could legally fly as far as Erzurum without any special permission, it was east of there that was the problem. Sakir called his friend and spoke with him for just a short time and the word came back as "YES"!

It was a verbal approval and in a few short minutes, due to the marvelous invention of the fax machine, we had written approval. The restrictions are that we won't be allowed to fly below 9,000 feet (so we won't get shot down), and we won't be allowed to take photographs. It will be a visual flight around Ararat only. It wasn't 11:00 a.m., it was mid afternoon, but we were on our way!

At 4:15 p.m. we left the hotel on the move – at last — after two weeks to the day from our arrival in Turkey. The Bible verse from Isaiah 40:31 spoke to me in a big way: "They that wait upon the Lord shall renew their strength; they shall mount up with wings as eagles."

At 5:08 p.m. we lifted off! In a nutshell, here's the brainstorm. Across the northeastern side of the mountain we would fly and visually search. So far there will be no touchdown and no photos, but we were on our way and certainly the plan would be revised en route. If a landing was to take place to confirm a sighting, we would drop a select team – the two Duces and myself – on the ice. We would leave the rest of the team in Kars, 50 miles northwest of Ararat, and if the opportunity presents itself, we would shuttle from there. That was the new revised plan — GOD WILLING.

I noticed something very special. The registration letters of the helicopter were TC-HER. I read it as "Touch Her". Mount Ararat is known by the Armenians as "Mother of the World." We wanted very much to touch her. I expected we would.

I got out of my seat and walked up to the cockpit and watched the crew perform their duties. The nomenclatures of the flight instruments, switches, and circuit breakers were written in Russian, so much of what I was looking at I couldn't quite figure out, but I did recognize the vertical speed indicator, the altimeter, and air speed indicator. The engine instrument needles were all registering in the green arc (or blue, as it was), and this told me both engines were performing very well.

We were climbing at about 145 km/hr, which equates to around 90 mph. We climbed to an indicated 4,450 meters, which is an altitude of approximately 14,685 feet above sea level. We were heavy, with three pilots up front, three relief pilots in the back, along with nine team members — that's 15 people plus a lot of heavy luggage and a full load of fuel. Sikar told me the helicopter was performing very well at this altitude. Our cruise speed is 180 km/hr or about 113 mph.

We landed at the Adona Airport at 7:15 p.m. It was still legal daylight and we could see a full moon. The rules specify we cannot fly at night, so we stay here, one night at the Sedef Hotel. It's prayers of thanksgiving, a dinner, and a short night's sleep. We're up by 4:15 in the morning. By 5:55 a.m. we're in the air again. It's nearly dawn, the moon is full, the sun is reaching to find its way above the horizon, and the sky is clear. I watch the blades of the blue and white MI-8 spin above me, lifting this mechanical grasshopper-shaped machine upward. Below the valleys are shrouded in fog that weaves its way into a blanket of white with specks of green sprinkled randomly as the trees try to claim the early dawn.

The sun shows itself in our eyes by 6:14 a.m. and I'm studying the blue on the dented fuel tank, which is in my view out the window. It is streaked like it was painted with a brush over some shade of brown, which was its former color. This particular machine was once configured inside with easy chairs and a desk. It was the private aircraft of the one-time Soviet President Brezhnev! Wouldn't it somehow be ironic if this machine, once operated by an atheist government, was the one to carry a Christian team and sight the structure of Noah's ark on the mountain called Ararat?

We ride above the top of an overcast; we're "on top" until mountain peaks pierce the blanket of white on either side. Then at 7:25 we see the green hills below, terraced like that of many farms, and there's a river. We touch down on at Elazig at 8:10 in the morning,

September 1. The fuel stop takes longer than anticipated, but we used that time to again modify the plan.

Originally we had planned the next leg of the flight to go from Elazig to Erzurum, then a fuel stop and on to Kars for a landing. I had wanted to fly around Ararat before landing in Kars. The legs would go Elazig to Erzurum to refuel, then Erzurm to Ararat on a fly-by, and on to Kars for a landing. The pilots had argued that the helicopter didn't have the range. They said what I wanted to do would have them landing at Kars with less than minimum fuel and the Russian pilot who was the aircraft commander said "no." (I remember his name to be Alexander.) They wanted to land in Kars first, refuel, and then fly the mountain. If a mistake was made, this could have been the place.

On this flight, Alexander, the Russian, was in command of the aircraft and Sikar, the Turkish pilot, was in charge of the flight and the associated handling. It is confusing, but the rules demanded a Russian captain on the Russian-made chopper. The Russian captain was in charge of flying the aircraft and he knows the machine. He is supposed to know the range it can fly and the distance to travel. He has to have a fuel reserve onboard when he reaches his destination and he has to plan the flight appropriately. I gave him that credit.

However, in retrospect, as I study the map and figure the distances involved, I believe his educated guess on how much fuel would be remaining after an Erzurum-Ararat-Kars leg of flight was an especially cautious one. The captain was extremely conservative, and he wanted a very safe and large reserve of fuel upon landing at Kars. I believe the flight I proposed which included a quick fly-by of Ararat and a landing at Kars, could have been made with an adequate reserve of fuel on board. The captain said "no." I think he and I should have discussed this a little further. Still, even if our discussion would have reached an intensified level, he is the captain; what he says is law. I certainly understand that.

I know this could get confusing, but please stay with me. Because the Erzurum-Ararat-Kars leg was given a thumbs down by the Russian captain, then bypassing Erzurum completely was sensible in that it saved time. The captain decided we had the fuel to fly from Elazig to Kars without a stop in Erzurum, rather than flying Erzurum, Ararat, Kars. There was some merit to this because I was concerned about the inspection we would face if we landed at Erzurum.

I knew also that a fuel truck had been dispatched to meet us in Kars and it should be waiting there when we arrived. To the best of my knowledge, the military authorities in Kars were not part of this permission game yet, so we would possibly get in and out of Kars en route to Ararat before they would stop us. Because the chopper captain had said "no" to the Erzurum-Ararat-Kars leg I had proposed, and because of the reasons just given, I decided to bypass Erzurum and go to Kars. I believed we would be able to do the job from Kars as long as we moved quickly.

At 9:30 a.m. we lifted off and climbed above the rugged terrain and experienced an eagle's eye view of eastern Turkey. A few puffy summer clouds accent the hot summer sky, then Gary and Barnett witnessed the flashes and smoke of artillery tank fire somewhere before us. We were about to touch down in bandit country. The PKK and the Turkish military were at war. At 11:46 a.m. we touched down at the Kars Airport. I had known the airport was reported to be secure so we hadn't tossed safety away, but I hoped the security police would leave us alone just long enough for us to refuel and take off.

We looked for the fuel truck, but it wasn't to be seen. Sakir went to phone the company in Antalya to find out its progress. Ersan told Sakir that the fuel had been dispatched out of Erzurum and was supposed to have left there by 8:00 this morning. The eastern Turkey highways would give the fuel truck a four-hour drive. We expected it at any time. We waited, and waited some more.

Time dragged on and then a problem developed between Sakir, the Turkish pilot, and myself. He said it was now too windy to fly. I disagreed. He said he had just talked with a police chopper pilot and the policeman told him it was too windy. Now we were getting the police involved. This was not a good sign. Sakir said it was getting too cloudy. Well, the summertime convectional buildups can be expected, but from here we couldn't see Ararat; we didn't know if it was covered or not. I didn't agree with that excuse, either. Then he said that the airport closes at 5:30 and that we could never get back by then. Sakir said that we would have to pay a fine.

I thought about that. In 1986, when two Turks, a Dutchman, and I flew Ararat in a Cessna 206 we arrived in Erzurum after the airport had shut down and that probably contributed to the authorities' closing down our flight and not allowing us to fly the next day.

Then, I quizzed Sakir on how much the fine would be. He didn't know, but he was tired and the flight was shut down for today. We had been awake since 4:15 in the morning, so he was probably tired. It was 3:00 p.m. and the fuel truck still hadn't arrived. A military officer who could speak some English walked up and asked to see all of our passports. I guess he was passport control. Then he asked to see my permission. I showed it to him. He looked at it, said it wasn't enough, then asked to take it. He promised to copy it and bring it back to me. I just smiled and said "Of course you may copy it." I gave it to him and said nothing else. He smiled and walked away — with our permit.

That evening when Mehmet Sakir showed up at the Turistik Hotel Temel in Kars, where our team had checked in, I was informed that the fuel truck had arrived and the helicopter was now about ready to go. The seats were being removed to lighten the aircraft and theoretically help our climb.

I was then informed that the base of the mountain we wanted to land on top of was under artillery fire from the Turkish military and that aircraft were bombing PKK targets in the same vicinity.

In the meantime, we were invited to have dinner at the Officer's Club. I'm told the military Officer's Club is an old Russian building. It was about a four-story structure with armed guards at the door. The service we received was very good. Young soldiers were doing their best to impress us and also their superiors. We ate chicken and onion and salads and melon and some things I couldn't identify, along with Baklava for dessert. I had always thought Baklava was a Greek dish and I was curious. The Turks told me the Baklava was Turkish and that there are six kinds of the sweet dessert. The Greeks just stole it. I initially understood that we were their guests, but later I found out there was a catch when I was presented with the bill to pay for the meal.

While we were enjoying our dinner, the military passport control officer who had taken our permit walked in with a couple of other officers. They sat together with Sakir and had a conference. After about half an hour of this, the military officer turned to me and said, "I don't think it is a good idea to fly. A military operation is starting and it's very dangerous and we cannot give security." I replied, "We fly." The military officer then handed back the permit and said, "No photos, no landing, visual okay." That meant that we could still fly. I thanked him, smiled, and shortly thereafter, thought it was best that while we were still ahead, the team leave and return to the hotel.

It turns out that on this day and the previous day, in addition to the killing of an unknown (at least to me) number of PKK, and perhaps several innocent people in the area of Ararat, several Turkish soldiers were also killed. Eighteen were killed in the border town of Aralik in an ambush and 12 more were killed, apparently by a mine, as their truck drove over it while they were on the way to help the 18. Also, 34 soldiers were killed in a fight, primarily by a missile, or missiles, fired from the hidden areas of Ararat's base.

Well, one thing for sure, our timing for this trip was really lousy.

During the night the local police chief had found out about us and arrived at the hotel demanding to see the pilots. Also during the night, and on a larger scale of events, Iran attacked Armenia in defense of Azerbaijan. This angered the Turks who were friends of Azerbaijan. If anyone were to help Azerbaijan, the Turks wanted it to be themselves, not Iran. The main reason the Turks hadn't come to the aid of Azerbaijan was that they were waiting for the go-ahead, or for some action, from the United Nations. That was slow coming.

The border of Iran and Armenia is only a short dozen or so miles from Mount Ararat. Turkish troops were pouring into the area and they were on alert. This was not good for us. What was good for us was that anticipation ran high, and we expected a great day — we were greatly excited about what we believed would happen. Also, Ron woke up without back pain. This was the first time this had happened since before he left the States to join us. This, too, was an answer to prayer by our team. Everyone felt great!

At 5:15 a.m. we reached the helicopter by means of three taxicabs (for all of us) and found it to be surrounded by armed policemen. We were then told that the governor of Kars had ordered the police chief to stop our flight. This wasn't legal, because we had prior permission, but that was only my point of view. The permission we had was from the army commander at Erzurum. If the fuel truck had been on time, if there had been no war, we could have flown yesterday.

However, this was today, there was war, and now we were in Kars. The governor of Kars had not been asked for his approval of our flight, and he didn't like that fact. I can assume the police chief had notified the governor that we were there. We were told to wait until 8:30 or 9:00 a.m. until the governor arrived. Sakir was in an argument with the policeman present, and then on the phone to the police chief (who later showed up), but all to no avail. We were not allowed to board the chopper and complete our mission.

It is 8:30, then 9:00 a.m. Time passed by, police came and went, and Sakir went with them to speak with the governor. We wait. Time passes.

The local military commander now shows up at the airport, apparently to see some people off on a THY flight (the only one of the day), which was en route to Erzurum and Istanbul. This commander took an interest in what was going on and decided he himself would see that we didn't go anywhere any time soon. Also, a telex or a message of some sort had come down from the powers that be in Ankara to order that our flight be stopped. Things were shaping up rather poorly by this time.

The orders given to us and our pilots were to fly back to where we came from and abandon the mission. They assured that we would do that by putting a policeman (plain clothes) on the chopper with us to be our on-board escort. I was convinced by then that it was time to pull back as far as Erzurum and regroup. Also, telephone contact out of Kars to Antalya in an attempt to reach Mehmet and Ersan was extremely difficult, while phone conversations in the larger city of Erzurum would have been better.

As the helicopter was being prepared for the return flight, I went back to the hotel, paid the bill, and returned. While I was gone, a policeman told the climbing team and pilots to leave, that I was not coming back. They waited, I came back, and we left. I wondered what that policeman thought was going to happen to me.

It was reported after we left the airport that there had been a gun battle, and that the PKK killed two policemen. It's not clear whether they were at the airport or had just left the airport on their way to a town named Idir, or were in town near the hotel — I heard all three stories.

We landed in Erzurum and I checked us into the Grand Erzurum Hotel. It's the best in the city, located in the center of the city and well protected. It's also a place I had stayed several times over the years on earlier expeditions. I recommend it. We stayed there that night and into the next day. We were then told by Attalos to return to Antalya. They want the helicopter back. We are informed that our permission has been revoked. All permissions will be denied for us to continue our search effort. The telex from Ankara stood. Our expedition was over.

On September 3, 1993, at 1:40 p.m., while en route from Elazig to Capadocia, fuel stops on our long journey back to Antalya, Ron Lane wrote a note and handed it to me. The note reads:

> Dick,
>   It just occurred to me to remind you of the trials and tribulations, the sufferings, the disease, the loss of family, etc. of the biblical character of Job. Never once did he question God's reasons for bringing so much hardship to him. In spite of everything, he kept the faith. Even though he did not understand why or what purpose God intended, Job remained strong. Sure enough God did reward him with greater

riches than he had previously. It occurs to me that we as a team are much like Job in that we have been continually tested as to our belief. Perhaps our sufferings have not been as great as Job's, perhaps some minor ridicule as to our beliefs.

Keep the faith. Ask only for wisdom to recognize what God's will for us is, and from the Lord's prayer — Thy will be done.

Your friend – Ron

2000 — TOO OLD TO CLIMB?

There is a bitter cold wind against our faces and the way is long, strenuous, and we're climbing. After a couple of hours, we reached the top of a rise where the travel toward Lake Kop promised to be relatively flat. It's the plain, or plateau, on the western side of the mountain where had we continued in the direction of Lake Kop, we would have passed the area where Kurdish shepherds had treated us to cay (tea) a little more than a week ago. As it is now, I expect to walk over the plateau, pass Lake Kop, climb up the steep and rocky hillside that follows, and then cross the few yards of relatively easy terrain which slopes down to a wide area of grass, and rocky morains — an extensive flat area of difficult terrain. The rocky terrain contains numerous glacial melt-water streams at elevations of approximately 11,000–11,500 feet. Then we will reach the place where we can begin our long and slow climb to pass by last year's camp at 12,000 feet and continue up (and I mean up) the most difficult area of the mountain I've experienced until now. I expect that we'll be at the 14,000-foot camp by late afternoon. We will spend the night there.

The plan is that Dave (Larsen, my climbing partner) and I will do just what Paul and I did, except we will push on past the place the weather stopped us on that previous climb. We will walk over and pass behind the upper part of the Ray Anderson site and continue up to Cakmak Peak at 16,500 feet. Then we will continue down and around the 16,000-foot peak to descend the east ridge (quickly) to a place we can descend (rappel, if necessary) into the gorge and investigate the three or four areas of interest. We will find a place in the gorge to spend another night. What we find along the way will influence our decision on how long we stay in the area. Our direction of departure will be over the same miserable terrain by which we left the mountain on the previous descent. That was the plan. However, as should by now be expected, the unexpected happened.

Kannot, our guide, said something about wanting to stop and

camp. We said, "No, we go to the ice." Although he was well aware of the plan, and since he was with me on the previous climb, Kannot certainly knew the way. In retrospect, perhaps I should have been more specific about the ice we go to. Then again, maybe not. He had his own plan. A short time later, Kannot says (in the motion of hand and only the few English words he knows), "We must go to the right of Kop and climb a ridge."

"Why?" I ask.

"Jandarma," he says. I argue that there are no jandarma and we will not be stopped. "Jandarma," he says, and turns to the right. I thought maybe he had a cell phone call when I wasn't paying attention and maybe there is something I don't know. Maybe our agreement with the authorities wasn't exactly solid as rock and he had found this out in a phone call. But if that is the case, then why wasn't I given this information? If the agreement had been breached, then Mahmut would have phoned Kannot and asked to speak with me. This had not happened, and Kannot was climbing fast away from us and going in a direction I was beginning to question.

We had little choice except to follow Kannot. He had the largest of my two packs on his back. That was his purpose on this trip — to carry the weight. I knew that even in this new direction we traveled that we could reach our destination. It would just be a longer and more difficult trip. The terrain ahead of us was steep and the rocks promised to be the kind that cause you to slide down a few steps for each few gained. They are loose and hard to climb over. So what's new?

Then Kannot, who at 23 years of age and strong, and far ahead of Dave and me, turns farther to the right and heads toward the ice cave — the "eye of the bird." I do not want to go there. That is entirely the wrong direction and takes us away from our objective. He has my pack and he moves quickly. He is way out in front and won't respond as we holler for him to stop. I need that pack and he is taking it in the wrong direction. Kannot has his mind set on the ice cave. We have to follow him; he has my stuff!

Something else is beginning to be of concern. The cloud cover is heavy and the weather is closing in. I realize that I am not able to see the ice cave much of the time, and the upper part of the mountain in front of us is obscured in clouds. What I don't seem to realize, however, is how close to vertical the ice and terrain is above the ice cave. The reason that is becoming important is because if Kannot continues in this direction, we'll have to climb the mountain to the ice cap from wherever Kannot decides to stop. We're on a time schedule and this new direction of travel is rapidly cutting into that schedule. We may not have time to retrace our steps and get back to the climb we had planned and, too, we may not be able to climb the ice or the rock above the ice cave in order to reach the ice cap.

Over rocks, sliding down rocks, falling down, getting back up and climbing over big and bigger rocks, splashing through a melt-water stream that has found its place between, over, under, and among the rocks. We're tired, aggravated, a little wet, and generally "ticked off." By the time Dave and I catch up with Kannot, he is resting on a ridge below the stretch of ice that leads to the ice cave. The pack he has been carrying is on the ground.

The argument (I'll call it a "discussion") that followed was one to behold. Kannot and I have a definite language problem but I endeavored to made myself completely understood as to how I felt about his direction of travel. Kannot says, "We camp here."

I said, "No, we go to our camp." I pointed back to my left, which was in the direction we had planned to climb.

He said :"No, we camp here."

In anger, I tossed my pack to the ground. Then I said (among other things), "We cannot camp here. We must go to the top."

He said, "No — cannot." He also replied with a few more things in his language which I couldn't understand. Kannot, who had wanted to camp shortly after we had begun the work of this day, had made up his mind to take charge of the events of the day and camp right on this spot and go no farther. As far as Dave and I were concerned, to agree with that decision was absolutely out of the question for the success of this mission.

Kannot, Dave, and I had a further "discussion." When I decided the discussion was over, I picked up the pack that Kannot had been carrying, removed his sleeping gear, leaving it with him, and put the pack on my back. Then in my right hand I took my other pack, the smaller one which I had been carrying and said to Kannot, "You go back to Dogubeyazit." He was fired! "We camp there." I pointed up beyond the ice cave to the top. After I made that statement and looked up in the direction above and beyond the ice cave, which I then could see were two identical caves, side by side, looking to me like a double-barrel shotgun pointing right at me. The heavy cloud cover gave way for a few seconds and the near vertical and seemingly "impossible to climb" terrain above the ice cave came into view. Then the clouds took over again. Everything above us was obscured.

Dave and I had a decision to make. Do we go back down the more than a thousand feet we had just gained (it took us nearly four hours to do that while we were trying to catch up to Kannot)? Do we climb the rocky ridge to the ice, put on crampons and walk up to the ice cave (or caves) and maybe camp there if a climb above the caves was out of the question? Do we attempt to climb the rocks well to the left of the ice cave till we reach the ice cap? Could we shortcut the distance and the time to the 14,000-foot campsite by climbing this direction among all these rocks? Certainly not by the end of the day. Then, would we find a suitable place to camp if we chose this latter direction? Would the weather get us before we were ready for it?

I knew we had wasted a lot of this day, and the mountain yet above us was enshrouded in a dense cloud cover. What was clear was that if we descended to the plain that takes us to Lake Kop then we could no longer reach the 14,000-foot camp we had initially intended to reach before dark. Most likely we could not even reach the 12,000-foot camp. It was now early afternoon. Over six hours had passed since we had left the four-wheel-drive truck. By choosing to descend and pick up on the planned route and continue past Lake Kop, it would take the rest of the day and all of tomorrow morning to get us to a place on the ice just above the campsite at 14,000 feet. We would be exhausted, and to go on the ice at that time could be suicide. There is also the fact that we now have more weight to carry. Kannot is no longer on the team. Could I even climb any higher, let alone to the 12,000 and 14,000 foot camps with this extra weight on my back? Another factor — the weather was closing in.

Dave and I divided the weight of the three packs into two, and proceeded to climb a ridge in front of us toward the ice cave. That was a bigger job then I ever thought it could be. Rocks of all sizes rolled when we stepped on them. That slowed us down when we were needing to hurry to accomplish something before the end of the day. Discouragement was lingering in the background as we continued toward the ice cave without a clear-cut plan. Then we reached a very deep vertical drop-off that completely changed our direction of travel.

Kannot had lied to me about the jandarma. There were none. Our way of travel, according to the original plan, would have been clear. In the middle of our "discussion" I had asked Kannot for his cell phone to call Mahmut. Kannot said, "No credit," meaning there was no credit left on the phone. We couldn't get Dave's cell phone to work, and I didn't have one. Then a few minutes later, Kannot was on the phone. Obviously he had "credit." I have no idea who he phoned on that call. Finally, he did call Mahmut and was told to do everything I told him to do. However, Kannot and I had a communications problem. I was angry and I told him to go back to Dogubeyazit. I couldn't depend upon him and that kind of relationship is the last thing we need on a mountain. Kannot had indicated we would have no problem reaching the ice below the ice cave, but there was a problem. It was inaccessible from this approach. The deep vertical drop-off that threatened to prevent Dave and I from climbing higher, extended as far in either direction that we could see.

Basically, Kannot did not know the terrain, and even though he was being paid for his help, he was too lazy to carry my expedition-size pack to the previously planned 14,000-foot camp. He saw ice that was "low down" and decided he would take my pack there and then lay down and sleep a few days while Dave and I figured out how to climb the near-vertical ice and rocks to the ice cap and beyond and back again.

Dave and I had our ropes and could have rappelled off of the ridge, but to climb out of the "pit" that rappel would have put us in just didn't seem to be an option. We turned to our left, paralleling the vertical drop, and continued to climb toward the far left of the glacial ice finger that surrounds the ice cave. It was at least in generally the correct direction toward the campsite at 14,000 feet. We crossed the glacial stream previously crossed when trying to catch Kannot, and we stopped long enough to fill our water bottles. We stumbled in the rocks and were blessed when we found a solid sandstone formation that provided us with good footing for a time that seemed all to short.

Dave and I reached the end of our uphill climb when a few raindrops promised that the rest of the day and probably the night would present us with a problem we really didn't care to face. There was going to be a storm. With the weather closing in all around us, we talked it over, prayed, and decided we had better head back down and find a reasonable place to camp and wait out the storm. Still, we were hesitant in doing so. In trying not to lose too much altitude we initially traveled to our left in the general direction of Lake Kop. We didn't want to quit this attempt to complete our job, and delayed our descent as long as we could. There was some hope (though not much) that we could find a sheltered place to sit out the storm while we were still on this part of the mountain. Then the rain and sleet began to fall and we did begin our descent. It was downhill, and I mean downhill. That was a trip I'll not forget anytime soon.

The mountain moved, and rocks of every size and description were on the mountain. Every step turned into an adventure, and not the kind that I thought I had "signed up" for. Rockslides were our constant companion. Dave and I slipped, fell, slid, rolled, and simply crashed at least 20 or 30 times each on the way down this treacherous and dangerous part of Ararat. It's a part of the mountain that I've never heard of anyone trying to climb up or down. There was the rain and sleet, then, too, there was the wind. I would guess it was blowing about 40–50 mph, and every time we'd try to stand — down we would go. Fortunately, the fall was usually backwards and I would land with my backpack protecting me from the jagged rocks, and I would slide till I stopped. Dave had similar experiences. On at least two occasions I went head over heals and I experienced a tumble or two that should have left me with broken legs, ankles, and arms. But, by the grace of God, I survived. I did pick up a new limp not unlike the one I "earned" on the previous climb a week and a half earlier. We "rolled" onto a fairly level place and tried to hide from the wind behind a row of rocks, and make some sort of a camp. We were beat-up and absolutely exhausted. Nine hours had passed since we had gotten out of the vehicle for what we had hoped and expected to be a profitable day. It was 3:15 p.m.

August 27. Last night we were treated to a wind that must have reached 60 mph, a drop in temperature, and a rain that we weren't really prepared for. I kept dry in my one-man tent, which I used as a bivy sack since I couldn't put up the tent in the wind. Dave's bibby sack turned out not to be as waterproof, yet he still laughed it off (at least I think he was laughing). The morning found us a bit chilled and ready to get off of that mountain. We had wasted a day of valuable time, and Dave and I each had a plane to catch. I believe that we could have completed our job and located the objects which we saw on my photographs and on Paul's video, and maybe even found the ark, had Kannot had given us a bad steer that cost us a day of valuable time. But it happened. If you consider the two attempts on the previous climb, as well as give credit to the serious consideration of the third attempt which was decided against due to reasons previously mentioned, then this could possibly be considered the fourth attempt this year to reach the top of the Ray Anderson site, Cakmak Peak, and now the east ridge. Again I am faced with the questions: Was the opposition just too strong, or is it just not the right time for a discovery? I choose to believe that the time wasn't right. The opposition is not too strong. God's in charge. He must be, He kept us alive.

At 8:15 a.m. we started another descent. From this part of the mountain, the remaining descent wasn't too difficult. It was just a walk down a very long, steep, and rocky hill. We did manage to find a couple of boulder fields to cross. I guess we just couldn't pass up those opportunities. But we also found the Lake Kop road, and that was a relief. Dave's cell phone worked just once, and that's all we needed. He reached a friend in the city, and Dave told him to send someone to find us. That was at 12:30 p.m., and by 2:00 p.m. Mahmut, with Hollywood driving, had reached us as we walked on the Lake Kop road. They somehow managed it in a two-wheel-drive car. Dave and I were on our way back to Dogubeyazit. Kannot was nowhere to be seen. Due to a decision by his employer, he will lose his job at least for such a period of time as it takes him to learn to do what he is told while employed. Is that fair? Maybe, and maybe not.

August 28. The expedition is over for now. Dave and I have to return to our responsibilities in the States.

On August 29, Dave and I left Murat Camping on our individual journeys back to the States. I returned to the States one month to the day since I left on this second trip of the year, the 19th since my 1st trip in 1984. Another "vacation" is over. This time I didn't come back completely empty — I have a limp. It's a temporary thing.

So here we have another report. When the facts are in, I'm sure we'll find the U.S. government knows all about the location of the object on Ararat which could well be the ark. If so, then they have purposely suppressed the information. There could be a couple of reasons for this action. One would be to protect their military interests and investments in Turkey. A find such as the ark would no doubt bring Christians, Jews, and Moslems from around the world to see this truth. The discovery of tremendous historical and scientific implications could bring about a religious revival, and in Turkey any increase in the Islamic party because of the discovery would possibly threaten the political arm of government as well as the military control over the country.

There is also the fact that educational institutions of the world would be threatened. In the battle of creationism versus evolution, consider if you will, the plight of the scientist, the teacher of "scientific" thought, and those whom he has influenced. Henry and John Morris say, "The evolutionary philosophy thoroughly dominates the curricula and faculties of secular colleges and universities today, as well as the schools of the large religious denominations. It is not well known, however, that this philosophy has also had considerable effect on many evangelical Christian colleges." "It is bad enough for theological 'liberals' to embrace evolutionism, but absolutely inexcusable for those who profess to believe the Bible and to follow Christ."[1] The key word here is "inexcusable."

I sat in church on two occassions this past year when I myself heard a preacher speak of long ages and, in so doing, indicated evolution with some rational for his belief. I confronted the preacher on each of the two occassions by letter, and what I thought to be a reasonable approach to a future discussion. Although I was complimented on what the pastor referred to as "a scholarly work" on my first contact, on the second I was ignored. I no longer attend that church, but that's not the point. The point is that he is a product of what he has been taught, and I'm of the belief that what he and others with a similar background and belief teach, is a compromise, and not the truth. "For the invisible things of him from the creation of the world are clearly seen, being understood by the things that are made; even his eternal power and Godhead; so that they are without excuse" (Rom. 1:20). The apostle Paul said:

> O Timothy, keep that which is committed to thy trust, avoid profane and vain babblings, and oppositions of science falsely so called: which some professing have erred concerning the faith (1 Tim. 6:20–21).

> For the time will come when they will not endure sound doctrine; but after their own lusts shall they heap to themselves teachers, having itching ears; And they shall turn away from the truth, and shall be turned unto fables (2 Tim. 4:3–4).

> Ever learning , and never able to come to the knowledge of the truth (2 Tim. 3:7).

Those of us who search for the truth realize the re-discovery of Noah's ark could be seen as a warning; perhaps a final warning of things to come. If God allows this to happen, then possibly a few people will be wise enough to pay attention, and choose to accept the gift. "For BY GRACE are ye saved THROUGH FAITH; and that NOT OF YOURSELVES: it is a GIFT of God: NOT OF WORKS, lest any man should boast" (Eph. 2:8–9).

ADDENDUM

In the search for the ark we have a conundrum. Where did it land? When I wrote *The Ark, A Reality?* I thought the evidence of my research put the ark on Ararat. In recent years I've entertained the thought of another possibility for the landing place of the ark.

My good friend Bob Cornuke, explorer, author, businessman,

and founder of the BASE Institute of Colorado Springs, Colorado, has accomplished a Herculean amount of research that tells us the ark landed in what is now modern Iran. Larry Williams, explorer, author, businessman, commodities expert, and good friend of mine, also thinks the landing site to be in Iran. There are others who are biblical scholars who believe the same thing. Much of this belief begins with the Scripture in Genesis 11:1–2 which says, "And the whole earth was of one language, and of one speech. And it came to pass, as they journeyed from the east, that they found a plain in the land of Shinar, and they dwelt there." It was "from the east" that the generation of Noah traveled after Noah died some three hundred and fifty years after the flood. The plain of Shinar is accepted by biblical scholars to be in modern-day Iraq. Bible atlases give me testimony to that belief. If the generations of Noah stayed in one place near the landing site of the ark for three hundred and fifty years until Noah's death, then moved "from the east," the landing site of the ark must have been west of the plain in the land of Shinar.

The city of Babylon is located on what is considered to be the plain in the land of Shinar. A question could be, "What is the extent of the plain, or of the land of Shinar?" A Bible dictionary tells me that Shinar (meaning two rivers) is the alluvial plain through which the Tigris and Euphrates pass, and probably inclusive of Babylon and Mesopotamia. It's the word "probably" that interests me. It indicates that there is a question pertaining to the extent — not of the plain, but of the land of Shinar. Could it extend to the mountainous area where the two rivers begin? Mesopotamia is the country between the two rivers. The Tigris is the great eastern tributary of the Euphrates, rising in the Armenian mountains and flowing southeastwardly 1146 miles. Between it and the Euphrates lay Mesopotamia. The Euphrates is a great river of western Asia, rising in Armenia and emptying into the Persian Gulf. Both rivers rise out of Armenia. Keep in mind that Mount Ararat is in Armenia.

If the ark landed on Ararat, could the generations of Noah have followed the Tigris River southeastward just a few hundred miles during the three hundred and fifty years of Noah's life after the Flood, then after his death, moved eastwardly till they came to the Euphrates, and built there on the plain that is within the land of Shinar? How about right after the Flood? Noah was a husbandman. Did Noah and his family leave the rugged mountains and follow that river until he found a place suitable to farm and plant a vineyard? The Bible does not say that he did, and one might question if the river was even in place immediately following the geological changes of the earth at that time. But if the river was in place, could he have followed it? More on this thought in a minute.

If he did not follow the river, then it would seem that the Zagros Mountains to the east of Babylon would have been the landing place of the ark. Bob's research indicates that these mountains are included in the Kingdom of Ararat. Therefore, this information suggests these are mountains of Ararat. When I spoke with Larry in March 2001, he had just returned from that particular region of Iran, and his search, which includes meeting with the locals of the area, leads him to think that this area is in fact where the ark landed. Among the many things he learned was a story of wood being found many years ago on a flat area on a fairly high mountain in that region. As of today however, nothing on the surface of the ground at that particular place remains to be seen of any structure.

I went with Bob, Larry, and their team to climb on Sabalon, a mountain in Iran, in 2000. By doing this, I think I've shown this is a search for truth; wherever it is. We've searched on Ararat, we've searched in Iran, and we continue to search. In my present opinion, Sabalon is the wrong place. If Shinar is in Iraq, and the generations of Noah traveled from the east; which would have been the Zagros Mountains, Sabalon is too far north. So, what were we doing there? It is thought by some that Ed Davis was on this mountain when he was taken to a broken structure he was told was the ark. Call it research.

When I was in Nachicevan and Azerbaijan a few years ago in the company of Dr. Salih Bayruktutan of Ataturk Univeristy, Erzurum, Turkey, and John McIntosh, explorer, teacher, and ark researcher from California, we visited with Dr. Isa Habibbeyli of Arazuste Universite and Nahcivan Devlet Universitiesi (local spelling). We were told of folklore pertaining to Noah's ark in that region. This would be north of Iran and east of Mount Ararat in Turkey. We were told that Noah's grave is in this region and they knew the spot. If this were true, then presumably the generations of Noah would have had to travel far to the south in order to turn west to go ("from the east") to the plain of Shinar. The Bible doesn't say they did that. Larry was told by the locals in Iran that Noah's grave was down there. So, where are we now?

In Turkey, there is a vast plain to the southwest of Ararat. On that plain there is a city by the name of Cinar. It is pronounced nearly like Shinar. According to an eyewitness from Australia, a doctor (I don't have permission at this writing to mention his name), there is what appears from a distance to be a large accumulation of rocks or something buried. The remains of a ziggurat? Is this the plain of Shinar, and did the generations of Noah travel from the east — from south of Ararat — from the land of Armenia? It sounds like a real stretch to think that would be the case; the result of an overactive imagination, if you will. The research of the scholars tell us that Bob and/or Larry are correct. I have recently spent time in research considering that possibility, and I admit, it seems as though they are, in fact, correct. The cities built and mentioned in Genesis 10:10 were built in Babylonia, on the plain of Shinar. I do not disagree. So, what's the point, and where does this leave us?

When Nimrod decided to build a city and a tower, the Lord saw the city and the tower and didn't like it (you know the story). "So the Lord scattered them abroad from thence upon the face of all the earth: and they left off to build the city" (Gen. 11:8). "They *stopped* building the city" (NIV, emphasis mine). "Therefore is the name of it called Babel; because the LORD did there confound the language of all the earth; and from thence did the LORD scatter them abroad upon the face of all the earth" (Gen. 11:9). They were scattered from the tower of Babel, they stopped the building of the city, and were scattered abroad upon the face of the earth. In other words, after the confusion with the language, they didn't stick around to build a city of Babylon near the tower. They all moved! So, does this mean that Babel and Babylon are not at the same place? This is the point of the previous paragraph. The tower of Babel has not been identified, and its exact location is in doubt. I'm not saying the tower is in Turkey. I'm saying that it is a mystery, and so is the location of the landing site of the ark. The scholars themselves may not yet have all the answers in regard to biblical history.

As mentioned, Noah, was a "husbandman" after the flood. He was a farmer. He tilled the soil. He planted a vineyard. Apparently he stayed in one place for a while. It's reasonable that he did not travel far from the ark. We do know that he found a place to grow a vineyard; wherever that was. Reportedly, there was a vineyard in the area of the Ahora on Mount Ararat. That's not the case now, and I don't know the report to be true. I am to understand there are vineyards in Iran near where the ark may have landed. My question is, where did Noah farm? If it was near where he landed, and if he landed on Ararat, and Bael is in Iraq, did Noah and all the generations of Noah stay in one place for three hundred and fifty years until

Noah died, or did they move around a bit? Did they follow the river southeastwardly till they were in place to move "from the east" to build Babel? The Bible doesn't say that they did. But the bible doesn't tell us much of what happened during those three hundred and fifty years. It does tell us that there will be seasons. "While the earth remaineth, seedtime and harvest, and cold and heat, and summer and winter, and day and night shall not cease" (Gen. 8:22). Could Noah have moved his farm? Isn't it a reasonable thought that the changing climate after the Flood, the cool temperatures and possibly snow in the winter in what is now eastern Turkey, could have encouraged Noah to follow the river to a warmer place where he could continue to farm?

The best scholarly research seems to indicate the ark did not land on what is now Mount Ararat. But if the ark landed in what is now Iran, and no longer exists, then I'm not sure how one could prove it landed there, or even floated to begin with. So, if this is the case, then why are we looking for it? The Scripture says, "And the ark rested in the seventh month, on the seventeenth day of the month, upon the mountains of Ararat" (Gen. 8:4). According to the scholars, the mountains of Ararat cover an extensive area and include the Zagros Mountains. My atlas of the Bible shows a map that names the Zagros Mountains in what would be a range extending from southern to northern Iran. But in the area between Lake Van in modern Turkey, and Lake Sevan in Armenia, the mountains depicted on the map are titled "Ararat Mountains." Mount Ararat is right in the middle of them.

The story of Noah, the ark, and the Flood is mentioned several places in Scripture. For instance, in Matthew 24:37–38, Jesus compares the time of Noah and the Flood to the time He will return. I find it interesting in 2 Peter 3:5–7, Paul says, "For this they are willingly ignorant, that by the word of God the heavens were of old, and the earth standing out of water and in the water: whereby the world that then was, being overflowed with water, perished: But the heavens and the earth, which are now, by the same word are kept in store, reserved unto fire against the day of judgment and perdition of ungodly men." The key here is being "willingly ignorant."

I believe it is true to a great extent that because of what we are taught in school about the history of the earth, that we are ignorant. Not necessarily are we "willingly ignorant" because of what someone told us. The earth has a cataclysmic history, and one that includes a global flood. Secular geology instructors prefer to teach a uniformitarian theory which has no mention of a great cataclysm such as the global flood. Thoughtful observation shows cataclysm by water to be a historical fact. It is my guess that the secular minded instructor doesn't consider "the world that was then" and "the earth that is now" (as per the preceding Scripture) to include a physical change to the earth. I doubt many of the secular instructors consider the Word of God at all.

To be "willingly ignorant," perhaps something more is necessary in order that each of us can choose how or what we believe. If the ark is found, that would allow us the opportunity to make the decision. One might also consider that because Jesus made a point to mention the story, that when it is found, it will be a warning by what had happened — to what is to come. I believe God will use the discovery to bring many people to salvation. If this is reasonable, then the ark survives to this day. Therefore, if so, and if the ark is to be found, and according to what we have just read, it probably will not be found in Iran. It would have to be resting in a place where it has been preserved until the proper time. Where is that? I might suggest in the ice-cap of Mount Ararat.

Consider the following, yet another reported account. Out of Santa Anna, California, comes a report from a 79-year-old lady by the name of Jeanne Marquette. She had met an Armenian gentleman by the name of John Derpaulian in 1961, who had told her that as a nine-year-old boy, he and a few other kids would climb Ararat, and stand upon the ark. He said that the ark was on the eastern slope, and that it had green moss on it. In reference to the moss, Hagopian had said the same thing. Derpaulian said the ark sat in front of a black crater, which in Armenian was called a "sieve". He said that there was not a lot of damage, and that it was not broken in two pieces as more recent reports suggest (i.e., Davis). If both the Derpaulian and Davis reports are correct, then the ark was in one major piece in, say 1915, and broken in two major pieces in 1943. We would now be looking for a broken ark. If the sighting of a broken ark is true, then it might be possible that an earthquake in this land of Anatilian faults could have caused the damage. The whereabouts of John Derpaulian is difficult at this point in time to determine. Rumor has it that he went to someplace in South America several years ago. There is an attempt now to locate him. At this writing, we're not sure this old man is still alive. He would be approximately 95 years old.

From March 2 until May 28, 2001, there was an exhibition at the British Library in London, England, entitled "Treasures from the

Ark." It was a celebration of 1,700 years of Armenian Christian art. I flew to London, and went to the exhibition.

Out of the Urartu nation, which dates back approximately 3,000 years, and was formed by "Arame," came the Armenian nation. Located about halfway between Lake Van in the southwest, which is Turkish Armenia, and Lake Sevan to the northeast, which is the Republic of Armenia, is Mount Ararat. The most natural feature of Armenia is Mount Ararat, the legendary resting place of Noah's ark. From the literature at the exhibition we read, "Armenia is the biblical home of Mount Ararat, where it is believed that Noah's ark finally came to rest after the flood. (We read earlier of this area being the Ararat Mountains.) In A.D. 301 the Armenians adopted Christianity as their official state religion, the first people to do so. Since then the Church has played a central role in Armenian art and culture. The exhibition was about the history and the art since A.D. 301. Artifacts from the ark, if they exist, were not shown.

A wonderfully interesting and spectacular display of ancient handwritten Bibles, tapestries, stone carvings, photographs of church building ruins, such as "Ani" (a place I once visited), and the art forms were presented. The exhibition was a magnificent record to the early beginnings of Christian Armenia.

There was something else, too. Over the three days I visited, I asked many questions. I won't mention the names of the people I spoke with, just the bottom line. The Armenians have had reason to believe the ark is on Ararat, and the Turkish authorities objected to the title of the exhibition. For political reasons, Noah was not mentioned. So the question I have is, "Why?" I can think of two possible answers. One, the Turkish authorities are tired of all the ark hunters, and the title would draw more of the same to eastern Turkey, and more requests to be allowed to climb Ararat. Two, the ark is there and the Turkish authorities know it and don't want it to be found and reviled. Perhaps it is a combination of both answers. The result? I'm encouraged. Do you suppose, to the Glory of God, we should climb that mountain — one more time?

ENDNOTES

Chapter 1 — What Has Been Found?

1. Clifford L. Burdick, "The Elliptical Formation in the Tendurek Mountains," *Creation Research Society Quarterly*, vol. 13 (September 1976): p. 96.
2. Ibid., p. 97.
3. William H. Shea, "The Ark-shaped Formation in the Tendurek Mountains at Eastern Turkey," *Creation Research Society Quarterly*, vol. 13 (September 1976): p. 91–92.
4. Will Durant, *Caesar and Christ* (New York, NY: Simon and Schuster, 1972), p. 464.
5. Ibid., p. 662.
6. Ibid., p. 654.
7. Ibid., p. 655.
8. Ibid., p. 663–664.
9. Robert W. Faid, *A Scientific Approach to Biblical Mysteries* (Green Forest, AR: New Leaf Press, 1994), p. 51.
10. William H. Shea, "A Review of Recent Data from the Region of the Ark-shaped Formation in the Tendurek Mountains of Eastern Turkey," Dr. Shea is Professor of Old Testament, Andrews University, Berrien Springs, MI, 1980.
11. Tim LaHaye and John Morris, *The Ark on Ararat* (Nashville, TN/New York, NY: Creation Life Publishers, Thomas Nelson, Inc., Publishers, 1976), p. 250, from "The Ark of Noah," Henry M. Morris, *Creation Research Society Journal*, 8:2 (September 1971): p. 142–144.
12. Violet M. Cummings, *Has Anybody Really Seen Noah's Ark?* (San Diego, CA: Creation Life Publishers, 1982), p. 224–225.

Chapter 2 — Russian Accounts

1. John C. Whitcomb Jr. and Henry M. Morris, *The Genesis Flood* (Philadelphia, PA: Presbyterian & Reformed Publishing Co., 1961).
2. Cummings, *Has Anybody Really Seen Noah's Ark?*, p. 62–66.
3. C. Allen Roy, "Was It Hot or Not?" *Bible Science Newsletter* (July 16, 1978), Loma Linda University Library, L.A. Sierra Campus.
4. Ibid.
5. LaHaye and Morris, *The Ark on Ararat*, p. 76.
6. Cummings, *Has Anybody Really Seen Noah's Ark?*, p. 25.
7. Ibid., p. 68–69.
8. Ibid., p. 77–81.
9. Ibid., p. 81–83.
10. Ibid., p. 85.
11. Guy Richards, *The Hunt for the Czar* (New York, NY: Dell Publishing Co., Inc., 1971), p. 134.
12. Cummings, *Has Anybody Really Seen Noah's Ark?*, p. 89–90.

Chapter 3 — Early Sightings

1. Cummings, *Has Anybody Really Seen Noah's Ark?*, p. 94–95.
2. Ibid., p. 96.
3. Ibid., p. 102.
4. Ibid., p. 103.
5. Ibid., p. 106.
6. *Koran, English and Arabic: The Holy Quran; Text, Translation and Commentary* (Al-Riyadh, Saudi Arabia: Al Malik Faysal, Street, 1938), p. 525, #1531.
7. Cummings, *Has Anybody Really Seen Noah's Ark?*, p. 107.
8. Ibid., p. 108.

9. LaHaye and Morris, *The Ark on Ararat*, p. 16.
10. James Bryce, *Transcaucasia and Ararat (Notes of a Vacation Tour in the Autumn of 1876)* (London: MacMillan and Co., 1877), p. 202–203.
11. LaHaye and Morris, *The Ark on Ararat*, p. 17.
12. Bryce, *Transcaucasia and Ararat,* p. 200.
13. LaHaye and Morris, *The Ark on Ararat*, p. 18.
14. Sir John Mandeville, *The Travels of Sir John Mandeville: The Version of the Cotton Manuscript in Modern Spelling* (London: MacMillan and Co., Ltd., 1915), p. 100.
15. Morris, "The Ark of Noah," p. 94.
16. LaHaye and Morris, *The Ark on Ararat*, p. 20.
17. Bryce, *Transcaucasia and Ararat,* p. 208.
18. LaHaye and Morris, *The Ark on Ararat*, p. 21.
19. Ibid., p. 22.
20. Ibid., p. 26.
21. John Montgomery, *The Quest for Noah's Ark* (Minneapolis, MN: Bethany Fellowship, 1972), p. 78.
22. Manuel Komroff, editor, *The Travels of Marco Polo (The Venetian)* (Garden City, NY: Garden City Publishing Co., Inc., 1930), p. 25.
23. Montgomery, *The Quest for Noah's Ark.*
24. LaHaye and Morris, *The Ark on Ararat*, p. 26.
25. Ibid., p. 19.
26. Ibid., p. 20.
27. Cummings, *Has Anybody Really Seen Noah's Ark?*, p. 112.
28. "A Remarkable Narrative," *Zions Watch Tower,* Allegheny, PA, Vol. XV, No. 16 (August 15, 1894): p. 1689. Printed by permission from *Watch Tower,* Bible and Tract Society of New York, Inc., Brooklyn, NY.
29. Cummings, *Has Anybody Really Seen Noah's Ark?*, p. 120.
30. R.W. Thomson, *Agathangelos — History of the Armenians* (Albany, NY: State University of New York Press, 1976), Introduction and Foreword.
31. Leon Arpee, *A History of Armenian Christianity* (Princeton, NJ: Princeton University Press, 1946), p. 15.
32. Thomson, *Agathangelos — History of the Armenians,* p. xiii.
33. Arpee, *A History of Armenian Christianity,* p. 25–31.
34. Thomson, *Agathangelos — History of the Armenians,* p. ixxx.
35. Michael J. Arlen, *Passage to Ararat* (New York, NY: Farrar, Straus & Giroux, 1975), p. 115–116.
36. Cummings, *Has Anybody Really Seen Noah's Ark?*, p. 120–122.
37. Ibid., p. 136.
38. Cummings, *Has Anybody Really Seen Noah's Ark?*, p. 127.
39. Ibid., p. 124–129.

Chapter 4 — Do the Locals Know?

1. LaHaye and Morris, *The Ark on Ararat*, p. 239–241.
2. Ibid., p. 56–58.
3. Ibid., p. 70.
4. Roy, "Was It Hot or Not?"
5. Cummings, *Has Anybody Really Seen Noah's Ark?*, p. 139.
6. World Book Encyclopedia, Vol. 15, p. 290.
7. Cummings, *Has Anybody Really Seen Noah's Ark?*, p. 139–140.
8. Roy, "Was It Hot or Not?"
9. Cummings, *Has Anybody Really Seen Noah's Ark?*, p. 218.

10. Edward Stevenson Murray "On the Turk's Russian Frontier," *National Geographic* (September 1941). Murray was a former professor at Robert's College in Istanbul, and was a roving editor for National Geographic Society.
11. Cummings, *Has Anybody Really Seen Noah's Ark?*, p. 229.
12. Ibid., p. 219.
13. LaHaye and Morris, *The Ark on Ararat*, p. 69–71.
14. Roy, "Was It Hot or Not?"
15. Cummings, *Has Anybody Really Seen Noah's Ark?*, p. 120.

Chapter 5 — World War II and Other Reports
 1. Cummings, *Has Anybody Really Seen Noah's Ark?*, p. 149.
 2. Ibid., p. 229.
 3. Ibid., p. 219.
 4. Ibid., p. 149–150.
 5. Ibid., p. 153–157.
 6. Ibid., p. 158–159.
 7. Ibid., p. 159–160.
 8. Ibid., p. 160–161.
 9. Robert Meyer Jr., *The Stars and Stripes Story* (New York, NY: David McKay Co., Inc., 1960).
10. Cummings, *Has Anybody Really Seen Noah's Ark?*, p. 161–162.
11. Ibid., p. 159.
12. Charles Berlitz, *Doomsday 1999 A.D.* (Garden City, NY: Doubleday & Company, Inc., 1981), p. 187–188.
13. Cummings, *Has Anybody Really Seen Noah's Ark?*, p. 143–144.
14. Charles E. Sellier Jr. and Dave Balsiger, *In Search of Noah's Ark* (Los Angeles, CA: Sun Classics Books, 1976), p. 161.
15. Montgomery, *Quest for Noah's Ark*, p. 121.
16. LaHaye and Morris, *The Ark on Ararat*, p. 135.
17. Cummings, *Has Anybody Really Seen Noah's Ark?*, p. 144–146.
18. *Aircraft Recognition Manual*, Department of the Army, Navy, Air Force, and Marine Corps. Issued by the Chief of Bureau of Naval Weapons, June 1962.
19. Ibid.
20. Bill Guston, editor, *Aviation: The Complete Story of Man's Conquest of the Air* (London: Octopus Books, Limited, 1978), p. 192.
21. Giorgio Apostolo, *The Illustrated Encyclopedia of Helicopters* (New York, NY: Bonanza Books, 1984), p. 22.

Chapter 6 — Pieces of Wood on a Treeless Mountain
 1. Fernando Navarra, *Noah's Ark, I Touched It* (London: Coverdale House Publishers; Plainfield, NJ: Logost International, 1974), p. 137.
 2. Douglas M. Considine, editor, *Van Nostrand's Scientific Encyclopedia* (New York, NY: Van Nostrand Reinhold Company, 1983), p. 2387–2388.
 3. Cummings, *Has Anybody Really Seen Noah's Ark?*, p. 340.
 4. Ibid., p. 340–341.
 5. Ibid., p. 339.
 6. Ibid., p. 331.
 7. Ibid., p. 331.
 8. Ibid., p. 221.
 9. Ibid., p. 300.
10. Navarra, *Noah's Ark, I Touched It*, p. 33–34.
11. Cummings, *Has Anybody Really Seen Noah's Ark?*, p. 302.
12. Navarra, *Noah's Ark, I Touched It*, p. 18.

13. Cummings, *Has Anybody Really Seen Noah's Ark?*, p. 302–303.

14. Ibid., p. 303.

15. Ibid., p. 306–307.

16. Navarra, *Noah's Ark, I Touched It,* p. 34–36.

17. Fernando Navarra, translated by Michael Legat, *The Forbidden Mountain* (London: MacDonald, 1956), p. 165–166.

18. Roy, "Was It Hot or Not?"

19. Cummings, *Has Anybody Really Seen Noah's Ark?*, p. 312.

20. Ibid., p. 123.

21. LaHaye and Morris, *The Ark on Ararat*, p. 101.

22. Navarra, *The Forbidden Mountain,* p. 130–131.

Chapter 7 — What Is Ararat?

1. Clifford L. Burdick, "Ararat — The Mother of Mountains," a report of observations on an expedition sponsored by the Archaeological Research Foundation of New York, p. 9.

2. LaHaye and Morris, *The Ark on Ararat*, p. 11.

3. James G. Moore, "Mechanism of Formation of Pillow Lava," *American Scientist*, vol. 63 (May–June 197): p. 269–276.

4. LaHaye and Morris, *The Ark on Ararat*, p. 11.

5. Richard Foster Flint, *Glacial Geology and the Pleistocene Epoch* (New York, NY: John Wiley and Sons, Inc.; London: Chapman & Hall, Limited, 1947), p. 514–515.

6. Henry M. Morris and Gary E. Parker, *What Is Creation Science?* (Green Forest, AR: Master Books, 1982), p. 231.

7. Bernard Kummel, *History of the Earth* (San Francisco, CA: W.H. Freeman and Company, 1961).

8. Whitcomb and Morris, *The Genesis Flood.*

9. Burdick, "Ararat — The Mother of Mountains," p. 10.

10. Kummel, *History of the Earth,* p. 14.

11. Burdick, "Ararat — The Mother of Mountains," p. 11.

12. Ibid., p. 9.

13. LaHaye and Morris, *The Ark on Ararat*, p. 10–11.

14. Sellier and Balsiger, *In Search of Noah's Ark*, p. 72.

Chapter 8 — Was There a Flood?

1. *Webster's New School and Office Dictionary* (Greenwich, CN: Fawcett Publications, Inc., 1960), p. 798.

2. Charles Lyell, *Principles of Geology* (New York, NY: D. Appleton and Company, 1887), 11th ed., Vol. 1, p. xi.

3. Henry M. Morris, "The Flood and The Genesis Record," a tape recording, Creation Life Publishers, San Diego, CA.

4. Morris and Parker, *What Is Creation Science?*, p. 129–133.

5. D.G.A. Whitten and J.R.V. Brooks, *The Penguin Dictionary of Geology* (New York, NY: Penguin Books, 1972), p. 457–458.

6. *The Fossil Record* (film), Films for Christ Association, Mesa, AZ.

7. Whitcomb and Morris, *The Genesis Flood*, p. 89.
Henry M. Morris and John D. Morris, *The Modern Creation Trilogy* (Green Forest, AR: Master Books, 1996).

8. Whitcomb and Morris, *The Genesis Flood*, p. 89.

9. Kummel, *History of the Earth*, p. 541.

10. Whitcomb and Morris, *The Genesis Flood*, p. 95.

11. Lyell, *Principles of Geology*, p. 298–299.

12. Ibid., p. 308, 318.

13. Cesave Emiliani, "The Great Flood," *Sea Frontiers*, International Oceanographic Foundation, vol. 22, no. 5 (1976): p. 258, 260.
14. Harold T. Wilkins, *Mysteries of Ancient South America* (London: Rider and Co., 1946), p. 55, 186, 190.
15. Whitcomb and Morris, *The Genesis Flood*, p. 161.
16. "Recent Paleontological Discoveries From Cumberland Bone Cave, Science of the March," *The Scientific Monthly*, vol. 76, no. 5 (May 1953): p. 301.
17. Whitcomb and Morris, *The Genesis Flood*, p. 159.
18. Ibid., p. 154.

Chapter 9 — Was the Flood Local or Universal?
1. Ellicott and Smith, *A Bible Commentary*, p. 40.
2. Ibid.
3. Ibid., p. 42.
4. Ibid., p. 40.
5. Charles Ellicott and R. Payne Smith, *A Bible Commentary* (New York, NY: Cassell and Company Limited, no date), p. 42.
6. John Gill, *Gill's Commentary* (Grand Rapids, MI: Baker Book House, 1980), p. 48.
7. Rev. J.S. Exell, *The Preachers Homeletic Commentary* (New York, NY: Funk & Wagnall's Company, 1892), p. 49.
8. Derek Goodwin, *Pigeons and Doves of the World* (Ithaca, NY and London: Comstock Publishing Associates, a division of Cornell University Press, 1977), p. 6–9, 195, 213.
9. Whitcomb and Morris, *The Genesis Flood*, p. 104; quoting *A Commentary on the Holy Scriptures: Genesis*, J.P. Lange, editor (Grand Rapids, MI: Zondervan Publishing House, no date), p. 301; quoting *A New Commentary on Genesis*, Sophia Taylor, trans. (New York, NY: Scribner & Welford, 1899).
10. Ibid., p. 105.
11. Arnold Krochman, "Olive Growing in Greece," *Economic Botany* (July–Sept. 195): p. 228–231.
12. Whitcomb and Morris, *The Genesis Flood*, p. 105–106.
13. Henrietta C. Mears, *What the Bible Is All About* (Glendale, CA: Regal Books Division, G/L Publications, 1980), p. 19–20.
14. Henry M. Morris, *The Genesis Record* (Grand Rapids, MI: Baker Book House Co., 1976), p. 25–28.
15. Sir J. William Dawson, *The Meeting Place of Geology and History* (New York, NY: Fleming H. Revell, 1894), p. 152.
16. Ellicott and Smith, *A Bible Commentary*, p. 42.
17. Ibid.
18. Ibid., p. 40.
19. Whitcomb and Morris, *The Genesis Flood*, p. 21–22.
20. Ellicott and Smith, *A Bible Commentary*, p. 16.
21. Whitcomb and Morris, *The Genesis Flood*, p. 113–114.
22. Ellicott and Smith, *A Bible Commentary*, p. 40–41.
23. William Smith, editor, *A Dictionary of the Bible* (New York, NY: Fleming H. Revell Company, no date), p. 462–463.
24. F.N. Peloubet, editor, *Peloubet's Bible Dictionary* (Philadelphia, PA: Universal Book and Bible House, 1947), p. 454–455.
25. *The Oxford English Dictionary* (London: Oxford University Press, 1970), Vol. III, E, p. 11, 316; Vol. XII, W, p. 300, 301.
26. Adam Clarke, *Clarke's Commentary* (Nashville, TN: PSA Abingdon, no date, authorized 1977), p. 73.

27. Joseph P. Free, *Archaeology and Bible History* (Wheaton, IL: Van Kampen Press, 1950), p. 41–43.
28. Karl Friedrick Keil and F. Delitzsh, *Bible Commentary on the Old and New Testament,*Vol. I, The Penlateach Trans. by Rev. James Martin (Grand Rapids, MI: Wm. B. Eerdmans Publishing Co., 1951), p. 145–146.
29. Ramm, *The Christian View of Science and Scripture*, p. 244.
30. Whitcomb and Morris, *The Genesis Flood*, p. 77.
31. Peter W. Stoner and Robert C. Newman, *Science Speaks* (Chicago, IL: Moody Press, 1976).
32. Burdick, *Ararat* — "The Mother of Mountains," p. 9–10.
33. Ramm, *The Christian View of Science and Scripture*, p. 244.
34. Whitcomb and Morris, *The Genesis Flood,* p. 11.
35. Ibid., p. 23–31.
36. *The International Standard Bible Encyclopedia*, Vol. II, "The Deluge of Noah," George F. Write, p. 824.
37. Ramm, *The Christian View of Science and Scripture*, p. 239–240.
38. Sellier and Balsiger, *In Search of Noah's Ark*, p. 107.
39. Berlitz, *Doomsday, 1999 A.D.*, p. 171.
40. Charles H. Hapgood, "The Mystery of the Frozen Mammoths," *Coronet Magazine* (September 1960): p. 72–78.
41. Robert Jamieson, *A Commentary, Critical, Experimental and Practical on the Old and New Testament* (Grand Rapids, MI: Wm. B. Eerdmans Publishing Co., 1945), Vol. I, p. 95.
42. Free, *Archaeology and Bible History*, p. 41–43.
43. *The International Standard Bible Encyclopedia*, p. 824.

Chapter 10 — Where Is the Water?

1. Kummel, *History of the Earth*, p. 555.
2. Sellier and Balsiger, *In Search of Noah's Ark*, p. 46.
3. Whitcomb and Morris, *The Genesis Flood,* p. 215.
4. Ibid.
5. Harold K. Blum, *Times Arrow and Evolution* (Princeton, NJ: Princeton University Press, 1951), p. 57.
6. Whitcomb and Morris, *The Genesis Flood*, p. 122.
7. Ibid., p. 230.
8. Ibid., p. 127–128.
9. Kummel, *History of the Earth*, p. 552–554.
10. Joseph Weisberg and Howard Parish, *Introduction to Oceanography* (New York, NY: McGraw-Hill Book Company, 1974), p. 65.
11. Ibid., p. 61.
12. Ibid., p. 66.
13. Ibid., p. 62.
14. *Genesis*, movie, Denver Imax Theater, Museum of Natural History, December 1984.
15. Weisberg and Parish, *Introduction to Oceanography*, p. 53.
16. Flint, *Glacial Geology and the Pleistocene Epoch*, p. 514–515.
17. Ibid., p. 128.
18. "A Geological Report from the Geological, Glaceological and Botanical Reports Taken During the 1964 and 1966 Expeditions to Eastern Turkey and Mount Ararat," Archaeological Research Foundation, by Clifford L. Burdick.
19. LaHaye and Morris, *The Ark on Ararat*, p. 11.
20. Whitcomb and Morris, *The Genesis Flood*, p. 292.
21. Kummel, *History of the Earth*, p. 550.

22. Whitcomb and Morris, *The Genesis Flood*, p. 295–298.
23. Flint, *Glacial Geology and the Pleistocene Epoch*, p. 210.
24. Maurice Gignoux, *Stratigraphic Geology* (San Francisco, CA: W.H. Freeman and Co., 1955), p. 626–627.
25. *Great Salt Lake and Past and Present* (David E. Miller Publishing Press, 1949), p. 7–8, 34–35, 41–42, 44.
26. Wallace S. Broecker, Maurice Ewing, and Bruce C. Heezen, "Evidence for an Abrupt Change in Climate Close to 11,000 Years Ago," *American Journal of Science*, vol. 258 (June 1960): p. 441.
27. Whitcomb and Morris, *The Genesis Flood*, p. 429.
28. Ibid., p. 304–311.
29. David G. Smith, *The Cambridge Encyclopedia of Earth Sciences* (Cambridge, MA: Cambridge University Press, 1979–1981), p. 291–312.
30. *World Book Encyclopedia* (Chicago, IL: World Book Inc., A Scott Felzer Co., 1984), Vol. 10.
31. Ibid.
32. Smith, *The Cambridge Encyclopedia of Earth Sciences.*
33. *World Book Encyclopedia,* Vol. 10.
34. Smith, *The Cambridge Encyclopedia of Earth Sciences,* p. 312.
35. Whitcomb and Morris, *The Genesis Flood*, foreword.
36. Kummel, *History of the Earth*, p. 554.

Chapter 11 — When Was the Flood?

 1. Whitcomb and Morris, *The Genesis Flood*, p. 43.
 2. Rodney Hoare, *The Turin Shroud Is Genuine* (London: Souvenir Press, 1995), p. 96–99.
 3. Ibid.
 4. Whitcomb and Morris, *The Genesis Flood*, p. 253.
 5. Gilbert N. Plass, "Carbon Dioxide and the Climate, *American Scientist*, vol. 44 (July 1956): p. 314.
 6. Kummel, *History of the Earth*, p. 554.
 7. Whitcomb and Morris, *The Genesis Flood*, p. 378.
 8. "The Age of the Universe," *Scientific Monthly*, vol. 77, Oct. 1953, p. 177.
 9. Whitcomb and Morris, *The Genesis Flood*, p. 382.
10. T.S. Jackson, "Review of Space, Time, and Creation," *Science*, vol. 128 (Sept. 3, 1958): p. 527.
11. Edmund Schulman, "Bristlecone Pine, Oldest Living Thing, *National Geographic*, vol. 113 (March 1958): p. 355.
12. Whitcomb and Morris, *The Genesis Flood*, p. 393.
13. Ibid.
14. LaHaye and Morris, *The Ark on Ararat*, p. 231–232.
15. Lewis Spence, *Myths and Legends — Babylonia and Assyria* (Boston, MA: David D. Nickerson & Company, no date), p. 154–155.
16. Theodore H. Guster, *Myth, Legend and Custom in the Old Testament* (New York, NY: Harper & Row Publishers, 1969), p. 82.
17. Spence, *Myths and Legends — Babylonia and Assyria,* p. 173–174.
18. Guster, *Myth, Legend and Custom in the Old Testament*, p. 83.
19. Spence, *Myths and Legends — Babylonia and Assyria,* p. 175–176.
20. Guster, *Myth, Legend and Custom in the Old Testament*, p. 84.
21. Ibid., p. 92.
22. Ibid., p. 92–93.
23. Ibid., p. 121.

24. William Eberhard, *Folktales of China* (Chicago, IL: University of Chicago Press, 1965), p. 161–173.

25. W. Ramsay Smith, *Myths and Legends of the Australian Aboriginals* (New York, NY: Farrar & Rinehart Publishers, 1936), p. 155.

26. Frank Waters, *The Book of the Hopi* (New York, NY: Viking Press, 1963), p. 3–22.

27. Ibid.

28. John Anthony West, "The Sphinx, Clue to a Lost Civilization?, *Conde Nast Traveler* (Feb. 1993).

Chapter 12 — Evolution? Creation?

1. *Webster's Encyclopedia of Dictionaries*, compiled by John Gage Allee (Ottenheimer Publishers, Inc. 1953-1981; Literary Press 1958), p. 133.

2. Sylvia Baker, *Bone of Contention — Is Evolution True?* (Queensland, Australia: Evangelical Press, 1983), p. 2.

3. Walter Karp, *Charles Darwin and the Origin of Species* (New York, NY: American Heritage Publishing Co. Inc., 1968), p. 69.

4. Ibid., p. 118.

5. Ibid., p. 140.

6. *Webster's New School and Office Dictionary* (Greenwich, CT: Fawcett Publications, Inc., 1960), p. 485.

7. Karp, *Charles Darwin and the Origin of Species*, p. 78, 82, 83, 102, 104, 106, 109.

8. Ibid., p. 74.

9. Ibid., p. 111.

10. Ibid., p. 99.

11. Paul S. Taylor, *A Young People's Guide to the Bible and the Great Dinosaur Mystery* (Brisbane, Australia: Printcraft, 1985), p. 8.

12. Baker, *Bone of Contention — Is Evolution True?*, p. 30–31.

13. "The Flood and The Genesis Record," A tape recording by Henry M. Morris, Creation Life Publishers, San Diego, CA, 1982.

14. Ibid.

15. "The Fossil Record," Origins Film Series, Films for Christ, Mesa, Arizona.

16. Morris, "The Flood and The Genesis Record."

17. Paul S. Taylor, *The Great Dinosaur Mystery and the Bible* (Green Forest, AR: Master Books, 1987), p. 45–47.

18. *Ripley's Believe It or Not!*, "Reptiles, Lizards, and Prehistoric Beasts" (New York, NY: Byron Press, Tom Doherty Assoc., 1992), p. 121.

19. A.E. Wildersmith, *The Natural Sciences Know Nothing of Evolution* (Green Forest, AR: Master Books, 1981), p. 160.

20. Ibid., pp. 161–162.

21. Wildersmith, *The Natural Sciences Know Nothing of Evolution,* p. 150.

22. Ibid.

23. Morris, *Modern Science and the Genesis Record.*

24. Paul G. Hewett, *Conceptual Physics* (San Francisco, CA: Little, Brown and Company Inc., 1971), p. 81–82.

25. Fred Hoyle, *The Intelligent Universe* (New York, NY: Holt, Rinehart & Winston, 1983), p. 172.

26. Hewett, *Conceptual Physics,* p. 21–27. Newton's Laws of Motion:

    Law 1. Every body continues in its state of rest, or of uniform motion in a straight line, unless it is compelled to change that state by forces impressed upon it.

    Law 2. The acceleration of a body is directly proportional to the net force acting on the body and inversely proportional to the mass of the body.

    Law 3. To every action force there is an equal and opposite reaction force.

27. Hoyle, *The Intelligent Universe*, p. 171.
28. Morris, *Modern Science and the Genesis Record*.
29. Jerry Adler and Gerald Labenow, "Reading God's Mind," *Newsweek* (June 13, 1988): p. 56–59.
30. Sharon Begley and Michael Rogers, "Where the Wild Things Are," *Newsweek* (June 13, 1988): p. 60–65.
31. Morris, *Modern Science and the Genesis Record*.
32. Ibid.
33. Wildersmith, *The Natural Sciences Know Nothing of Evolution*, p. 3–4.
34. Ibid., p. 4.
35. Ibid., p. 5.
36. Ibid., p. 12–14.
37. Hoyle, *The Intelligent Universe*, p. 25.
38. Ibid., p. 48.
39. Wildersmith, *The Natural Sciences Know Nothing of Evolution*.
40 Ibid., p. 149–150.
41. Morris and Parker, *What Is Creation Science?*, p. 5.
42. *The Origin of Life* (film).
43. Morris and Parker, *What Is Creation Science*, p. 5, 7, 15.
44. *The Origin of Life* (film).
45. Morris and Parker, *What Is Creation Science*, p. 37, 60.
46. Ibid., p. 63.
47. *The Origin of Life* (film).
48. Morris and Parker, *What Is Creation Science*, p. 63.
49. Ibid., p. 145.
50. Wildersmith, *The Natural Sciences Know Nothing of Evolution*, p. 5–6.
51. Morris, *The Flood and the Genesis Record*.
52. Hoyle, *The Intelligent Universe*, p. 43.
53. Wildersmith, *The Natural Sciences Know Nothing of Evolution*, p. 6.
54. Mr. Ken Ham, lay speaker, Creation Outreach Seminar, Denver, Colorado, March 15, 1986.
55. Morris, *Modern Science and the Genesis Record*.
56. Ibid.
57. Morris, *Modern Science and the Genesis Record*.
58. *Webster's Encyclopedia of Dictionaries*, p. 250.
59. Stoner and Newman, *Science Speaks*, p. 33.
60. Lloyd R. Bailey, *Genesis, Creation, and Creationism* (Mahwah, NJ: Paulist Press, 1993), p. 122–123.
61. Ibid., p. 125.
62. Stoner and Newman, *Science Speaks*, p. 35–37, 39.
63. Ibid., p. 39–40.
64. *Prophecy Reference Bible*, Morris Cerullo World Evangelism Special Edition King James Version (San Diego, CA: Salem Kirban, Inc., 1979), Revelation visualized commentary, p. 85.
65. Stoner and Newman, *Science Speaks*, p. 40–41.
66. Ibid., p. 39–44.
67. Ibid., p. 62, 64.
68. Kummel, *History of the Earth*, p. 14, Table 1.1; 60; 61.
69. Walter T. Brown, *In the Beginning* (Phoenix, AZ: Center for Scientific Creation, 1989), p. 89.
70. Barry Setterfield, *Creation and Castastrophe* (Adelaide, S.A., Australia: Adelaide Crusade Center, 1993), p. 15.

71. Brown, *In the Beginning,* p. 89.
72. Setterfield, *Creation and Castastrophe,* p. 26.
73. Ibid., p. 29. The * refers to chronology in the pages of his work.
74. Ibid.
75. Ibid., p. 29–30.
76. Brown, *In the Beginning,* p. 90.
77. Lambert Dolphin, *Jesus: Lord of Time and Space* (Green Forest, AR: New Leaf Press, 1988), p. 110.
78. Ibid., p. 125.
79. "Research and Exploration," *National Geographic,* vol. 10, no. 4 (Autumn 1994).
80. *Fingerprints of Creation,* video, American Portrait Films, Alpha Productions, Cleveland, Ohio, 1994–1996.
81. Morris, *The Genesis Record.*
82. Ibid., p. 54–55.
83. Whitcomb and Morris, *The Genesis Flood,* p. 232–233.

Chapter 13 — A Summarizing Thought of Evolution, and a Look at the Size of the Ark

1. Stoner and Newman, *Science Speaks,* p. 67–68.
2. Josh McDowell and Don Stewart, *Reasons Skeptics Should Consider Christianity* (San Bernardino, CA: Here's Life Publishers, Inc., 1981), p. 184–187.
3. "Puzzling Out Man's Ascent," *Time,* Nov. 7, 1977, p. 66–67.
4. McDowell and Stewart, *Reasons Skeptics Should Consider Christianity,* p. 192.
5. Clifford Wilson, *The Bible Comes Alive,* Vol. I (Green Forest, AR: New Leaf Press, 1997), p. 27–32.
6. Rick Gore and Kenneth Garrett, "The First Europeans," *National Geographic* (July 1997): p. 98–103.
7. LaHaye and Morris, *The Ark on Ararat,* p. 244–246.
8. Ibid., p. 246.
9. World Book Encyclopedia, p. 207.
10. Whitcomb and Morris, *The Genesis Flood,* p. 73–74.
11. Morris, *The Flood and the Genesis Record.*
12. Steve Austin, *Mount St. Helens, Explosive Evidence for Catastrophe,* video, Institute for Creation Research, El Cajon, CA, 1996.

Chapter 14 — The Question of God

1. A.E. Wildersmith, *Why Does God Allow It?* (Costa Mesa, CA: The Word for Today, Inc., 1980), p. 10.
2. Ibid., p. 51–52.
3. Ibid.
4. Morris, *The Genesis Record,* p. 176.
5. Wildersmith, *Why Does God Allow It?,* p. 53.
6. Ibid., p. 36.
7. Ibid., p. 37.
8. Ibid., p. 35.
9. Pastor Del Roberts, Grace Community Chruch, Aurora, Colorado.

Chapter 15 — Expeditions

1 Henry M. Morris and John D. Morris, *The Modern Creation Trilogy,* Vol. 3 (Green Forest, AR: Master Books, 1996), p. 186 and 185.